★★

★ EARLIEST COUNTY COURT RECORDS ★
★   OF   ★
★   BEDFORD COUNTY, TENNESSEE   ★

★★★

1985

COMPILED

BY

HELEN CRAWFORD MARSH
TIMOTHY RICHARD MARSH
SHELBYVILLE, TENNESSEE

This volume was reproduced from
an 1986 edition located in the
publishers private library.
Greenville, South Carolina

Please direct all Correspondence & Orders to:

Southern Historical Press, Inc.
P.O. Box 1267
375 W Broad Street
Greenville, S.C. 29602-1267

Originally published: Greenville, S.C. 1986
Copyright: Southern Historical Press, Inc. 1986
ISBN #8-89308-568-5
Printed in the United States of America

FOREWORD

Abstracted here are the oldest surviving Minutes of the County Court
of Bedford County, Tennessee [1848-1860], all minutes prior to this date
were destroyed in the Courthouse fire in 1863. This destruction also
included Wills, Probate Records and Marriages, Guardian Accounts and
Settlements of Estates. Chancery Court and Land Deed Records fared much
better. These Court Records are presented in abstract form, focusing on
material of a genealogical or historical nature. Those desiring to see
the originals may do so by contacting the Tennessee State Library and
Archives in Nashville, Tennessee, where the originals are stored on micro-
film, Roll # 78, of the Bedford County, Tennessee Records. At this writing
the original Book is in the clerk's office in the Bedford County Court
House in Shelbyville, Tennessee. Be assured these are the oldest existing
Minutes of the Court of Pleas and Quarter Sessions of Bedford County, Tennessee or generally known as the Quarterly County Court.

The Marshs, 1985

BEDFORD COUNTY COURT MINUTES, BOOK 1848 - 1852
ABSTRACTS

1848 October Term

Page 1 - Amzi D. Anderson petitioned Court to examine Eliza Jane Gambill
and report is she is mentally capable of taking care of herself.

Page 1 - William Potter, admr. of estate of George W. Whitsell, deceased.

Page 3 - Joseph Anderson, exr. of estate of Peter Crowel, deceased.

Page 3 - Henry Killingsworth, admr. of Joel Pitts, deceased.

Page 3 - Mary S. Elkins, widow of William P. Elkins, deceased.

Page 4 - Lewis Gaunt appointed admr. of estate of Mary Gaunt.

Page 5 - Patsey Batten appointed admr. of estate of William G. Batten,
deceased.

Page 5 - John S. Brown, Henry Killingsworth and Joshua Hall, appointed
Commissioners to lay off support for widow and family of Lewis G.
Ray, deceased.

Page 14 - Isaac Patterson is over 50 yrs old, of the 3rd District.

Page 14 - Thomas Shearin, Jr., Jesse Morris and John W. Mayfield, Commissioners
for support of widow and family of William G. Batten.

Page 14 - David J. Norville, admr. of Elizabeth Norville, deceased.

Page 14 - John W. Cobb, admr. of James H. Cobb, deceased.

Page 15 - Sterling Newsom resigned as guardian of minor heirs of Thomas
Newsom, deceased. Randolph Newsom appointed in his place, of
his own minor children by his first wife.

Page 15 - Leroy W. Barrett, exr. of John Barrett, deceased.

Page 15 - Mary Ann Hime guardian of Cyntha Hime.

Page 15 - Edmund Word guardian of William and Mary Jane Hastings.

Page 15 - James E. Webb admr. of estate of Bushrod Webb, deceased.

Page 15 - John A. Moore guardian of Elizabeth Snelling, an idiot and heir
of Hugh Snelling, deceased.

1848 November Term

Page 16 - John J. Shriver admr. of estate of Frances W. Daniel.

Page 17 - George W. Buchanan appointed admr. of George W. Whitesell, deceased,
instead of William Potter.

1848 November Term

Page 19 - James Harris guardian of Ann Harris, a lunatic.

Page 19 - L. B. Knott guardian of Thomas B. and Henry S. Ledbetter, minor heirs of Willie Ledbetter, deceased.

Page 19 - George Kimbro guardian of Samuel D. Coble, minor of Jacob Coble, deceased.

Page 19 - H. L. Davidson guardian of Emily, Rachel and Hugh L. Brittain, minor heirs of William Brittain, deceased.

Page 19 - Meshack Hale guardian of his minor son Joseph H. Hale.

Page 19 - David Wagster guardian of Mary B. Thogmorton, a minor heir of Robert Thogmorton, deceased.

Page 20 - Rachel Gilbert appointed guardian of Susan M., Mary Ann, Artemisa and John C. Gilbert, minor heirs of John Gilbert, deceased.

Page 20 - Power of Attorney by Haywood Oakley and Eliza Oakley his wife, to Elijah E. Hester of Granville County, North Carolina.

Page 20 - Power of Attorney by John Overcast to Caleb Phifer of Cabarrus County, North Carolina.

Page 20 - Commissioners to lay off support of widow and family of Willis Baucom, deceased.

Page 21 - Commissioners to lay off support for widow and family of John Younger, deceased.

Page 21 - Commissioners to lay off support for widow and family of Frederick Shofner, deceased.

Page 21 - Jury decided that Eliza Jane Gambill is not able to take care of herself.

Page 22 - Joshua Woosley guardian of Willie, Cinthia Ann, James and Amy Johnson, minor heirs of William Johnson, deceased.

Page 22 - Barnet Stephens appointed admr. of Erwin Stephens, deceased.

Page 23 - Commissioners to lay off support for widow and family of Erwin Stephens, deceased.

Page 23 - Enoch D. Rushing guardian of Martha Little, Alsea Little, Rebecca C Little, Jemima D. and Amanda T. Little, minor heirs of William Little, deceased.

Page 24 - James Foster guardian of minor heirs of John Taylor, deceased.

1848 November Term

Page 24 - George Kimbro guardian of Samuel D. Coble, minor heir of Jacob
Coble, deceased.

Page 24 - James B. Reagor guardian of Martha Ann Cross, minor heir of James
M. Cross, deceased.

Page 24 - Asa York guardian of his minor son Terril York.

Page 24 - William Rucker guardian of Violet A. Kimmons and Margaret A.
Kimmons, minor heirs of Joel Kimmons, deceased.

Page 24 - John Eakin guardian of Mary Jane Strickler, Ann E. Strickler, and
Christiana Strickler, minor heirs of Benjamin Strickler, deceased.

Page 24 - William Potter admr. of George W. Whitesell, deceased.

Page 24 - James H. Graham exr. of estate of Lawson Harris, deceased.

Page 25 - E. D. Rushing failed to renew his guardianship of minor heirs of
William Little, deceased.

Page 25 - Jane Russell failed to renew guardianship of minor heirs of James
Russell, deceased.

Page 25 - Joseph R. McKinley failed to renew guardianship of minor heirs of
Joseph L. Word, deceased.

Page 25 - Daniel Stephens failed to renew guardianship of Henry Meadows.

1848 December Term

Page 27 - Robert Allison guardian of minor heirs of George W. Nash.

Page 27 - Hezekiah Bennett applied in Court that Robert C. Daniel be appointed guardian of minor heirs of William Bennett, deceased.

Page 27 - Edmund Word renewed guardianship of William and Mary Jane Hastings.

Page 28 - Paschal Brown guardian of Robert A. Brown.

Page 28 - Herbert Smith applied to Court that he be guardian of Sarah Elizabeth Smith, minor heir of Thomas Smith, deceased.

Page 28 - N. P. Modrell appointed guardian of Harriett, Levina, Charles,
Nelson and Elizabeth Harris, minor heirs of Alsey Harris, deceased.

Page 28 - William J. Hill guardian of James W. Hill and William C. Hill.

Page 28 - Amzi D. Anderson appointed guardian of Eliza Jane Gambill, a
lunatic.

1848 December Term

Page 28 - Robert M. Whitman admr. of estate of Daniel Whitman, deceased.

Page 29 - John F. Norman admr. of estate of Sarah Hubbard, deceased.

Page 29 - Numrod Burrow admr. of estate of Henry Webster, deceased.

Page 29 - Widow of John Trice, deceased, relinquished her right as admr. of her deceased husbands estate. Joseph Trice, Jr. appointed admr.

Page 29 - William K. Ransom admr. of estate of John Deason, deceased.

Page 29 - Richard Warner admr. of Will of Shadrack S. Brown, deceased.

Page 30 - Lewis Gant admr. of Sarah Gant, deceased.

Page 30 - B. W. Nowlin and J. W. Nowlin, exrs. of estate of Jabus Nowlin, deceased.

Page 30 - Barnet Stephens admr. of estate of Erwin Stephens, deceased.

Page 30 - Commissioners to lay off support for Elizabeth Trice, widow of John Trice, deceased, and her family.

Page 30 - Commissioners to lay off support for widow Mary Adcock and family.

Page 30 - Edward A. Moseley guardian of Sarah H., Ann and Amanda J. Martin, minor heirs of Henry C. Martin, deceased.

Page 30 - James Stallings, John Stephenson and Ransom Stevens, commissioners appointed to value the School Land in Sinking Creek, Range 3, Section 5.

Page 31 - Isaac Shook admr. of estate of Jonathan Shook, deceased.

Page 31 - Daniel Hooser admr. of estate of James H. Cobbs, deceased.

Page 31 - John Noblitt admr. of estate of Thomas Noblitt, deceased.

Page 31 - William Boone exr. of estate of M. A. Reagor, deceased.

Page 31 - Wiley Riggins admr. of estate of Archibald Caruthers, deceased.

Page 31 - Edward T. Haley surviving exr. of estate of James Haley, deceased.

Page 31 - Newcum Thompson, Jr. admr. of estate of William R. Looney, deceased.

Page 31 - John T. Neil guardian of Sarah Ray, minor heir of William R. Ray, deceased.

Page 31 - Robert Allison guardian of G. W. Nash's minor heirs.

1848 December Term

Page 31 - Samuel Doak guardian of Sarah Carter, minor heir of William
         Carter, deceased.

Page 32 - F. F. Fonville guardian of Sarah C. Parkes, minor heir of John B.
         Parkes, deceased.

Page 32 - Alfred Ransom guardian of Martha E. Cooper.

Page 32 - John Noblitt guardian of Nancy and John Noblitt, minor heirs of
         Thomas Noblitt, deceased.

Page 32 - Daniel Stephens guardian of Henry Meadows.

Page 32 - Sarah, Hannah, Ann and Amanda J. Martin, minor heirs of Henry C.
         Martin, deceased, made choice of James Mullins as their guardian.

Page 33 - The children of D. B. Shepperson are in suffering condition, the
         father having abandoned them and ceases to support his children.
         Court appointed Charles Phelps to take possession of the two
         children _____ and Rufus. Melchisadec Tribble to take one child,
         William Shepperson.

1849 January Term

Page 35 - Mary Whitesell appointed guardian of William and Mary S. Whitesell,
         minor children of George W. Whitesell, deceased.

Page 35 - Catharine Lee appointed guardian of Mary Lee and Peter Lee, minor
         children of Peter Lee, deceased.

Page 35 - Mary Purvis guardian of Josephine, Henry C., Archibald, Francis and
         Elizabeth Purvis, minor children of Tarlton J. Purvis, deceased.

Page 35 - Frederic F. Fonville guardian of Sarah Caroline Parks.

Page 36 - James C. Russell guardian of Robert B. and James K. Looney, minor
         heirs of William R. Looney, deceased.

Page 36 - Jackson Nichols guardian of Violet A. Kimmons.

Page 36 - William Carlisle guardian of Benjamin, James, William, John and
         Joseph Phillips.

Page 36 - On application of Isham H. Lane, that widow of John H. Lane,
         deceased, relinquishes her rights as admr. of her husband's
         estate. Isham H. Lane appointed admr.

Page 38 - Mrs. _____ Wright, a poor and aged woman, be allowed $10.00.

Page 38 - Benjamin Allen, a pauper, be allowed $20.00.

1849 January Term

Page 39 - Julius Terry be emancipated, January Term 1846, he was permitted to remain in Bedford County, Tennessee for 3 years. This is the County of his birth and that his wife and child, Mother and Brothers are living here, he wants to support his mother who is advanced in years. Feb 4, 1842. Court allowed him to stay in Bedford County 3 years. Also, a case of Dolly Terry who had also been emancipated at the same time Julius was on a like bond executed by her with Sarah Terry and William Word her securities. She was permitted to remain in Bedford County for 3 years.

Page 40 - Barclay M. Tilman applied for license to practive law.

Page 40 - Court says that a female child, daughter of D. B. Shepperson, of the age of 10 years, is living with Charles Phelps. Court ordered for the good of the child that she remain with Phelps. Also, that Elizabeth Margaret Shepperson be and hereby bound to Charles Phelps to learn the occupation of housewife until she arrives at age of 18 years.

Page 41 - Allen Wallis guardian of Pheribe L. Cathey, a minor heir of James Cathey, deceased.

Page 41 - Abram Terry, a free man of color who was at January Term 1846, emancipated and asked to remain in Bedford County.

Page 42 - Settlement with Richard Harris, guardian of the minor heirs of William B. Sutton, deceased.

Page 42 - Settlement with Sterling Newsom former guardian of minor heirs of Thomas Newsom, deceased.

Page 42 - Settlement with James Harris guardian of Ann Harris.

Page 42 - Settlement with Jacob W. Swift, admr. of estate of Henry Williams, deceased.

Page 42 - Settlement with R. P. Thogmorton, exr. of Robert Thogmorton, deceased.

Page 42 - Settlement with Jas. Foster, admr. of Hugh Allen, deceased.

Page 42 - Settlement with Richard H. Sims, admr. of Lewis A. Boyd, deceased.

Page 42 - Settlement with E. A. Moseley, guardian of Amanda H., Sarah H. A. Martin, minors of Henry C. Martin, deceased.

1849 February Term

Page 43 - Hiram Daniel, McKemsey Arnold and Jeremiah Hold(Holt), elected Commissioners for upper Thompson's Creek tract of School Land.

1849 February Term

Page 45 - Joseph Anderson appointed admr. of Jane Anderson, deceased. Robert Ray, John C. Wilson and Alexander B. Moore appointed to lay off support to two orphans of Jane Anderson, deceased.

Page 46 - Henry Dean appointed guardian of Mary Lipscomb, Henry Lipscomb, and Tapenus Lipscomb, minor heirs of _____ Lipscomb, deceased.

Page 46 - John P. Steele guardian of Priscilla Ann Wheeler.

Page 46 - William Webb guardian of his minor children. Benjamin F. Webb and J. M. Hix, securities.

Page 47 - Joseph Trice, Jr. admr. of estate of John Trice, deceased.

Page 47 - Willie Perry, James Mankin and W. T. Thomason appointed to lay off support to Emily Weaver, widow of A. Weaver, deceased.

Page 47 - William Little, E. D. Winsett and James Mankin appointed to lay off support to the widow and family of Richard C. Garrett, deceased.

Page 47 - Thomas Williams, John Powell and P. L. Shofner, commissioners of the upper Tract of School Land on Thompson's Creek.

Page 47 - Wilkins Blanton by his Attorney Edmund Cooper, in the case of Joseph Holt, exparte petition in relation to the lunacy of Elizabeth Kimbro. Commissioners found that she was capable, mentally at the time of the filing petition and that she does not need a guardian. Case dismissed.

Page 48 - Settlement with H. L. Davidson guardian of H. L. Brittain, a minor heir of William Brittain, deceased.

Page 48 - Settlement with A. B. Moon guardian of Thomas C. Allison, minor heir of Robert Allison, deceased.

Page 48 - Settlement with John Wilhoite guardian of John B. Wilhoite, a minor heir of William Wilhoite, deceased. Also, of Jacob Wilhoite a minor of William Wilhoite.

Page 48 - Settlement with John E. Scruggs guardian of William Waite, Mary A. Waite, Frances P. Waite, minor heirs of William Waite, deceased.

Page 48 - Settlement with Thomas B. Moseley guardian of Rebecca M. and Sarah A. Eddins, minor heirs of Lewis Eddins, deceased.

Page 48 - Settlement with John T. Neil guardian of John R. Ray, minor heir of William R. Ray, deceased.

Page 48 - Settlement with John T. Neil guardian of William, Eliza J., John A. Gant, minor heirs of John Gant, deceased.

1849 February Term

Page 48 - Settlement with Robert Allison guardian of minor heirs of George W. Nash.

Page 49 - Settlement with John McGuire guardian of Benjamin, William, and John McGuire, minor heirs of William and Mary McGuire, deceased.

Page 49 - Settlement with Herbert Smith guardian of William S. Stephens, minor heir of Willie Stephens, deceased. Also, guardian of Leander Stephens.

Page 49 - Settlement with B. F. Whitworth guardian of Tennessee F. Bell, Mary Ann Bell, minor heirs of Samuel A. Bell, deceased.

Page 49 - Settlement with B. F. Whitworth guardian of Thomas B. Whitworth, minor heir of Edward Whitworth, deceased. Also, guardian of McEwen H. Whitworth.

Page 49 - Settlement with John Claxton guardian of Mary Claxton.

Page 49 - Settlement with James J. Miller admr. of estate of Caswell High, deceased.

Page 49 - Settlement with John Hastings admr. of estate of John Sutton, deceased.

1849 March Term

Page 50 - Absalom Arnold guardian of William Coble, a lunatic, renewed his bond.

Page 50 - James Vannatta guardian of James R. Nash, minor heir of John Nash, deceased, renewed his bond.

Page 50 - John F. Norman admr. of estate of Sarah Hubbard, deceased.

Page 50 - Edmund Cooper, Esq., appointed admr. of estate of Joshua P. Scott, deceased. The father and mother relinquished their right to admr. upon the estate. Support for widow and family was laid off.

Page 51 - Matthew Shearin and Lewis Gaunt appointed admrs of estate of Thomas Shearin, deceased. Also, support was laid off to widow and family.

Page 51 - Sarah Shearin appointed guardian of Willie Frances and Edward M. Shearin, minor heirs of Thomas Shearin, deceased.

Page 51 - William Shearin guardian of Andrew J. and John W. Shearin, minor heirs of Thomas Shearin, deceased.

Page 51 - Thomas Shearin guardian of Newton C. and Hugh L. Shearin, minor heirs of Thomas Shearin, deceased.

1849 March Term

Page 52 - Elisha Bobo relinguished his right as admr. upon application of Robert H. Terry and he is hereby appointed admr. on estate of Franklin D. Bobo, deceased.

Page 52 - William K. Ransom admr. of estate of Mary Deason, deceased.

Page 52 - The widow of Thomas Primrose, deceased, relinguishes her right as admr. of the estate of Thomas Primrose, deceased, and that John G. Primrose was appointed admr. of the estate.

Page 53 - Alexander McLean, James Foster and Roland Landers and William S. Puckett laid off support to widow and family of Thomas Primrose, deceased.

Page 53 - John Nance, J. Cunningham and Thomas J. Gambill laid off support to widow and family of John Trice, deceased.

Page 53 - Martha Batten admr of estate of William G. Batten, deceased, brought list of inventory of sales.

Page 53 - James Foster, William Putman and Thomas Bullock laid off support to widow and family of John H. Lane, deceased.

Page 53 - Larkin Turman is a pauper and a fit subject for the poorhouse.

Page 54 - Settlement with John Eakin guardian of Sarah L. Pearson, minor of William Pearson, deceased.

Page 54 - Settlement with L. B. Knott guardian of Thomas and Henry Ledbetter, minor heirs of Willie Ledbetter, deceased.

Page 54 - Settlement with L. B. Knott guardian of Abner, Francis, Augustus, Grandison and Lafayette Nash, minor heirs of Travis C. Nash, deceased.

Page 55 - William Wood, James McCutcheon and John Larue laid off support to widow and family of Kimbro O. Chapman, deceased.

Page 55 - James G. Barksdale and his wife Mary Ann Barksdale, that they executed a Power of Attorney from them to John G. Berry, dated 6 March 1849. Berry is to act for them in regard to the estate of Isaac Holeman, Anna Holeman and John W. Holeman for the purpose therein contained, and Mary Ann Barksdale was also examined in open court apart from her husband and acknowledged she executed said Power of Attorney without knowledge of her husband.

Page 56 - Widow of John Sharp, deceased, relinguished her right as admr. of her deceased husband's estate. G. B. Sharp was appointed admr.

Page 56 - John Tillman, John E. Scruggs and Richard M. Stephens laid off support to widow and family of John Sharp, deceased.

1849 March Term

Page 56 - Isaac Shook clerk of the Board of School Land Commissioners of
        Flat Creek tract made report.

1849 April Term

Page 57 - John Lacy guardian of Rebecca Jane Reagor and Levi Reagor, minor
        heirs of A. W. Reagor, resigned and James B. Reagor was appointed
        guardian.

Page 60 - Alexander B. Moore, Robert Ray and John C. Wilson laid off support
        to minor children of Jane Anderson, deceased.

Page 61 - Isham H. Lane admr. of estate of John H. Lane, deceased, inventory
        list submitted.

Page 61 - Robert M. Whitman admr. of Daniel Whitman, deceased.

Page 64 - In September 25, 1848 in San Augustine County, Texas - Guardianship
        of Charles H. Robinson and James A. Robinson. Charles H. Robinson
        being over the age of 14 years and made choice of Richard O.
        Robinson as his guardian also James A. Robinson, minor heirs of
        Alexander Robinson, deceased.

Page 70 - John Fisher admr. of Rebecca Fisher, deceased.

Page 71 - Settlement of James T. Arnold, exr. of Nancy Arnold, deceased.

Page 71 - Settlement with Bartlett Bird admr. of Mary Bird, deceased.

Page 71 - Settlement with David J. Ozment guardian of Charles L. Batte.

Page 71 - Settlement with John Jakes guardian of Sarah P. Morrow.

Page 71 - Settlement with John Jakes guardian of Matty Jakes.

Page 71 - Settlement with Joseph Couch guardian of Rhoda F. Couch.

Page 71 - Settlement with Joseph Couch guardian of Isaac N. Couch.

Page 71 - Settlement with Joseph Couch guardian of Reubin W. Couch.

Page 71 - Settlement with Anderson Rucker guardian of B. F. Kimmons.

Page 71 - Settlement with P. C. Steele guardian of minor heirs of William
        Short, deceased.

Page 71 - Settlement with Smith Arnold guardian of minor heirs of William
        Mullins, deceased.

Page 71 - Settlement with Juliett M. Caruthers guardian of minor heirs of
        Archibald Caruthers, deceased.

1849 April Term

Page 72 - The widow of Lewis F. Thompson, deceased, relinquished her right
as admr. of his estate. Thomas Thompson was appointed admr.

Page 72 - Green T. Neeley, Hiram Harris and Benjamin Lentz laid off support
for widow and family of Lewis F. Thompson, deceased.

1849 May Term

Page 73 - Neely Coble guardian of Martha Catherine Coble.

Page 73 - John Fisher appointed guardian of his minor children, Sarah E.
and Michael Fisher.

Page 73 - William W. Miller guardian to Benjamin F. Bowers, Victoria Josephine
Bowers and Eliza Evans Bowers, minor children of Benjamin F. Bowers.

Page 73 - Widow of Michael F. Parsons, deceased, relinquished her right as
admr. of her husband's estate. Jacob M. Parsons appointed admr.

Page 73 - P. C. Steele, James W. Head and Thomas Wheeler laid off support
to the widow and family of Michael F. Parsons, deceased.

Page 74 - Widow of William Blackburn, deceased, relinquished her right as
admr. and James H. Locke appointed admr.

Page 74 - John T. Neil guardian of Mary R. Sharp and Margaret E. Sharp, minor
heirs of William Sharp, deceased.

Page 74 - Thomas B. Moseley, Sr., admr of his wife Rebecca Moseley, deceased.

Page 74 - Edward A. Moseley admr. of his deceased wife Betty M. Moseley's
estate.

Page 76 - Hiram Harris, Green T. Neeley and Benjamin Lentz laid off support
for widow of Lewis F. Thompson, deceased.

Page 77 - John Larue, James McCutchen and William Wood laid off support to
widow and family of Kimbro O. Chapman, deceased.

Page 77 - Ziza Moore and Anderson Landers, exrs. of George S. Landers' estate
brought in an inventory list.

Page 77 - Noah Smith, Jr. admr. of Noah Smith, Sr., deceased.

Page 78 - Power of Attorney executed by Nancy Landers, Moses Clark, Thomas
Landers, Elizabeth Damron, Mary Clark, Richard Landers, Jackson
Landers, James Damron and William C. Evans to John P. Steele.

Page 78 - Eliza F. Evans, wife of William C. Evans, is unable from bodily
infirmity to come into Court. John L. Cooper, Esq., is to take
the acknowledgement from her to a Power of Attorney of John P.
Steele, to attend to business in North Carolina.

11

1849 April Term

Page 78 - Sarah Shearin guardian of Willie Francis Shearin and Edward
         Shearin, resigned as their guardian. John F. Thompson was
         appointed guardian of the two, minor heirs of Thomas Shearin,
         deceased.

Page 78 - Joseph Holt admr. of estate of Elizabeth Kimbro, deceased.

Page 79 - Widow of Matthis Davis, deceased, relinguished her right to admr.
         his estate. James R. Terry appointed admr.

Page 80 - Robert H. Majors admr. of William P. Elkins, deceased. Widow
         Mary S. Elkins, and son David S. Elkins is an idiot or weak in
         mind. John Norvill, Samuel M. Gentry and Styers Marsh appoint-
         ed to lay off support for widow and family.

Page 80 - James C. Russell guardian of Robert B. and James K. Looney, minor
         heirs of William R. Looney, deceased, resigned.

Page 80 - Power of Attorney by Paschal Brown for himself and as guardian
         of Robert Brown, Jesse W. Brown for himself and as guardian for
         John F. Brown, H. L. Brown, Thomas Brown, Joel Whorley and
         Cynthia Whorley his wife to William Brown.

Page 81 - R. C. Daniel guardian of Hicks Bennett, minor heir and orphan of
         William Bennett, deceased, stated Hicks Bennett was about 12 years
         old to be bound as apprentice to William Goosby to learn occupation
         of a farmer.

Page 81 - Settlement with Willie B. Snell guardian of Jane and William Cross.

Page 81 - Settlement with Horatio Claggett guardian of J. W. C. Waters,
         minor heir of Zachariah Waters, deceased.

Page 81 - Settlement with William C. Blanton and John W. Tilford, admrs of
         David Tilford, deceased.

Page 82 - Jesse Phillips has been bound to present term of Court on charge of
         Bastardy. Case continued.

1849 June Term

Page 83 - Price C. Steele, Thomas Wheeler and James W. Head laid off support
         to widow and family of Michael F. Parsons, deceased.

Page 83 - Joseph Looney guardian of minor heir of William R. Looney, deceased,
         in place of James C. Russell former guardian.

Page 83 - Alexander B. Moon, Jackson Nichols and David W. Thompson laid off
         support for widow and family of William Blackburn, deceased.

Page 83 - Widow of William S. Wade, deceased, relinguished her right as admr.
         Newton C. Thompson appointed admr.

1849 June Term

Page 83 - Power of Attorney, 15 May 1849, executed by Thomas G. Bates and Jonathan C. Bates to James Powell.

Page 85 - Widow of Abram Myers, deceased, relinguished her right as admr. John R. Eakin appointed admr. A. M. Holt, John Q. Davidson and Jeremiah Cleveland laid of support.

Page 86 - Robert H. Terry admr. of estate of Franklin D. Bobo, deceased.

Page 86 - State of Tennessee vs Jesse Phillips, Charge of Bastardy, case squashed.

Page 86 - Settlement with Lovicey Covington guardian of minor heirs of Jesse Covington, deceased.

Page 86 - Settlement with George Davidson guardian of Jane R. and Mary B. Coldwell, minor heirs of N. E. Coldwell, deceased.

Page 86 - Settlement with Louisa M. Rankin guardian of James C., Amanda F., Nancy E., Eleanor J., and Ermina L. Rankin, minor heirs of Thomas C. Rankin, deceased.

Page 86 - Joseph R. McKinley, Jeremiah B. Boothe and Isaiah Webb laid off support for widow and family of Hugh McCrory, deceased.

Page 86 - Robert Matthews guardian of Harriett N. Clark, minor heir of Newton Clark, deceased.

Page 88 - Widow of John Lacy, deceased, relinguished her right as admr. James B. Reagor appointed admr.

Page 88 - Jury to inquire into the idiocy or lunacy of David S. Elkins. They found he was not capable to taking care of his property &c.

Page 88 - D. D. Hix, J. C. Hix and Thomas Word laid off support for widow and family of John Lacy, deceased.

1849 July Term

Page 89 - Elizabeth Anderson relinguished her right as admr. of her deceased husband, James Anderson. Jos. Anderson appointed admr.

Page 90 - Gabriel Shofner guardian of Mary M. Roane, Virginia Elizabeth and Albert Wesley Webster, minor heirs of Henry Webster, deceased. Newton K. Shofner and Hezekiah Shofner, securities.

Page 90 - Newton K. Shofner guardian of Julia Lydia, Eliza Jane, and Milly H. Webster, minors of Henry Webster, deceased. Nimrod Burrow and Gabriel Shofner, securities.

Page 90 - William D. Elkins guardian of David Elkins who is a lunatic. Securities, Mary S. Elkins and H. H. Elkins.

1849 July Term

Page 93 - G. W. Heard, Robert B. Maupin and Elijah Parker laid off support
to widow and family of Henry Webster, deceased.

Page 93 - William D. Elkins, Exr. of Will of William D. Elkins, deceased
vs James M. Elkins, Harrison H. Elkins and Benjamin F. Brown.

Page 97 - Settlement with Robert Matthews guardian of Harriet N. Clark,
minor heir of Newton Clark, deceased.

Page 97 - Settlement with John ONeal guardian for James K. ONeal, minor
heir of Willie ONeal, deceased.

Page 97 - Settlement with James B. Reagor guardian of Rebecca and Lewis S.
Reagor, minor heirs of A. W. Reagor, deceased.

Page 97 - Settlement with Milton A. Reagor guardian of Benjamin F., Sally A.,
Hampton P., Amanda, James B., Anthony W., and Rhoda M. Reagor,
minor heirs of A. W. Reagor, deceased.

Page 98 - O. H. Bigham guardian of minor heirs of Robert Bigham, deceased.

1849 August Term

Page 100 - Robert M. Whitman admr. of estate of Alfred Anthony, deceased.

Page 101 - Mary Jane Hopkins, widow of Eli Hopkins, deceased, relinguished
her right as admr. of said Eli Hopkins' estate. William W.
Hopkins, admr.

Page 102 - Orville Muse admr. of estate of Isaac Muse, deceased.

Page 103 - John J. Shriver admr. of Frances W. Daniel, deceased.

Page 103 - William W. Whitesell appeared in open Court to give information
of the lunacy or idiocy of Lewis Whitesell of Bedford County.

Page 103 - Old William Trollinger, a very aged and poor woman is in indigent
circumstances &c. Court allowed her $15.00.

Page 104 - A Deed executed by Charles L. Cannon to Thomas B. Cannon for the
undivided one half of 2214 acres in State of Texas, Nacogdoches
County.

Page 105 - Settlement with Magdalen Waite guardian of Sarah P. and Magdalen
B. Waite, minor heirs of Robert Waite, deceased.

Page 105 - Settlement with James L. Armstrong guardian of Amanda M. Bradford,
minor heir of John Bradford, deceased.

Page 105 - Settlement with James G. Neeley guardian of minor heirs of Joseph
McElwrath, deceased.

14

1849 August Term

Page 105 - Settlement with John S. Frazier guardian of William P. and
Jane T. Temple, minor heirs of Dempsey P. Temple, deceased.

Page 105 - Settlement with Joseph Trice guardian of Mary K. Gambill, minor
heir of Alfred H. Gambill, deceased.

Page 105 - Settlement with Robert Ray guardian of Permelia and John Tucker.

Page 105 - Settlement with Lemuel Broadway guardian of his own children.

Page 106 - Thomas A. Talbert admr of estate of Nancy Talbert, deceased.

1849 September Term

Page 107 - Daniel R. McAdams, late of Bedford County, is dead. Thomas
McAdams appointed admr.

Page 107 - William Raney admr. of estate of John Wray, deceased. William H.
Wisener, William Taylor and David Potiller witnesses.

Page 107 - Power of Attorney executed by Alexander Gill and Jane Leftwich
to Lucian B. Coggin.

Page 108 - William T. Tune guardian of Tempey B. Hickman and Margaret J.
Hickman, minor heirs of George W. Hickman, deceased.

Page 109 - Thomas Kimmons guardian of Barkley Kimmons and William Kimmons,
minor heirs of Edward Kimmons, deceased.

Page 109 - William W. Whitsell guardian of Lewis Whitsell.

Page 110 - John Rushing guardian of Parthenia Elizabeth, Sarah Ann, Talitha
Jane, and Mary Palestine Rushing, minor heirs of Asa Rushing,
deceased.

Page 110 - Sarah Deason, widow of John Deason, deceased, in the 5th District
be released from double tax.

Page 112 - P. C. Steele admr. of James Burns, deceased.

Page 112 - Joshua Hall admr. of estate of George W. Whitesell, deceased.

Page 113 - Settlement with Henry Dean guardian of minor heirs of William
Noblett, deceased.

Page 113 - Volney H. Steele guardian of Eliza Minerva and Mary Steele, minor
heirs of Wilson Steele, deceased.

Page 113 - Samuel McMahan guardian of Malinda McMahan, minor heir of John
McMahan, deceased.

15

1849 September Term

Page 113 - Settlement with Thomas Couch guardian of Susan J. Couch, minor heir of Isaac Couch, deceased.

Page 113 - Settlement with B. S. Hoover guardian of Jane R. Dillard, minor heir of Joel Dillard, deceased.

1849 October Term

Page 114 - William T. Myers guardian of Lorenzo, Elizabeth, Mary, Elvira, Frances, Thomas, and Andrew Myers, minor heirs of Abram Myers, deceased.

Page 114 - James B. Reagor guardian of Nancy E. Cross, resigned and James Cheshire appointed her guardian.

Page 115 - (From the affidavit of William Bearden, Sr.) that the widow of William Bearden, Jr., deceased, relinguished her right to admr. upon her husband;s estate. James C. Tribble appointed admr.

Page 116 - John J. Shriver admr. of estate of Nancy A. Cobb, deceased.

Page 116 - Claiborne W. Black guardian of minor children of George J. Black, deceased.

Page 117 - William Mallard guardian of minor grandchildren of Joseph A. Arnold, deceased, to wit, William Arnold, Felix Arnold, Lucy A. Arnold, and Harris Tomlinson, Nancy and Elvira Andrews.

Page 117 - The petition of Nelly, Nancy, Lewis, Jefferson, Jackson, Julia, Richard, Houston, Emiline, Salina, Harriett, Franky, Phil, and Sam for and on behalf of themselves and of Polly, for and on behalf of herself and her daughter Calfina who is under 15 years of age, and of Paulina for and on behalf of herself and her six children who are under 15 years of age, and of Polly for and on behalf of herself and her four children who are under 15 years of age, Angeline for and on behalf of herself and her three children who are under age of 15 years of age, and of Caroline for and on behalf of herself and her three children who are under 15 years of age, and of Charlotte and her two children who are under 15 years of age, showeth to your Worshipful that their late Master, Peter Singleton, to whom they owed perpetual servitude, previous to his death which transpired in 1839, entitled them to their freedom at the death of Sally Brooks Singleton, who died in March 1848.

Page 120 - Samuel Jones be allowed $20.00 for care of his idiot son.

Page 121 - Orphan girl named Rhoda Wise, age 9 years, was bound to Barnett Stephens until she arrives at age of 18 years.

Page 124 - Thomas Eakin guardian of Mary Jane, Eliza Ann, and Christiana Strickler, minor heirs of Benjamin Strickler, deceased.

16

1849 October Term

Page 124 - John Knott guardian for Eliza, Minerva, and Mary Steele.

Page 124 - John P. Steele, Esq. guardian of estate of Joseph Steele, deceased.

Page 124 - Settlement with John A. Moore guardian of Elizabeth Snelling, a lunatic and heir of Hugh Snelling, deceased.

Page 125 - An orphan boy by name of William R. Wise, age 13 years, was bound to William M. Evans, until age of 21 years, to learn farming.

1849 November Term

Page 127 - James H. Miles guardian of William T. and Henrietta Miles, minor heirs of John Miles, deceased.

Page 127 - Willie B. Snell admr. of Salome Cross, deceased.

Page 127 - Alfred Ransom brought a written statement of the widow of James H. Floyd, deceased, relinguishing her right to admr. on his estate. Alfred Ransom appointed admr.

Page 127 - James Mankin, Stephen Woodard and William Taylor laid off support to Martha L. Floyd.

Page 128 - Power of Attorney by G. P. Baskett to Henry W. Baskett.

Page 128 - Robert E. Haile guardian of Newton J., James S., William J., and Mary J. Haile, minor heirs of Samuel S. and Stephen E. Haile, deceased.

Page 128 - John T. Neil guardian of Mariah C. and Phillip D. Collins, minor heirs of Henry H. Collins, deceased.

Page 129 - Augustine Wilson and John C. Wilson, exrs. of estate of Nancy Wilson, deceased.

Page 129 - James H. Miles, John Stanfield, and John Evans laid off support for Nancy Bearden, widow of William Bearden, deceased.

Page 129 - John Hastings and Isham Reaves, exrs. of estate of Robert Morgan, deceased.

Page 130 - State of Tennessee vs Jesse Phillips. Charge against him for bastardy. Court overruled motion to squash the charge. Court ordered that Jesse Phillips is the father of a bastardy child begotten of the body of one Helen Freeman of which she was delivered on the 18th day of November 1848. He is to pay support.

1849 November Term

Page 131 - George Davidson, John T. Neil and William Galbreath laid off support for Elizabeth Brasfield, widow of Isaiah C. Brasfield, deceased.

Page 131 - Settlement with Price C. Steele and George W. Bell admr of Samuel Bell, deceased.

Page 131 - Settlement with Williamson Haggard admr of Samuel Haggard, deceased.

Page 131 - Isham H. Lane admr of John H. Lane, deceased, made settlement.

Page 131 - Settlement with Needham King admr. of David Pearson, deceased.

Page 131 - Settlement with Thomas Eakin guardian of Ann E. and Mary J. Strickler, minor heirs of Benjamin Strickler, deceased.

Page 131 - Settlement with Jordan Rucker guardian of Joseph E. Kimmons, minor heir of Joel Kimmons, deceased.

Page 131 - Absalom Reavis guardian of Mary Jane, Martha Ann and William J. Johnson, minor heirs of Samuel Johnson, deceased.

Page 131 - John Q. Davidson guardian of Mary L. and Lucy A. Campbell, minor heirs of William P. Campbell, deceased.

Page 131 - Samuel Doak guardian of Joseph A. Whitney.

1849 December Term

Page 132 - Benjamin Pollock, father of Lewis Pollock, deceased, relinquished his right as admr. of his son's estate. James H. Miles appointed admr. James W. Proby and John Evans, securities.

Page 132 - Jesse Phillips paid $250.00 to State of Tennessee. He is to support his child to keep it from becoming ward of the County.

Page 133 - James L. Woods guardian of Martha P. Muse, minor heir of George P. Muse, deceased.

Page 133 - Alfred Campbell admr. of George Reaves, deceased.

Page 133 - John Norvill, Charles F. Sutton and William McGrew laid off support for Martha Cunningham, widow of Richard Cunningham, deceased.

Page 134 - Settlement with David J. Norville admr. of estate of Elizabeth Norville, deceased.

Page 134 - Settlement with Augustine Wilson and Leonard Bullock, exrs of estate of William Ogilvie, deceased.

18

1849 December Term

Page 134 - Settlement with William Webb guardian of his minor children, Silas
          W., Sarah Jane, and Melissa T. Webb.

Page 134 - Settlement with Edmund Word guardian of William and Mary Jane
          Hastings, minor heirs of Willis Hastings, deceased.

Page 134 - Settlement with Hugh C. Hurst guardian of William L. and Mary
          Jane Brown, minor heirs of Thomas Brown, deceased.

Page 134 - Settlement with Samuel Knight guardian of Sophronia Knight.

Page 134 - Benjamin F. Whitworth guardian of Tennessee F. and Mary Ann Bell.

Page 135 - Widow of Edward H. Popejoy, deceased, relinquished her right to
          admr. to said estate. Daniel Stephens was appointed admr. John
          S. Davis, Benjamin Beachboard and William D. Clark laid off support
          to Elizabeth Popejoy, widow of Edward H. Popejoy, deceased.

1850 January Term

Page 136 - Edmund Cooper and Hugh L. Davidson admr of estate of Ervin J.
          Frierson, deceased. He left family and a widow.

Page 136 - Samuel Ewing admr. with Will annexed of Asa Fonville, deceased.

Page 137 - Elizabeth A. Martin, widow of Thomas J. Martin, deceased, relin-
          guished her right as admr. Absalom Power appointed admr. Alfred
          Ransom, William Taylor and Noah Putman laid off support for widow
          and family.

Page 137 - Robert B. Davidson guardian of William, Albert, Robert, John and
          Ervin Frierson, minor heirs of E. J. Frierson, deceased.

Page 137 - William Shaw guardian of Susanna Stammers, resigned. John
          Stammers appointed guardian.

Page 138 - Ephraim B. Jones admr. of estate of Zadoc Wood, deceased. Stephen
          Galleghy, security.

Page 143 - Settlement with Miles Phillips guardian of Edward Davis, minor
          heir of William Davis, deceased.

Page 143 - Settlement with Paschal Brown guardian of Robert A. Brown, minor
          heir of Jesse Brown, deceased.

Page 143 - Settlement with H. L. Davidson admr. of L. V. Brittain, deceased,
          also guardian of Hugh L. and Emily R. Brittaon, minor heirs of
          William Brittain, deceased.

Page 143 - James W. Pennington admr. of Benjamin F. Pennington, deceased.

1850 January Term

Page 143 - George Capley, deceased, widow relinguisged her right as admr.
Jacob Moulder appointed admr.

Page 145 - George W. Cunningham guardian of William Cortner, minor heir of
Levi Cortner, deceased.

Page 145 - Allis Cooper, widow of Peyton Cooper, deceased, relinguished her
right as admr. She wants her father Matthew Dixon as Admr. John
Rutledge and Hillard Dixon, his securities. Willie Perry, Thomas
Cheatham and E. P. Wynn laid off support for widow and family of
Peyton Cooper, deceased.

1850 February Term

Page 146 - Lucretia Eakin guardian of George M., Albert and Charles Eakin,
minor heirs of John Eakin, deceased, and William S. Eakin guardian of Julia A., eakin, Sarah J. Eakin, Alexander E. Eakin,
Thomas Eakin, and James Eakin, minor heirs of John Eakin, deceased.

Page 148 - William Woosley guardian of William and Elizabeth Hubbard.

Page 148 - John S. Brown guardian of Nancy Catherine Ray, a minor heir of
John Ray, deceased.

Page 148 - Richard H. Stem guardian of Cary H. and Stephen A. Garrett, minor
heirs of Stephen and Elizabeth Garrett, deceased.

Page 148 - James Mullins admr. of estate of Polly Miller, deceased.

Page 148 - John Jackson relinguished his right to admr. upon the estate of
John S. Jackson, his deceased son. Kimbrough T. Allison appointed
admr.

Page 149 - Robert Hurst, late a citizen of Bedford County, departed this life
on the 9th of December 1849. John H. ONeal appointed admr.

Page 149 - Joseph Morton and Jesse Brown, exrs. of Joshua Yates, deceased,
estate.

Page 149 - James H. Miles, John Gardner and John Evans laid off support for
Sarah C. Loyd, widow of John H. Loyd, deceased.

Page 150 - Power of Attorney executed by Richard H. Stem to Thomas S. Jenkins
in Granville County, North Carolina, dat 1 Feb 1850.

Page 150 - Settlement with Herbert Smith guardian of Leander and William S(L).
Stephens, minor heirs of Willie Stephens, deceased.

Page 150 - Settlement with William T. Tune guardian of Tempey B. and Margaret
J. Hickman, minor heirs of George W. Hickman, deceased.

1850 February Term

Page 151 - Settlement with James Harris guardian of Ann Harris, a lunatic.

1850 March Term

Page 151 - Thomas S. Mays admr of estate of Lewis G. Ray, deceased.

Page 153 - Widow of Robert McFarland, Sr., deceased, relinguished her right as admr. of her deceased husband's estate. Joseph Hastings appointed admr.

Page 153 - Elizabeth Musgraves, widow of Richard Musgraves, deceased, relinguished her right as admr. of her deceased husband's estate. Joel Stallings appointed admr. William K. Glenn, Michael Moore, and Thomas Smith laid off widow's support.

Page 154 - James P. Couch guardian of Thomas R., James C., Isaac A., and Christopher C. Couch, minor children of James Couch, deceased.

Page 154 - Elizabeth Thompson guardian of Sarah Jane, John, Benjamin, William, Elizabeth, Judah, and Lavenia Thompson, minor heirs of L. C. Thompson, deceased. John Thompson her security.

Page 154 - James W. McCrory guardian of minor heirs of Sarah Springer, deceased.

Page 155 - Jacob Moulder admr. of George Capley, deceased.

Page 155 - John W. Norvill be released from the bond of security David J. Norvill admr of Elizabeth Norvill, deceased.

Page 155 - Calvin Hunt, an orphan boy, age 17 years, was bound to Joseph B. Bomar until he arrives at the age of 21 years. He is to learn Schooling and Farming.

Page 156 - Settlement with William Woosley guardian of William and Elizabeth Hubbard, minor heirs of John Hubbard, deceased.

Page 156 - Settlement with Robert B. Davidson guardian of Peter and Mary Jane Proby, minor heirs of Thomas Proby, deceased.

Page 156 - Settlement with John McGuire guardian of minor heirs of William and Mary McGuire, deceased.

Page 156 - Settlement with John Wilhoite guardian of John B. and Jacob Wilhoite, minor heirs of William Wilhoite, deceased.

Page 156 - Settlement with Horatio Claggett guardian of Zachariah J. W. C. Waters, minor heir of Zachariah Waters, deceased.

Page 156 - Settlement with Asa York guardian of Terril York his minor heir.

1850 March Term

Page 157 - Francis V. Story admr. of Jane Story, deceased.

Page 157 - Edmund Cooper guardian of Susanna M. and Daniel W. Dollar.

1850 April Term

Page 179 - Thomas Holland, Jr. guardian of James M. Flint, minor heir of Thomas G. Flint, deceased.

Page 182 - James L. Heazlett guardian of James M. Flint, minor heir of Thomas G. Flint, deceased. Nathaniel Porter his security.

Page 182 - J. L. Couch guardian of Elizabeth C. Bearden, minor heir of John T. Bearden, deceased.

Page 184 - G. G. Osborne guardian of John S. Morrison, a minor.

Page 185 - Settlement with John Jakes guardian of Sarah P. Morrow.

Page 185 - Settlement with John Jakes guardian of Matty Jakes.

Page 185 - Settlement with Amzi D. Anderson guardian of Eliza Jane Gambill, a lunatic.

Page 185 - Settlement with Jacob Troxler guardian of William Troxler.

Page 185 - Settlement with Joseph P. Thompson guardian of his own minor children.

Page 185 - Lucy Hudlow admr. of estate of George W. Hudlow, deceased.

Page 186 - John P. Steele admr. of Mary Steele, deceased, and Joseph Steele, deceased.

Page 186 - Jordan Rucker admr. of estate of William Rucker, deceased. The widow had relinquished her right as admr. of said estate. Alfred Ransom, William Taylor and James Mankin laid off support for the widow and family.

Page 187 - John B. and Jacob Wilhoite vs John Wilhoite, guardian. Case to be continued.

Page 187 - William Galbreath and Nathan Ivey resigned as Trustees of a Deed of Trust made by Thomas Holland.

Page 187 - Peter Cortner guardian of Mary Catherine Cortner, his minor child.

Page 187 - John D. Gilmore, Joseph Smith and Jacob Siveley elected School Land Commissioners of the Wartrace Fork Tract for 1850. Elnathan Davis, security.

1850 April Term

Page 187 - William Kingree guardian of Nancy McLaughlin and Jos. L. Burgess, minor heirs of William Burgess, deceased. Rescinded next day of Court. Next day, Jordan C. Holt appointed guardian.

Page 188 - Settlement with John E. Scruggs guardian of Phill Dedmon's heirs.

Page 190 - Power of Attorney by Matthew Kirkland to Thomas Kirkland, Jr. of Chesterfield District of South Carolina.

1850 June Term

Page 190 - This day, June 3, 1850, satisfactory evidence was produced to the Court from the affidavit of John W. Brian, Margaret A. R. Brian, Nancy E. Brian and J. P. Brian, taken before Meredith Blanton, a Justice of the Peace for Bedford County, that Hezekiah Briant, late a citizen of Marshall County in the State of Tennessee and Soldier of the Revolutionary War had departed this life on the 30th day of January 1850 and that he left a widow whose name is Mary Bryant.

Page 190 - William T. Tune guardian of William Thomas and Clement Nance, minor heirs of Clement Nance, deceased.

Page 191 - Joseph Anderson admr. of William C. Ray, deceased. Meredith Blanton, security.

Page 191 - Robert Pate guardian of minor heirs of William Litle, deceased. Alfred Ransom and Robert Terry, securities.

Page 191 - Jasper N. Felps guardian of Jacob Anthony and Elizabeth Anthony, minor heirs of Alfred Anthony, deceased.

Page 191 - John Cortner guardian of Martha Cortner, his minor child.

Page 192 - William Word guardian of George W. Anthony, minor heir of Alfred Anthony, deceased.

Page 192 - Settlement with Lovicy Covington guardian of minor heirs of Jesse Covington, deceased.

Page 192 - Settlement with Alexander Ray guardian of Barbara and Rhoda Davis, minor heirs of William Davis, deceased.

Page 192 - Settlement with Lemuel Broadaway guardian of Rhoda Adelaide and Polly, his minor children.

Page 192 - Settlement with James A. Lentz admr of Malinda Lentz, deceased.

Page 192 - Settlement with James Mullins, admr. of Peter Miller, deceased.

23

1850 July Term

Page 195 - John Koonce guardian of minor heirs of Jesse Koonce, deceased.

Page 196 - Price C. Steele guardian of Ann C. Springer, minor heir of
Sarah Springer, deceased.

Page 196 - Benjamin F. Greer guardian of Lewis Whitesell, a lunatic (in the
place of William W. Whitesell).

Page 196 - John W. Mayfield admr. of estate of Thomas W. Smith, deceased.

Page 200 - Widow Morrison be allowed $30.00 for caring for a helpless child.

Page 200 - Widow of Jackson Rackley, an aged woman be allowed $15.00.

Page 200 - Mrs. Trolinger, a very aged and helpless woman be allowed $15.00.

Page 201 - Catherine Armstrong be allowed $20.00 for caring for an infant
child whose mother has abandoned it.

Page 203 - Hugh L. Davidson guardian of Martha Jane Sharp, a minor of William
Sharp, deceased.

Page 203 - John T. Neil guardian of Mary Ann and Margaret E. Sharp, minor
heirs of William Sharp, deceased.

Page 203 - John Bennett guardian of his minor children.

Page 203 - John B. and Jacob R. Wilhoite, minors, who petition by their next
friend, A. A. Robinson, supported by affidavit, and it appearing
to the Court that said minors reside in Marshall County and are
now without legal guardian in Bedford County. The former guardian John Wilhoite having been removed by order of the Court, and
A. A. Robinson appointed guardian.

Page 203 - Settlement with Price C. Steele admr. of estate of Hugh McCrory,
deceased.

Page 203 - Settlement with Henry Killingsworth admr. of estate of Joel Pitts,
deceased.

Page 203 - Settlement with William C. Work admr. of estate of Alexander W.
Williams, deceased.

Page 204 - Settlement with L. D. Stockton admr. of estate of John J. Noblitt,
deceased.

Page 204 - Settlement with William M. Shaw admr. of estate of James Haskins,
deceased.

Page 204 - Settlement with William Meadows exr. of estate of Elias Yates,
deceased.

1850 July Term

Page 204 – Settlement with William Hoover guardian of Joseph Loyd's minor heirs.

Page 204 – Settlement with Francis Jackson guardian of Abel Litle, deceased, minor heirs.

Page 204 – Settlement with Wilson Turrentine guardian of James Thompson, deceased, minor heirs.

Page 204 – Settlement with Samuel Phillips guardian of Sarah E. and Quarles T. Sutton, minor heirs.

Page 204 – Settlement with Stephen Freeman guardian of Jane C. Freeman's minor heirs.

Page 204 – Settlement with John Cortner guardian of John Ray, minor heir of Lewis G. Ray, deceased.

1850 August Term

Page 205 – Widow of John Wilhoite, deceased, relinquishes her right as admr. Jordan C. Holt was appointed admr.

Page 206 – Martha M. McCrory guardian of Rebecca Ann and Sarah Jane McCrory, her minor children and heirs of Hugh McCrory, deceased.

Page 206 – Richard Warner guardian of Richard B., Narcissa, John, and Huldah B. Wilhoite, minor heirs of John Wilhoite, deceased.

Page 206 – Edwin B. Hord admr. with Will annexed, of Edmund Hord, deceased. John Q. Davidson, Coleman F. Hord and William M. Hord, his securities. Also, William M. Hord admr. of estate of Mary Hord, deceased.

Page 207 – William Rone admr. of Unity Staggs, deceased. Jesse Davis, security.

Page 207 – Preston Frazier admr. of William Guy, deceased.

Page 207 – William C. Work admr. of his minor son Robert DePreist Work.

Page 207 – Hazardy Oliver and Thomas A. Oliver admr. of estate of Wright Oliver, deceased. Andrew Neill and John H. Larue, securities.

Page 208 – James Mankin admr. of estate of Thomas J. Martin, deceased.

Page 208 – Thomas C. Whiteside guardian of Margaret B. Sharp, minor heir of William Sharp, deceased.

Page 208 – H. L. Davidson guardian of Sarah A. Sharp, minor heir of William Sharp, deceased.

25

1850 August Term

Page 209 - Widow of Giles Lamb, deceased, relinguishes her right to admr. upon her deceased husband's estate. William Elmore appointed admr. Stephen Wood, James Mankin and Waddy S. Taylor laid off support for widow and family.

Page 209 - Rezin England of the 19th District be released from working on the road or pay a poll tax.

Page 210 (2nd page) - Augustine Wilson and J. C. Wilson exrs. of estate of Nancy Wilson, deceased.

Page 210 - Mrs. Margaret Muse of District No. 2, be released from double tax.

Page 211 - Allen Morris guardian of William H., Alexander D., Margaret Jane, Mary Matilda, Martha Virginia, and Eli James Hopkins, minor heirs of Eli H. Hopkins, deceased.

Page 211 - Robert S. Dwiggins guardian of William W. Lacy, minor heir of John Lacy, deceased.

Page 212 - Settlement with W. W. Caldwell admr. of estate of James B. Craig, deceased.

Page 212 - Settlement with Jacob M. Parsons admr. of estate of Michael F. Parsons, deceased.

Page 212 - Settlement with Jordan C. Holt guardian of Lafayette and Hiram Stephens, minor heirs of John Stephens, deceased.

Page 212 - L. B. Knott guardian of Thomas and Henry Ledbetter, minor heirs of Wiley Ledbetter, deceased.

1850 September Term

Page 213 - James W. McCrory guardian of minor heirs of Sarah Springer, deceased. The minors, Robert, John and Sarah.

Page 213 - Jonathan J. Cooper exr. of estate of Josiah Springer, deceased.

Page 214 - Sarah Permelia Tucker and John Tucker, minors who petition by their next friend Marinda Tucker. This day, Marinda Tucker, as the mother and next friend of Sarah Permelia Tucker and John Tucker presented her petition, desiring the guardianship for her children should be removed from the County of Bedford, to the County of Hickman. The children are at present residents of Hickman County, and they intend to reside there. Robert Ray was their Bedford County guardian.

Page 214 - D. B. Frierson guardian of Mary A. Frierson, a minor heir of E. J. Frierson, deceased.

Page 215 - Elizabeth Hubbard, widow of James M. Hubbard, deceased, relinguishes her rights as admr. Newton C. Thompson appointed admr.
Joseph Anderson, Charles L. Byrn and Jacob M. Parsons laid off
support for the widow.

Page 215 - William J. Barrett guardian of Duncan and Lewis Barrett, minor
heirs of John and Frances Barrett, deceased. Also on page 216,
George W. Cunningham guardian of Huldah Jane Cummings, a minor
heir of John and Frances Barrett, deceased.

Page 216 - Elizabeth Morgan guardian of her minor children.

Page 217 - William P. Temple guardian of Hannah M. Wilhoite, widow of John
Wilhoite, deceased, and a minor heir of Dempsey P. Temple,
deceased.

Page 217 - John Bomar guardian of Thomas S. Sharp, minor heir of William
Sharp, deceased. B. B. Bomar and Michael Dixon, securities.

Page 217 - Court to appoint Commissioners to settle the estate of John C.
McCuistion, deceased, with W. W. Coldwell as admr.

Page 218 - Settlement with William J. Hill guardian of minor heirs of
John D. Hill, deceased.

Page 218 - Settlement with John Knott guardian of minor heirs of Wilson
Steele, deceased.

Page 218 - Settlement with Elizabeth Morgan guardian of minor heirs of
Moses Morgan, deceased.

Page 218 - Settlement with Peter Cortner guardian of Mary C. Cortner, his
minor child.

Page 218 - Mariah E. Phillips guardian of Mary Catharine Hooser Phillips,
a minor orphan of B. L. Phillips, deceased.

Page 219 - Charles H. Pennington, Eliza Pennington and others - Exparte -
Petition for the sale of land. 60 acres. Benjamin J. Pennington
died intestate, seized of a tract of land in Bedford County on
waters of Little Sinking Creek adjoining Andrew Neill and others.
Benjamin J. Pennington had neither wife or children at the time
of his death and that the petitioners, Charles H. Pennington,
Hawkins Henden, Eliza Pennington, James W. Pennington, Mary
Pennington, and Narcissa Pennington are the only brothers and
sisters of the deceased.

Page 219 - Thomas Hensley guardian of Mary Mason, John T. Mason, and Clara
Jane Mason. Benjamin Merritt and Harris Hensley, securities.

1850 October Term

Page 220 - Jordan C. Holt admr. of estate of John T. Muse, deceased. The widow of the deceased relinguishes her right as admrix.

Page 220 - Coleman L. Randolph admr. of estate of William B. Randolph, deceased.

Page 221 - Preston Frazier guardian of John S. Frazier, minor heir of John S. Frazier, deceased.

Page 221 - Franklin P. McElwrath guardian of Joseph and David McElwrath, heirs of Joseph McElwrath, deceased. James Purvis, K. L. McElwrath and Thomas McAdams, securities.

Page 221 - G. B. Sharp guardian of Kattita Sharp, minor heir of William Sharp, deceased.

Page 221 - Louisa M. Rankin guardian of the minor heirs of Thomas C. Rankin, deceased. Jos. R. McKinley and James Hart, securities.

Page 222 - Nancy Parker, widow of Charles Parker, and Daniel Parker, a brother to Charles, guardian to Samuel Parker, James Parker, Nancy Parker, Amos Parker, Daniel Parker, William Parker, and Priscilla Parker, minor heirs of (blank) , deceased. NOTE: In 1850 Census, Charles Parker. Thomas L. Roberts, security.

Page 223 - Hugh C. Hurst admr. of estate of Roger Snell, deceased. Samuel Doak and Robert C. Jennings, securities.

Page 223 - Thomas B. Marks and wife Tennessee F. and Mary Ann Bell - Exparte - Petition for partition of land and division of slaves. Tennessee F. and Mary Ann are the owners of a tract of land, about 316 acres. Court ordered a division of the land and slaves between the petitioners.

Page 224 - Samuel Jones be allowed $20.00 for taking care of his idiot son.

Page 233 - Samuel Anderson, Thomas Gambill and William Collier appointed to lay off support to Rachael Muse, widow of John T. Muse, deceased.

Page 235 - James M. Neeley admr. of estate of Henry Bledsoe, deceased.

Page 235 - Absalom L. Landis admr. of estate of Leighton Ewell, deceased.

Page 235 - Robert Moffatt guardian of Mary R. Highland, minor.

Page 236 - Charles H. Pennington, Hawkins Hendon and others - Exparte - To sell land on waters of Little Sinking Creek. James W. Pennington bid on tract and purchased same.

Page 238 - Settlement with Isaac Shook admr. of estate of Jonathan Shook, deceased.

28

1850 October Term

Page 238 - Settlement with Price C. Steele and John A. Webb admrs. of estate
of Bushrod Webb, deceased.

Page 238 - Settlement with George Kimbro guardian of Samuel D. Coble, minor
heir of Jacob Coble, deceased.

Page 238 - Settlement with Edmund Word guardian of William and Mary Jane
Hastings, minor heirs of Willis Hastings, deceased.

Page 238 - Settlement with David Wagster guardian of Mary B. Thogmorton,
minor heir of Robert and Mary Thogmorton, deceased.

Page 238 - Settlement with Garrett Phillips exr. of estate of Matthew Phillips,
deceased.

Page 238 - Settlement with William W. Coldwell admr. of estate of John C.
McCuistion, deceased.

Page 238 - Settlement with Elijah Parker admr. of estate of Charles H.
Parker, deceased.

Page 238 - Settlement with Joseph Couch guardian of Isaac N. and Reuben W.
Couch, minor heirs of Isaach Couch, deceased.

Page 238 - Settlement with Thomas Kimmons guardian of Barkley and William P.
Kimmons, minor heirs of Edward Kimmons, deceased.

Page 238 - Settlement with N. P. Modrell guardian of minor heirs of Alsea
Harris, Sr., deceased.

1850 November Term

Page 240 - The widow of Thomas Culverhouse, deceased, relinguished her right
as admr. John L. Cooper was appointed admr. Edward Tarpley,
Thomas D. Tarpley and John E. Haskins laid off support for the
widow and family.

Page 241 - William K. Ransom guardian of Edmund, Kinnard, John, and Lucy
Deason, minor heirs of John Deason, deceased.

Page 241 - James W. Wallace guardian of Samuel M. and Mary M. Harper, minors
of William Harper, deceased.

Page 242 - G. G. Osborne admr. of estate of Stephen Garrett, deceased. Jeremiah Cleveland, Kinchen Stokes and Edward Smith laid off support
to Susan Garrett and family, widow of Stephen Garrett, deceased.

Page 244 - William Galbreath, Esq. admr. of Will of Square Thompson, a free
man of color, asking Court to emancipate Patsey his wife. Court
agreed.

Page 245 - Andrew Neill and wife Ann, Thomas W. Harper and others. Exparte - Petition to sell land. Thomas W. Harper and Benjamin B. Harper, states that Samuel Harper, late of Bedford County, departed this life in said county, intestate, and they were appointed admrs. of his estate. At the time of Samuel Harper's death, he owned a negro woman Nicy and her child. Samuel Harper left 11 children.

Page 246 - Thomas B. Marks and wife Tennessee F. and Mary Ann Bell by her guardian Benjamin F. Whitworth - To sell land and slaves. Mary Ann Bell to get slaves and Thomas B. Marks and his wife Tennessee Frances, formerly Tennessee Frances Bell gets Lot No. 2 and slaves. (Plot of land on page 248).

Page 249 - Leah Mason, widow, and Mary E., John T., and Clara Jane Mason, only children and heirs of John F. Mason, deceased. Exparte - Petition to sell land, Warrant No. 62229, dated 26 June 1849. To Leah Mason and heirs of John F. Mason, deceased, who was late a Private in Captain Gaither's Company, 3rd Regiment, United States Dragoons. Thomas Hensley appointed guardian of Mary E., John T., and Clara Jane Mason, the minors. 160 acres of land to be sold.

Page 250 - James Russ, Sr., guardian of Mary E. Johnson, a minor heir of James M. Johnson, deceased.

Page 250 - Jordan C. Holt admr. of John T. Muse, deceased. Exparte - Petition to sell slaves to pay his debts.

Page 250 - Eliza Jane Frazer and John S. Frazer, Jr. Exparte - Petition for Dower. Eliza Jane Frazer is entitled to the dower lands of John S. Frazer, deceased.

Page 251 - James B. Reagor admr. of John Lacy, deceased. John Lacy died in Bedford County, intestate, and was owner of slaves.

Page 252 - Settlement with Richard Warner admr. woth Will annexed of Shadrack L. Brown, deceased.

Page 252 - Settlement with Martha Batten admr. of William G. Batten, deceased.

Page 252 - Settlement with Barnet Stevens (Stephens) admr. of Ervin Stephens, deceased.

Page 252 - Settlement with John Rushing guardian of minor heirs of Asa Rushing, deceased.

Page 252 - Settlement with Cyrus N. Allen guardian of Martha F. Russell, minor heir of William M. Russell, deceased.

Page 252 - Benjamin Reynolds, one of the minor heirs at law of estate of James and Sally Reynolds, deceased, by his guardian William M.

1850 November Term

Page 252 - (continued) Wolf, who reside in Izzard County, Arkansas, for an
order upon Alfred Campbell the admr. upon the estate of Jane
Reynolds, deceased, late of Bedford County, to pay to said
guardian such monies as belongs to Benjamin Reynolds.
Upon application of William, Thomas, and Andrew Reynolds, Rachel,
Hugh, and Charlotte Reynolds, minor heirs at law of James and
Sally Reynolds, deceased. Benjamin G. Adams appointed their
regular guardian and reside in Izzard County, Arkansas. James
and Sally Reynolds, deceased, who was one of the heirs of Jane
Reynolds, deceased.

Page 254 - William G. Nivens made the following Declaration: He declares
by oath that he was born in the County of Antrim in the Kingdom
of Great Britain and Ireland on the 1st day of April in the year
1827, that he now owes Allegiance to her Majesty, Victoria, Queen
of the United Kingdom of Great Britain and Ireland, that he emig-
rated from Ireland to the United States in the year 1844, that he
has been residing in the United States, and within the State of
Tennessee since sometime in the year 1844, and that is now and
always been since he has resided therein as aforesaid bonafide
his intention to become a citizen of the said United States, and
to renounce forever all allegiance and fidelity to any foreign,
Prince, Potentate, State or Sovereignty whatever and particularly
to renounce forever all allegiance and fidelity to her said
Majesty the Queen of Great Britain and Ireland.
                                    Signed: W. G. Nivens

1850 December Term

Page 254 - Demarcus D. Hix admr. of estate of William Heazlett, deceased.

Page 255 - William Bearden admr. of estate of Mary Fuller, deceased.

Page 255 - William J. Hill guardian of minor heirs of John D. Hill, deceased.

Page 255 - Paschal Brown guardian of Robert A. Brown. Renewed guardianship.

Page 255 - George W. Heard guardian of James K., Lucy E., Mary M., Martha M.,
Richard S., Susan C., M---ha A., Thomas, Sarah A., and Phillip
Elkins, minor heirs of Anna Elkins, deceased.

Page 255 - Robert Allison guardian of Jane Nash's heirs.

Page 256 - Jeremiah Culverhouse guardian of Elizabeth and Jane Culverhouse,
minor heirs of Jesse Culverhouse, deceased.

Page 256 - Joshua Coleman guardian of Rilley(or Billey), Arguile, Lawson H.
L.W., and Sarah C. Bearden, minor heirs of John T. Bearden, deceased.

Page 256 - William D. Clark guardian of Mary C., Sarah J., and John R. Muse,
minor heirs of Richard Muse, deceased.

1850 December Term

Page 257 - Coleman L. Randolph admr. of estate of William B. Randolph, deceased. James H. Curtiss, Miles Phillips and John T. Medearis laid off support for Eliza Randolph, widow of William B. Randolph, deceased.

Page 258 - Edward Smith and Kinchen Stokes laid off support to Susan Garrett, widow of Stephen Garrett, deceased.

Page 258 - Andrew Neill and wife Ann, John M. Gibson and wife Martha, Miles Phillips and wife Mary, James D. Neill and wife Sarah, Thomas J. Bartley and wife Elizabeth, Thomas W. Harper, Benjamin B. Harper, John M. Harper, Andrew N. Harper, William England, John England, Jr., Elizabeth England, and Jane England, the four last being minors sue by their next friend Thomas W. Harper, and Samuel M. Harper and Mary M. Harper, minors who sue by their guardian James W. Wallace. Exparte - Petition for sale of land. Benjamin B. Harper bid on lands and purchased same.

Page 260 - Eliza Jane Frazer and John S. Frazer, Jr. Exparte - Petition for Dower. Eliza Jane Frazer, widow of John S. Frazer, deceased. (Plat on page 261)

Page 262 - N. P. Modrell guardian of minor heirs of Alsea Harris, deceased.

Page 262 - Settlement with Lewis Gant admr. of Mary Gant, deceased.

Page 262 - Settlement with James M. Neeley admr. of estate of Henry Bledsoe, deceased.

Page 262 - Settlement with Matthew Dixon admr. of estate of Peyton Cooper, deceased.

Page 264 - Nancy Culverhouse vs Jeremiah Culverhouse, Moses, Thomas, Barham Lamb and wife Lucy, William Primrose and wife Elizabeth, Jane Culverhouse, Elizabeth Culverhouse, and John L. Cooper, admr. of Thomas Culverhouse, deceased. Decree for Dower. Jane and Elizabeth Culverhouse are children of Jesse Culverhouse, deceased, who has no guardian.

Page 265 - Edm'd Cooper, admr. of estate of Frances Yancey, deceased. He is also guardian of Jane and Rebecca Yancey, minor children of Kavanaugh Yancey.

Page 265 - William H. Wisener appointed admr. of estate of Lucy G. Bradford, deceased.

1851 January Term

Page 266 - Power of Attorney executed by Asa York to John G. York of Franklin County, State of Georgia.

1851 January Term

Page 267 - Jesse Clanton, a blind man, be allowed $20.00.

Page 267 - Polly Sharp be allowed $15.00 for support of her affected son.

Page 268 - Samuel Hill be allowed $5.00 for making a coffin for Miss Hensley, an indigent woman.

Page 268 - James Mullins guardian of Amanda J. J. and Sarah H. A. Martin.

Page 268 - James W. Neely guardian of Frances, Amos, John, and D---son Blecher, minor heirs of Henry Blecher, deceased.

Page 269 - Thomas H. Coldwell, Esq., admr. with Will annexed, of Moses H. Kinney, deceased.

Page 269 - William Campbell admr. of estate of James Reynolds, deceased.

Page 270 - Power of Attorney by Sarah Moppin (Maupin) to John Jimerson (Jameson). Witness: D. P. T. House and Gabriel Maupin.

Page 270 - Lousina Pounds exrix of estate of John Pounds, deceased.

Page 270 - William Tailor, A. Ransom and Noah Putman laid off support of widow and family of Thomas J. Martin, deceased.

Page 271 - James M. Elliott and wife, John P. Dromgoole and wife Mary T. and Clement C. Ashburn. (James M. Elliott's wife is E. S.). Exparte - Petition for division of slaves. Petitioners are entitled each to one third of the (4) slaves.

Page 272 - Nancy Culverhouse vs Jeremiah Culverhouse and others, heirs &c. of Thomas Culverhouse, deceased. Dower. (Plat on page 272).

Page 273 - Power of Attorney by William M. Gogin to William L. Gogin of Bedford County, Virginia, dated 6 Jan 1851.

Page 273 - Joel Stallings admr. of Richard Musgrave, deceased. Richard Musgrave died intestate and being owner of a slave. Court ordered slave to be sold.

Page 273 - Daniel L. Barringer in behalf of Samuel Jones, a free man of color, residing in Bedford County, desires to remain with his wife in Bedford County. Page 275 - Permission granted.

Page 275 - Robert Denniston guardian of Martena S. Denniston, a minor heir of Robert Denniston, deceased.

Page 275 - George W. Buchanan guardian of John N. McAdams, minor heir of Dan C. McAdams, deceased.

Page 276 - John and Permelia Tucker, minors who petition by their guardian Miranda Tucker. Land to be sold, dated 7 Jan 1851.

33

1851 January Term

Page 277 - Andrew Neill and wife Ann, Thomas W. Harper and others. Exparte -
Petition to sale land and slaves. Thomas W. Harper, Benjamin B.
Harper and others, appointed admrs. of Samuel Harper, deceased,
late of Bedford County. Samuel Harper left a large number of heirs.

Page 277 - George W. King and Nicholas Burns et als. Exparte - Petition to
sell land. George W. King and wife Lovina, Nicholas Burns, Jesse
Chockley and wife Charlotte, John Blagg and wife Judey, are the
children and heirs at law of William Staggs, deceased. C & M to
examine the land &c. Also examine Nicholas Burns to the interest
of Isaac Rone and Eliza Jane his wife and Ezekiel Burns and
Lucinda his wife. Nathaniel White and Thomas Dryden, witnesses.
There are six heirs for land to be equally divided. They stated
that William Staggs died in Bedford County on the head waters of
Sugar Creek.

Page 279 - Settlement with Thomas Warren exr. of estate of John Warren,
deceased.

Page 279 - Settlement with Edmund Cooper as agent of Joshua Hall, admr. of
the estate of George W. Whitesell, deceased.

Page 279 - Settlement with Presley Jones admr. of estate of Richard C.
Garrett, deceased.

Page 279 - Settlement with John W. White admr. of estate of Bluford Davidson,
deceased.

Page 279 - Settlement with John F. Norman admr. of Sarah Hubbard, deceased's
estate.

Page 279 - Settlement with William Taylor exr. of estate of Caleb Cox,
deceased.

Page 279 - Settlement with Isham Reaves and John Hastings exrs. of estate of
Robert Morgan, deceased.

Page 279 - Settlement with Samuel C. Evans guardian of minor heirs of Thomas
Robinson, deceased.

Page 279 - Settlement with John Stammer guardian of Susanna Stammer.

Page 279 - Settlement with Neeley Coble guardian of Martha C. Coble.

Page 279 - Settlement with James L. Wood guardian of Martha P. Muse, minor
heir of George P. Muse, deceased.

Page 279 - Settlement with Nimrod Burrow guardian of Martin W. Webster.

Page 279 - Settlement with Gabriel Shofner guardian of Mary M. and Virginia
Webster, minor heirs of Henry Webster, deceased.

1851 January Term

Page 279 - Settlement with Newton K. Shofner guardian of Julia L., Eliza Jane, and Milley H. Webster, minor heirs of Henry Webster, deceased.

Page 279 - Settlement with John P. Steele guardian of Priscilla Ann Wheeler.

Page 280 - Airy E. Kincaid appointed guardian of her minor children, heirs of Joseph Kincaid, deceased.

Page 280 - James H. Miles guardian of minor heirs of Stephen B. Johnson, deceased.

Page 281 - Settlement with M. A. Rogers guardian of minor heirs of A. W. Rogers, deceased.

Page 281 - James M. Elliott and wife, John P. Dromgoole and wife, and Clement Ashburn. Petition for division of slaves (4). Mary Dobson guardian of her minor son Clement C. Ashburn.

1851 February

Page 283 - Price C. Steele admr. of estate of Robert F. Springer, deceased.

Page 283 - William G. Height admr. of estate of Elvira Harrison, deceased.

1851 February Term

Page 285 - L. B. Knott guardian of Henry S. Ledbetter.

Page 285 - William J. Peacock guardian of Thomas E. Peacock, Virginia G. Peacock, and Mary E. Peacock, his minor children.

Page 285 - John Jakes guardian of Sarah P. Frizzell formerly Sarah P. Morrow.

Page 288 - James M. Elliott and wife Justine E. L. Elliott, John P. Dromgoole and wife Mary T. Dromgoole, and Clement C. Ashburne. Decree to sell slaves. James M. Elliott bid and purchased some of the slaves. James R. Terry, agent for Mary Dobson, bid for negro Salley and became purchaser. Mary T. Dromgoole formerly Mary T. Ashburne and Justine E. L. Elliott formerly Justine E. L. Ashburne.

Page 290 - Nicholas P. Burns, George W. King and wife, Jesse Chockley and wife, John Blagg and wife Judah. Petition to sell land. Land in Bedford County on headwaters of Sugar Creek, a south branch of Duck River. Court ordered that George W. King and wife Lovina formerly Lovina Staggs, John Blagg and wife Judah formerly Judah Staggs, John Baker and wife Mary formerly Mary Staggs, be invested unto Nicholas P. Burns.

1851 February Term

Page 292 - Settlement with William Mallard guardian of minor grandchildren of Joseph Arnold, deceased.

Page 292 - Settlement with William Jenkins and Martin Euless exrs. of estate of Adam Euless, deceased.

Page 292 - Settlement with W. B. Nowlin and J. W. Nowlin exrs. of estate of John Nowlin, deceased.

Page 293 - James B. Reagor, admr. of John Lacy, deceased. Exparte - Petition to sell slaves.

Page 294 - John and Permelia Tucker, minor heirs &c. Exparte - Petition to sell land. C & M to sell land.

Page 294 - W. W. Miller guardian of Mary S. Bowers, William P. Bowers, and Henry C. Bowers, minor children of Benjamin Bowers, deceased.

Page 295 - William Kingree appointed guardian of Nancy McLaughlin and Joseph L. Burgess at May Term 1850. Court, for reasons, having resended as guardian.

Page 295 - Jordan C. Holt resigned as admr. of estate of Carlton Davidson, deceased. The estate having been settled.

Page 295 - Joseph M. Larue who had been charged of having begotten a bastard child of the body of Catharine Campbell, a single woman, and had been bound over to the present Term of this Court, came into Court and entered bond &c.

1851 March Term

Page 297 - William Burns guardian of John H., Robert L., Thomas K., and James P. Burns, minor heirs of Thomas P. Burns, deceased.

Page 298 - Deed executed by L. D. Winsett and Sarah Jane Winsett his wife, and E. B. Kelley was produced. The affidavit of Sarah Jane Winsett stated she alone executed the said Deed.

Page 298 - Power of Attorney executed by Asa York to John G. York of Franklin County, Georgia, dated 3 March 1851.

Page 298 - Power of Attorney executed by Robinson H. Lynch to John I. Harris of Brunswick County, Virginia, dated 3 March 1851.

Page 298 - Jeffery Goodrich Clarke, a free man of color, petitioned to remain in the State. He having been emancipated by the County Court of Lincoln County where he had resided for 16 years before he moved to this county, where he resided for the last 18 months. Granted.

1851 March Term

Page 299 - Woodly Dickerson, a free man of color, petition to remain in this State. He was emancipated by this County. Granted.

Page 299 - George Porter, a free man of color, petition to remain in this State. Continued to next Court.

Page 300 - Settlement with Thomas B. Moseley, Jr., guardian of Sarah Ann Edins, deceased.

Page 300 - Settlement with Edward Cooper admr. of William S. Watkins, deceased.

Page 300 - Settlement with William S. Eakin guardian of Julia A., Sarah J., Alexander E., James H., and Thomas L. Eakin, minor heirs of John Eakin, deceased.

Page 300 - Settlement with Lucretia Eakin guardian of Albert , Charles, and George N. Eakin, minor heirs of John Eakin, deceased.

Page 300 - Settlement with Joseph Anderson admr of estate of Jane Anderson, deceased.

1851 April Term

Page 302 - Thomas Shearin guardian of Newton C. and Hugh L. W. Shearin, minor heirs of Thomas Shearin, deceased.

Page 302 - William Shearin guardian of John W. Shearin.

Page 302 - John Claxton guardian of Mary E. Claxton. James Claxton and James Gregory, securities.

Page 305 - David M. Kaar (Kerr) appointed admr. of William Kaar, deceased, after widow of said Kaar's estate. George Huffman, Moses Ayers, and Middleton Holland laid off support to Jane Kaar, widow of William Kaar, deceased.

Page 305 - George W. Heard admr. of estate of John S. Hight, deceased. George Cortner, Alexander Kimbro and Lodwick Holt laid off support to widow and family of John S. Hight, deceased.

Page 305 - Price C. Steele admr. of estate of Thomas G. Watkins, deceased.

Page 305 - John S. Thompson guardian of Sarah J. Brown.

Page 306 - Thomas B. Jeffries, Alexander B. Moore and Calentine F. Lentz laid off support to Priscilla Jackson, widow of Avery Jackson, deceased.

Page 308 - J. A. Reed be allowed $5.00 for making a coffin for Jackson Gentry, deceased.

1851 April Term

Page 309 - James R. Terry admr. of estate of Matthias Davis, deceased.

Page 309 - Samuel C. Evans guardian of Thomas J. Robertson and John W. Robertson, minor heirs of Thomas Robertson, deceased. Appointment of admr. was made in Court in Lawrence County, Tennessee 1st March 1851, for the purpose of removing his guardianship from this county to that county where the guardian and his wards all reside.

Page 309 - Settlement with Price C. Steele guardian of minor heirs of William Short, deceased.

Page 310 - Settlement with George Kimbro guardian of Samuel D. Coble.

Page 310 - Settlement with Amzi D. Anderson guardian of Eliza J. Gambill.

Page 310 - Settlement with A. J. Greer and Catharine R. Greer Exrs. of estate of Thomas Greer, deceased.

Page 310 - Orphan boy, James R. Nix, age 13 years, was bound at Paton (Peyton) H. Coats to learn farming.

Page 311 - C. B. King, John McQuiddy and James S. Newton laid off support to widow and family of Franklin Holland, deceased.

Page 311 - Jason Winsett guardian of Newton A. and David G. Winsett.
1851 May Term
Page 314 - Augustine Rowland and Elizabeth C. Rowland guardian of James M. and Martha E. Watkins, minor heirs of Thomas G. Watkins, deceased.

Page 314 - John and William Beaty, minors, petitioning by their guardian Sherwood W. Beaty. Bushrod Webb died intestate some years ago in Bedford County and that John A. Webb and Price C. Steele appointed admrs. and that they have settled the administration with the Clerk of County Court. Petitioners John and William Beaty as two of the children of Sherwood W. Beaty and Sarah Beaty who was a daughter of Bushrod Webb, deceased, and they reside in Murry County, Georgia.

Page 316 - Settlement with John P. Steele admr. of estate of Mary Steele, deceased.

1851 June Term

Page 317 - Hugh L. Davidson guardian of Sarah A., William H., James B., and Robert T. Lane, minor heirs of Robert Lane, deceased.

Page 317 - Mariah Bigger and James R. Bigger admrs. of estate of James Bigger, deceased.

Page 317 - Orville Hensley guardian of Sarah Ann Hensley, a minor heir of Asa Hensley, deceased.

1851 June Term

Page 318 - Thomas Coffey admr. of John Dawdy, deceased. Howel M. Dawdy and
James Davis, securities.

Page 319 - Jordan C. Holt admr. of John Wilhoite, deceased, and others,
distributees of said John Wilhoite. Exparte - The (16) slaves
belonging to the estate of John Wilhoite, deceased. Distributees:
To Stegall and wife, 1/5; to Richard M. Wilhoite, Narcissa
Wilhoite and Huldah Wilhoite the other 4/5 jointly.

Page 320 - Price C. Steele admr. of Thomas G. Watkins with Will annexed.
John H. Watkins, William Wood and wife Mary S. Wood, Martha E.
Watkins and James M. Watkins, minors, by guardian Augustine
Rowland and Elizabeth C. Rowland. Petition for division of
slaves.

Page 321 - William P. Bowers and others by their guardian, W. W. Miller.
Report. To sell land.

Page 322 - Settlement with E. W. Dunaway and Matthew T. Cunningham, exrs. of
estate of John Dunaway, deceased.

Page 322 - Settlement with F. F. Fonville guardian of Sarah Caroline Parkes.

Page 323 - James R. Terry admr. of estate of Isaac Patterson, deceased. John
Shofner, John Chandler and James Mullins laid off support to
widow and family.

Page 324 - William D. Elkins guardian of David S. Elkins, a lunatic and
heir of William P. Elkins, deceased.

1851 July Term

Page 325 - William Houston appointed guardian of Harriet N. Clark, minor heir
of Newton Clark, deceased.

Page 325 - Annice L. Fisher and Eli H. Stephens admrs. of estate of John
Fisher, deceased. Alfred Mallard and Price C. Steele and Grayson
H. Stewart laid off support to the widow and family.

Page 325 - Ordered by the Court that John Evans be attached to the Flat
Creek Township, and hereafter his children be numbered therein.

Page 326 - James C. Gambill and Thomas J. Gambill admrs of estate of Aaron
Gambill, deceased. James Stallings, Samuel Anderson and Samuel
Doak, securities.

Page 326 - David W. Anglin guardian of Martha Jane Anglin, minor heir of
John C. Anglin.

Page 327 - Thomas Coffey admr. of estate of Mary Dawdy, deceased.

1851 July Term

Page 327 - Thomas Coffey admr. of estate of John Dawdy, deceased.

Page 327 - That since the death of Peter R. Proby, a suit was threatened by
John Hufman against the heirs of Peter Proby, and one of said
heirs, namely, James W. Proby. James W. Proby compromised said
claim with Hufman and agreed to pay and did pay him $100.00 for
and on behalf of himself and his co-heirs. All Co-heirs have
refunded James W. Proby. Their respective shares of said compromise money, except Mary Jane Proby and Peter Proby, who are
minors and have for their guardian Robert B. Davidson.

Page 334 - John T. Neil admr. of estate of Lewis Shappard, deceased.

Page 334 - Robert T. Searcy guardian of Lewis James Searcy, his minor child.

Page 335 - Eli H. Stephens and Annice Fisher, admrs. &c, John Fisher, deceased.
Exparte - Petition to sell slaves. John Fisher departed this life
intestate on the __ day of June 1851 in Bedford County. He died
seized of slaves. Eli H. Stephens was appointed to sell slaves.

Page 335 - James C. and Thomas J. Gambill, admrs. of Aaron Gambill, deceased.
Exparte - Petition to sell slaves. Aaron Gambill departed this
life intestate on the __ day of June 1851 in Bedford County. He
died seized of slaves. He left 11 distributees. Court ordered
slaves to be sold.

Page 337 - Price C. Steele, Alfred Mallard and Grayson H. Stewart laid off
support to widow and family of John Fisher, deceased.

Page 337 - James B. Bigger admr. of estate of James Bigger, deceased.

1851 August Term

Page 338 - E. P. Winn, J. R. Haskins, Wilie Perry and Richard Bandy laid off
support to widow and family.

Page 338 - Amos Hays admr. of estate of Stephen Stancell, deceased. William
Word, security.

Page 338 - W. W. Reese admr. of estate of D. J. Leathers, deceased. Nicholas
Burns, security. Thomas Conwell, George Castleman and David
Rozar laid off support to widow and family.

Page 339 - Joseph H. Looney guardian of Robert B. and James K. Looney, minor
heirs of William R. Looney, deceased. William Word and John S.
Brown, securities.

Page 339 - E. A. Covington guardian of Richard and Mary Jane Anderson, minor
heirs of James Anderson, deceased. James H. Locke and John W.
Allison, securities.

1851 August Term

Page 340 - John Stammers guardian of Robertson Bigger, Mary Bigger, Davis A.
         Bigger, Joseph T. Bigger and William J. Bigger, minor heirs of
         James Bigger, deceased.

Page 340 - John Stammers guardian of Mary Jane Stammers, his minor child.

Page 341 - Settlement with Edmund Cooper guardian of Susanna M. and
         Daniel W. Dollar, minor heirs of John Dollar, deceased.

Page 341 - Settlement with Edmund Cooper guardian of Jane and Rebecca Yancey,
         minor heirs of Kavanaugh Yancey, deceased.

Page 341 - Settlement with John Barrett guardian of Huldah J. Cummings,
         formerly Huldah J. Barrett.

Page 341 - Power of Attorney executed by Adam and Sarah Anthony to Daniel A.
         Montgomery in Alamance County, North Carolina.

Page 342 - William P. Bowers and others, minors by guardian W. W. Miller.
         Commissioners Report. Petition to sell land. On 19 July 1851,
         sold land to Harrison H. Elkins. Lands in the estate of William
         P. Elkins, deceased.

Page 343 - William G. Cowan admr. of Briant W. Nowlin, deceased. Alexander
         Eakin, security.

Page 344 - Widow of Richard Muse, deceased, relinguished her right to admr.
         upon estate. James L. Armstrong appointed admr.

Page 344 - Robert Allison and others. Exparte - Petition to sell slaves
         and land. Report. Estate is the late residence of Elizabeth
         Allison.

1851 September Term

Page 346 - Abram Reagor guardian of Hampton P. and Amanda Reagor, minor
         heirs of A. W. Reagor, deceased.

Page 346 - Lemuel Broadaway guardian of Rhoda M., minor heir of A. W.
         Reagor, deceased.

Page 347 - Newton C. Thompson guardian of James H. Hubbard and Malvina
         Hubbard.

Page 347 - Martha A. Stephens guardian of Michael B. Fisher, a minor heir
         of John Fisher, deceased.

Page 347 - Randolph Newsom guardian of Thomas, Martha, Nancy J., and Mary
         Newsom, minor children of Green B. Newsom, deceased. William J.
         Barrett and Edward Newsom, securities.

1851 September Term

Page 347 - R. S. Thomas admr. of estate of Lydia Boaz, deceased.

Page 347 - Edmund Cooper admr. of estate of John W. Hamlin, deceased. John
T. Neil, William Galbreath and Thomas Lipscomb laid off support
for widow and family.

Page 348 - Matthew Moss admr. of estate of Matthew Moss, Sr., deceased.
George Cortner, George Hufman and George W. Heard laid off support
to widow and family.

Page 348 - John T. Medearis admr. of estate of John Medearis, Sr., deceased.

Page 350 - A Deed, executed by William Boone and Margaret Boone his wife to
Milton A. Reagor for 690 acres of land in Washington County,
Arkansas, was produced and Margaret Boone being examined apart
from her husband and she axknowledged the execution of the Deed.

Page 350 - Power of Attorney executed by John T. Medearis to John P. Duval
of Tallahassee, Florida.

Page 350 - Sarah E. Eddins and Lewis James Searcy. Petition to sell slave.

Page 351 - James R. Bigger and others. Exparte - Petition to sell slaves.
James R. Bigger, John Bigger, John Stammer and wife Lettitia
Stammer formerly Lettitia Bigger, William H. Adams and wife Jane
Adams formerly Jane Bigger, William Bigger, Joseph Bigger, Davis
Bigger, Mary Bigger, Roberson Bigger, and Mary Jane Stammer, the
last six are minors and petitioners by their guardian John
Stammer, and Mariah Bigger widow of James Bigger, deceased, are
all and the only distributees of the said James Bigger who
departed this life in the month of April 1851. James Bigger died
seized of slaves. Mariah Bigger and James R. Bigger admrs. of
estate of James Bigger, deceased. The slaves are to be divided
between the petitioners.

Page 352 - James C. and Thomas J. Gambill, admrs., to sell slaves of Aaron
Gambill, deceased. Purchasers were N. C. Gambill and Newcum
Thompson.

Page 353 - E. H. Stephens and Annis Fisher, admrs. &C. Petition to sell
slaves of John Fisher, deceased. Sold to: C. W. Black, Alex.
Wood, William J. Whitthorne, M. B. Hamilton, H. Harris, sr., and
M. B. Fisher.

Page 354 - Robert Allison and John W. Allison and others. Petition to sell
land and slaves. Land sold to Sarah Allison.

Page 357 - N. C. Thompson and others. Petition to sell land. Land of
James M. Hubbard, deceased. Elizabeth, James H. and Malvina
Hubbard have interest in the land in Bedford County. Land sold
to Newton C. Thompson.

1851 October Term

Page 360 - James R. Bigger and others. Division of slaves to heirs.

Page 361 - Randolph Newsom guardian of Henry W., Margaret P., Eliza F., and George R. Newsom, his minor children. William J. Barrett and Edward Newsom, securities.

Page 363 - Power of Attorney executed by Sterling Abbott of Bedford County to _____ _____ of Dallas County, Texas.

Page 363 - John Reed admr. of estate of James Reed, deceased.

Page 363 - Benjamin Merritt admr. of estate of Mary McClure, deceased. James Haile and William T. Tune, securities.

Page 363 - Joseph N. Card admr. of estate of Allen S. Musgroves, deceased. Martin Sims, Fielding Bell and Joseph Click laid off support to widow and family.

Page 363 - Robert C. Daniel guardian of minor heirs of William Bennett, deceased.

Page 364 - Mrs. _____ Morrison be allowed $30.00 for taking care of her idiot child.

Page 364 - Levi Underwood and his wife be allowed $20.00 to support them.

Page 365 - Sarah A. Eddins and Lewis James Searcy. Exparte - Petition to sell slave. Sold to Samuel Davidson.

Page 365 - Samuel Ewing admr. of Asa Fonville, deceased.

Page 366 - Power of Attorney executed by Thomas Bullock to Haywood Oakley.

Page 366 - Power of Attorney executed by Eliza Oakley Bullock to Haywood Oakley.

Page 368 - Settlement with James Vannatta guardian of James R. Nash, minor.

Page 368 - Settlement with Joseph Holt admr. of Elizabeth Kimbro, deceased.

Page 368 - Power of Attorney executed by Robert Moffatt to John B. Parker of the District of Spring Garden and County of Philadelphia in Pennsylvania.

Page 368 - Levi Shook guardian of Sarah C. Parker for the removal of the guardianship from this county and State to the State of Missouri, Lawrence County, where Sarah C. Parker now resides.

Page 370 - John H. Floyd guardian of John W., William H., and James A. Floyd, minor heirs of James H. Floyd, deceased. James Mankin and Alfred Ransom, securities.

Page 370 - Julia Ann Holland guardian of Mary Jane, Martha Ann, Moses A., Matilda C., Mitchel B., and William A. Holland, minor heirs of Franklin Holland, deceased. Moses Ayers, security.

Page 370 - James Cheshire guardian of Nancy Elizabeth Cross, renewal.

Page 371 - James L. Armstrong admr. of estate of Richard Muse, deceased. G. G. Osborne, W. D. Clark, and John S. Davis laid off support for Margaret Muse, the widow, and her family.

Page 371 - James H. Graham elected Justice of the Peace of 7th District of Bedford County to fill the vacancy of John W. Hamlin, who has died.

Page 372 - Benjamin K. Coble to replace Richard J. Williams as guardian of Neely Coble, a minor heir of Jacob Coble, deceased. Alexander Kimbro and Gabriel Maupin, securities.

Page 372 - Robert Buchanan guardian of William A. and Sarah L. Campbell, minor heirs of L. D. Campbell, deceased.

Page 372 - Robert E. Haile guardian of Newton J., James S., and Mary J. Haile, minor heirs of Samuel S. and Stephen E. Haile, deceased. Meshack Haile and James H. Elmore, securities.

Page 373 - Augustine Rowland, who at May Term was in connection with Elizabeth C. Rowland, guardian of James M. and Martha E. Watkins, minor heirs of Thomas G. Watkins, deceased.

Page 373 - William Bearden admr. of estate of Mary Fuller, deceased.

Page 374 - William M. Cross by his next friend Young W. Allen. Petition to remove guardianship. William M. Cross, minor who now resides in Carroll County, Tennessee and that Young G. Allen be appointed guardian of William M. Cross. Guardianship of Wilie B. Snell to be replaced by Young W. Allen.

Page 374 - Alfred Ransom and others. James H. Floyd departed this life, intestate, some years ago, being seized of considerable real and personal estate, and leaving Martha L. Floyd his widow and John M., William H., and James R. Floyd his only heirs at law and that Alfred Ransom was appointed admr. He also had slaves, which will have to be sold. Martha L. Floyd had not received her Dower.

Page 376 - A Deed of Conveyance executed by James W. Oakley, Elsby Oakley and William Y. Oakley to Edward Jones for 164 acres of land in Granville County, North Carolina, was produced in Court.

1851 November Term

Page 377 - John T. Neil guardian of Mariah Caroline Collins and Phillip D. Collins, minor heirs of Henry H. Collins, deceased.

1851 December Term

Page 378 - Benjamin Moseley admr. of estate of Jonathan Moseley, deceased.

Page 378 - Robert H. Barnes guardian of Granville S., Edward T., Daniel W., and Lucy J. M. Barnes, minor children of Daniel and Susanna Barnes.

Page 379 - Allen Kimbro guardian of Thomas L. Kimbro, his minor son.

Page 379 - Washington P. Goodwin guardian of William Evans and Harrel Evans, minor heirs of George Evans, deceased.

Page 379 - Hiram Ede guardian of Patience P. _____, Jane L. Ede, France M. V. J. M. Ede, Moses P., Elizabeth Ede, and Candis J. Ede and Nancy Edde.

Page 380 - James L. Armstrong admr. of Richard Muse, deceased. Exparte - Petition to sell slaves. Richard Muse departed this life at the time mentioned in petition, in Bedford County. He left 6 distributees. He was the owner of 3 slaves. Slaves to be sold.

Page 380 - Margaret Muse. Exparte - Petition for Dower. Margaret Muse, widow of Richard Muse, deceased. Her Dower tract had not been laid off to her. Heirs are Richard Muse now of age, John R. Muse and Sarah J. Muse being minors, with no guardian, Joseph C. Muse, Mary C. Sumner and her husband Dr. George B. Sumner, Narcissa A. Coffey and her husband Wiley D. Coffey, and Dr. James L. Armstrong is the admr. of Richard Muse, deceased.

Page 381 - Abraham F. Smith, George Smith and Martha Frances Smith &c. Exparte - Petition to divide slaves. John E. Smith departed this life many years ago, leaving petitioners, Abraham F. Smith, George Smith and Martha F. Smith, his only heirs at law. Abraham F. Smith has arrived at the age of 21 years and that George Smith will soon arrive at the same age.

Page 382 - Richard Warner, admr. with Will annexed, of Shadrack Brown, deceased. Exparte - Petition to sell slaves. Sell on 24 Nov 1851.

Page 384 - Robert B. Davidson admr. of estate of James B. Laine, deceased.

Page 385 - Alfred Ransom and Martha L. Floyd and others. Petition for Dower. Plat in page 385.

Page 386 - John P. Steele guardian of Joshua Edde, minor heir of Hiram Edde.

1952 January Term

Page 388 - Mary Sharp be allowed $35.00 for supporting her afflected son.

Page 388 - Mrs. _____ Morrison allowed $30.00 for careing for her idiot daughter.

Page 388 - John Dean, Sr. and wife, very aged and poor people, be allowed $20.00 support.

Page 388 - R. H. Farrar be allowed $10.00 for 2 coffins, one for Jacob Noblett and one for Samuel Price, who has no means to pay for them.

Page 392 - Stephen Hart guardian of Elizabeth V. Beaty, minor heir of John Beaty, deceased.

Page 393 - George W. Brown guardian of Frances M. Wynn, minor heir of Francis M. Winn, deceased.

Page 393 - Robert Allison resigned as guardian of minor heirs of Jane Nash, deceased. Jane M. Nash guardian of William T. Nash, her minor son.

Page 393 - Harry M. Oneal guardian of Amanda Batten, minor heir of William G. Batten, deceased.

Page 393 - William A. Loyd guardian of William T. Miles and Henrietta Miles.

Page 393 - Jos. P. Thompson admr. of estate of Elizabeth Allison, deceased.

Page 394 - Samuel H. Card admr. of estate of William H. Card, deceased.

Page 394 - Robert Dixon admr. of estate of Clement C. Dixon, deceased.

Page 396 - Joseph Click, Fielding Bell and Martin Sims laid off support to Elizabeth Card, widow of William H. Card.

Page 396 - Fielding Bell, Joseph Click and Martin Sims laid off support to widow and family of A. S. Musgrove, deceased.

Page 397 - Margaret Muse vs Jos. H. Muse and others. Petition for Dower. Margaret Muse is widow of Richard Muse, deceased. Plat on page 398.

Page 399 - James A. Heazlett and others. Exparte - Petition to sell land. Clerk and Master to report.

Page 399 - Jane A. Nash, William Nash and others. Petition to divide slaves.

Page 400 - Elizabeth Myers, Lorenzo S. Myers et als. Abram Myers departed this life intestate some years ago, leaving his widow and William T. Myers and the petitioners his only heirs at law, and being owner of large number of slaves. Widow and his eldest son, W. T.

46

Page 400 - (continued) Myers have already received their portion of the same. Elizabeth and Lorenzo S. have already arrived at age of 21 years and desire their share of slaves.

Page 402 - Joel Stallings guardian of William E., James R., and Nancy _?_. Musgrave, minor heirs of Richard Musgrave, deceased.

Page 402 - Elizabeth Moss. Petition for Dower. Elizabeth Moss, widow of Matthew Moss, deceased. Alexander Kimbro and George Cortner appointed commissioners to allot and set off to said Elizabeth her dower of 1/3 in value &c. of land for her late husband Matthew Moss, in Bedford County.

Page 402 - Samuel D. Morgan and Susan F. Morgan, Granville Barnes, Edward Barnes, Daniel W. Barnes, and Lucy Jane Barnes, the two first by their guardian William Morgan and the four last by their guardian Robert Barnes. Petition to divide slaves.

Page 403 - Madison L. Burrow admr. Petition to sell slaves. Slaves of Ephraim Burrow, deceased. Ephraim Burrow leaves his widow Eve Burrow. Eve Burrow has recently departed this life.

Page 404 - Susanna Hutson. Petition for Dower. Susanna Hutson, widow of Cutty B. Hutson, deceased. All the heirs are over the age of 21 years, namely, William M. Hutson, Thomas Hutson, James T. Williams and his wife Mary C. Williams formerly Mary C. Hutson, did on 22 Dec 1851 acknowledge that Susanna Hutson would have her dower assigned to her. Cutty B. Hutson died intestate and no admr. That William M. Stephens, Sarah Stephens, Pleasant A. Stephens and Jefferson G. Stephens are heirs at law of Cutty B. Hutson and in right of their mother Elizabeth Stephens and they have no guardian and are all minors. Charles T. Philpot and James C. Tribble are to lay off dower.

Page 405 - William M. Hutson and others, heirs at law of Cutty B. Hutson, deceased. Request land to be sold. Cutty B. Hutson left 3 children and one dead child.

Page 405 - The Heirs of Thomas Newsom. Petition to sell land. Petition of John Pearson and wife Jane Pearson formerly Jane Newsom, Tarlton Newsom, James Newsom, Virginia Newsom, and Nancy Caroline Newsom, the last four of whom petition by their guardian Randolph Newsom. Thomas Newsom departed this life intestate leaving the petitioners, his only children and heirs at law, widow Mary Newsom has a dower.

Page 408 - Randolph Newsom admr. and Mary Newsom admrx. and Randolph Newsom guardian &c. Petition for division of slaves. John Pearson and wife Jane Pearson to be allotted their share.

Page 409 - James L. Armstrong admr. of Richard Muse, deceased. Petition to sell slaves.

1852 January Term

Page 409 - Deed executed 25 Oct 1851, by Samuel L. Davidson to Samuel B. McCuistion, for one half of a league of land situated in Anderson County, Texas. Land of 900 acres of land situate upon Pine Island Bayou in Liberty County, Texas.

1852 February Term

Page 412 - James C. Gambill admr. of estate of Aaron Gambill, deceased.

Page 413 - John W. Rucker admr. of estate of Elliott P. Rucker, deceased.

Page 413 - Benjamin F. Greer admr. of Charles R. Moore, deceased.

Page 413 - Richard H. Stem guardian of Stephen A. Garrett, minor heir of Stephen and Elizabeth Garrett.

Page 413 - Henry Brown guardian of Martha Elizabeth Mae Peak, minor heir of Franky Mae Peak formerly Franky Thorn, now deceased.

Page 414 - Power of Attorney executed by James Thorn, Theophilus Williams and his wife Leah Williams, and Joseph Pickle and his wife Emaline Pickle to Henry Brown.

Page 414 - James Edde and others vs Hiram Edde and others. Petition to sell land.

Page 415 - Settlement with Samuel McMahan guardian of Malinda McMahan.

Page 415 - Settlement with James L. Heazlett guardian of James M. Flint.

Page 415 - Settlement with James L. Woods guardian of Martha P. Muse.

Page 415 - Settlement with John Rushing guardian of Mary Palestine Rushing.

Page 415 - Settlement with H. L. Davidson guardian of H. L. and Emily R. Brittain.

Page 415 - Settlement with James Foster guardian of minor heirs of John Taylor, deceased.

Page 415 - Susannah Hutson vs William M. Hutson and others. Dower. Plat on page 415.

Page 416 - James L. Armstrong admr. of Richard Muse, deceased. Petition to sell slaves.

Page 418 - Jane Nash and others. Exparte - Petition to divide slaves. Slaves to go to Jane Nash, to Newton B. Parsons and wife Louiza, and to William T. Nash.

1852 February Term

Page 419 - Widow and heirs of Thomas Newsom. Petition to divide slaves.
To set apart to John Pearson and Jane formerly Jane Newsom.

Page 420 - James Edde and others vs Hiram Edde, Moses Edde and others.
Petition to sell land.

1852 March Term

Page 421 - Widow of George W. Wadley, deceased, relinguished her right to
admr. upon the estate. Jennings Moore appointed admr. Alexander
B. Moon, William A. Shaw and William Collins laid off support to
widow and family.

Page 421 - Henrietta W. Miles guardian of Amy Johnson, James M. Johnson, and
Cynthia Ann Johnson, minor heirs of Stephen Johnson, deceased.

Page 422 - Abram F. Smith, George Smith, and Martha Smith. Petition to
divide slaves. Slaves of John E. Smith, deceased.

Page 423 - Madison L. Burrow. Exparte - Slaves to be divided among heirs
of estate of Ephraim Burrow, deceased. Slaves sold.

Page 424 - Samuel D. Morgan and others. Exparte - Division of slaves.

Page 425 - William M. Hutson, Thomas Hutson and others. Exparte - To sell
land.

Page 427 - John Pearson and wife Jane Pearson, Tarlton Newsom, James Newsom,
Virginia Newsom, and Nancy Catharine Newsom, the last four of
whom are minors by their guardian Randolph Newsom. Exparte -
Petition to sell land.

Page 429 - James A. Heazlett and others. Exparte - Petition &c. To sell
land of William Heazlett, deceased. Several tracts.

Page 432 - Power of Attorney, dated 11 Sept 1851, executed by Andrew Burns
to Elliott Ivins. James S. Ervin and Solomon Womack, securities.

Page 434 - Joel Bromfield vs James Cheshire and others. To amend his Bill.

Page 434 - Wilie B. Snell guardian of William M. Cross, states that the
guardian is now removed to another guardian in Carroll County,
Tennessee.

1852 April Term

Page 435 - Orphan girl by the name of Minerva Stone was bound to Solomon
Stone to learn housewifry until she is 18 years old.

Page 458 - James B. Reagor admr. of estate of Joshua R. Hix, deceased.

1852 April Term

Page 458 - Alexander B. Moon guardian of Granville Wadley and Mary Jane Wadley, minor heirs of George W. Wadley, deceased.

Page 459 - Frederick Batt guardian of Sarah E. Batt formerly Sarah E. Wadley, a minor heir of George W. Wadley, deceased.

Page 459 - John H. Oneal guardian of Mary Ann and Amanda America McCuistion, minor heirs of John C. McCuistion, deceased.

Page 459 - Jason T. Brittain, J. M. Parsons and Valentine Lentz laid off support to Martha Thompson, widow of Calvin Thompson, deceased.

Page 459 - H. F. Holt, B. F. Wiggins and William Barrett laid off support to widow of Joshua R. Hix, deceased.

Page 460 - Joseph Loyd and others. Exparte - Petition to sell land.

Page 460 - Daniel Hooser exr. of Mary Elkins, deceased.

Page 461 - O. H. Mobley be allowed $5.00 for coffin for Henderson Adcock, deceased, a pauper.

Page 462 - Willis Jackson be allowed $5.00 for making coffin for Jefferson Lamb, deceased.

Page 464 - Joseph Loyd and others. Petition to sell land &c.

Page 465 - A. L. Landis admr. of Maxwell Ewell, deceased, Thomas Ewell, deceased, and Anna Elkins, deceased.

Page 465 - Settlement with Louisa M. Rankin guardian of her minor children, heirs of Thomas C. Rankin, deceased.

Page 465 - Settlement with George W. Cunningham guardian of William Cortner, minor heir of Levi Cortner, deceased.

1852 May Term

Page 467 - Elizabeth Card, widow of William H. Card, deceased, petitioned for her dower.

Page 468 - Leander Hickerson resigned as guardian of Catharine and Allen Coble, minor heirs of Jacob Coble, deceased. Benjamin K. Coble appointed guardian.

Page 468 - Charity Denson, widow of William Denson, deceased, admrix. of the estate with David G. Denson.

Page 469 - Susan Newsom and her son George W. H. Newsom petitioned the Court to bind the said G. W. H. Newsom to James M. Johnson until he arrives at the age of 21 years, to learn husbandry.

1852 May Term

Page 469 - Peter Cortner guardian of his minor daughter Mary Catharine Cortner.

Page 469 - Alexander Ray guardian of the minor heirs of William Davis, deceased.

Page 469 - E. A. Moseley, one of the exrs. of Rachel Martin, deceased.

Page 470 - Samuel Phillips admr. of Wilson Coats, deceased. Petition to sell slaves. Wilson Coats departed this life intestate in Bedford County of which he was a citizen, in June or July 1822 and that the (blank) Term 1822 of the Court of Pleas and Quarter Sessions, Petitioner was duly appointed admr. of the estate of the said deceased and qualified. In the estate, the four slaves were to be divided between the widow and other distributees of said deceased. Court said there were eight distributees to share the slaves. Court ordered the slaves to be sold.

Page 470 - James Ede and others vs Hiram Ede and others. To sell land.

Page 472 - Settlement with M. P. Modrel guardian of Alsey Harris.

Page 472 - Power of Attorney, 4th May 1852, executed A. H. Dashiell and his wife Ann Dashiell to R. Radgeley, Esq. of Baltimore, Maryland.

1852 June Term

Page 473 - James H. C. Scales admr of estate of Noah Scales, deceased.

Page 473 - Robert B. Maupin admr. of estate of Sarah Maupin, deceased. James S. and Gabriel Maupin, securities.

Page 473 - James S. Maupin admr. of estate of Jane B. Maupin, deceased. Robert B. and Gabriel Maupin, securities.

Page 474 - Samuel Doak, George W. Cunningham and George W. Greer laid off support to the family of Noah Scales, deceased.

Page 474 - James F. Shearin admr. of estate of William Hammill, deceased. Thomas S. Shearin and Lewis Gant, securities.

Page 474 - Jonas Sutton admr. of estate of Hugh Gault, deceased. Isaac Williams, security.

Page 474 - Benjamin Lentz guardian of Elliott Bussey and Michael Bussey, minor heirs of Daniel Bussey, deceased.

Page 474 - John Cortner guardian of his minor child, Martha Cortner.

Page 474 - Stephen Freeman guardian of John R., Lewis A., Bailey P., and Martha Jane Freeman, his minor children.

1852 June Term

Page 474 - George W. Greer guardian of minor heirs of Noah Scales, deceased.

Page 475 - John Cortner guardian of John A. Ray, minor heir of Willis Ray, deceased.

Page 475 - G. W. Black guardian of minor children of George J. Black, deceased.

Page 476 - Commissioners appointed to sell lands mentioned in the petition of John Pearson and wife Jane Pearson and the minor heirs of Thomas Newsom, deceased. Land sold to Alfred Campbell, 64 acres.

Page 477 - Robert B. Maupin admr. of Sarah Maupin, deceased. Petition to sell slave who belongs to the estate of Sarah Maupin, deceased.

Page 477 - Power of Attorney, 15 May 1852, executed by Rebecca Williams to John A. Williams in Isle of Wight County, Virginia.

Page 478 - Elizabeth Moss and others. Petition for dower. Land in 25th District of Bedford County, 35 acres. (Plat on page 478)

Page 479 - Joel Bromfield vs Alfred Campbell and others. Case continued.

Page 479 - Andrew Venable and wife vs Benjamin F. Greer. Not enough proof in this case. Estate of Charles R. Moore, deceased.

Page 479 - Power of Attorney, May 1852, executed by Washington G. McCombs, Elizabeth White and Frances West of Bedford County to John R. McCombs of Bedford County. Elizabeth West and Hetty Martin, witnesses.

Page 480 - Samuel Phillips admr. of Wilson Coats, deceased. Petition to sell slaves. Sold 15 May 1852.

Page 480 - Joseph Loyd and others. Exparte - Petition to sell land. 3 Lots.

Page 483 - William Boone did not qualify as exr. of Rachel Stewart, deceased. Lemuel Broadaway was appointed exr.

Page 483 - Settlement with Thomas Shearin guardian of N. C. and H. L. W. Shearin, minor heirs of Thomas Shearin, deceased.

Page 483 - Settlement with John F. Thompson guardian of Willie F. and E. M. Shearin, minor heirs of Thomas Shearin, deceased.

Page 483 - Settlement with Jasper N. Felps guardian of minor heirs of Alfred Anthony, deceased.

Page 483 - Settlement with Lemuel Broadaway guardian of his minor daughters.

Page 483 - Settlement with William D. Elkins guardian of David Elkins, a lunatic and heir of William P. Elkins, deceased.

1852 June Term

Page 483 - Settlement with John Bomar guardian of Thomas S. Sharp, minor
heir of William Sharp, deceased.

Page 484 - James Edde and others vs Hiram Edde and others. Petition to
sell land. Court ordered land to be sold and divided.

Page 485 - J. G. Barksdale and William Brown appointed Trustees of Thomas
Holland, sr. and wife in place of William Galbreath and Nathan
Ivey who has resigned said Trust, which had been made to them
by Thomas Holland, Sr. by Deed bearing date 22 day of January
1849.

Page 485 - E. A. Covington was removed as guardian of Richard and Mary Jane
Anderson, minor heirs of James Anderson, deceased. James H.
Locke was appointed guardian of the same.

Page 487 - Hardy Dunham and wife Nancy, James Jones and wife Phebe, Margaret
Craig, Leroy Warren and wife Elizabeth, Joel Bradley and wife
Mary M., William O. Price and wife Sarah, and Thomas Coffee, admr.
Exparte - Petition to sell slaves. Report slaves sold.

Page 488 - Phillip Hodges and John H. Watkins, Petition to sell land. Phillip
Hodges gets his 1/4 share of the land.

Page 488 - Power of Attorney by William Hughes to Thomas J. Penn of Patrick
County, Virginia, dated 5 July 1852.

Page 489 - Paten, still a very poor and afflicted man, be allowed $15.00.

Page 490 - Charles M. Norvell guardian of John E. and Eugene Norvell, his
minor children. H. J. H. Norvell and William B. Norvell,
securities.

Page 490 - John McGuire guardian of William Benjamin and John McGuire, minor
heirs of William McGuire, deceased.

Page 492 - Alexander Ray vs Bennet Right, Griffin Randle, A. Freeman, James
Calton, Jesse Thompson, P. J. Thompson, Martin Thompson, W. G.
Thompson, B. C. Cook, Henry Holder, James Moore, R. D(?).
Cummings, John F. Leech, Samuel Moore, John Reavis, Absalom Williams,
James Helton, John J. Hanie, Gabriel Davis, William Hill, and
John Williams. Petitioned Court to grant them a road from Rich-
mond in Bedford County to Harts Mill in Bedford County. Alex. Ray
stated he would be injured and damaged by the road running through
his land. Court ordered it to be examined.

1852 August Term

Page 494 - Hannah Harrison and John W. Greer admrs. of estate of John Harrison,
deceased. Samuel Doak and Benjamin F. Greer, securities.

1852 August Term

Page 494 - Widow of Robert Arnold, deceased, relinguished her right as admr. of his estate. William S. Arnold appointed admr.

Page 494 - Benjamin F. Whitworth admr. of estate of Thomas B. Whitworth, deceased.

Page 494 - Leroy W. Barrett, Randolph Newsom and George W. Greer laid off support for widow and family of Thomas B. Whitworth, deceased.

Page 495 - Wilkins Blanton, Presley Prince and H. C. Ferguson laid off support to widow and family of Robert Arnold, deceased.

Page 496 - Richard Warner admr. of estate of John Wilhoite, Jr., deceased.

Page 497 - Martha A. Gant petitioned the Court to issue notice to Jonas Sutton, who at a former Term of Court, was appointed admr. of estate of Hugh M. Gault, deceased, for him to appear and show cause why his letters of administration should not be recalled and Court ordered him injoined from further action as admr.

Page 497 - Joshua Hall, admr. of George W. Whitesell, deceased, be removed as admr. because he has removed from Tennessee, place of residence not known. Henry Moore appointed admr.

Page 498 - Phillip Hodges and others. Bill for division of land. (Plat on page 498)

1852 September Term

Page 502 - Widow of John Streeter, deceased, relinguishes her right as admr. of her husband's estate. John S. Davis appointed admr.

Page 502 - William Word admr. of estate of Julius Terry, deceased, a free man of color.

Page 503 - Leonard Bullock admr. of estate of Richard C. Ogilvie, deceased.

Page 503 - H. C. Ferguson admr. of estate of Margaret Ferguson, deceased.

Page 503 - Joseph Hiles admr. of estate of Alfred Hiles, deceased.

Page 503 - George Huffman admr. of estate of Garland Ayres, deceased.

Page 503 - Rencher Spence admr. of John W. Spence, deceased, estate.

Page 504 - Barnet Stephens admr. of estate of Sarah Hutson, deceased.

Page 504 - Joseph W. Couch guardian of Susan J. Couch, minor heir of Isaac Couch, deceased.

Page 504 - Jackson Nichols guardian of Thomas J. Deason and Amanda C. Deason, minor heirs of William Deason, deceased.

Page 505 - Iveson Knott guardian of Louisa Owens, minor heir of Sterling
Owens, deceased.

Page 505 - Edmund Cooper admr. of Ann Thompson, deceased, estate.

Page 506 - Neill, Harper and others. Exparte - Petition to sell land.
Land sold by Clerk and Master. John M. Harper sold by Deed to
B. F. Greer.

Page 506 - Jos. Anderson, A. B. Moore and William Shaw laid off support to
widow and family of R. C. Ogilvie, deceased.

Page 507 - Charity Allison, widow of William Allison, deceased.

Page 507 - Martha A. Gault and others vs Jonas Sutton. Motion to recall
letters. Jonas Sutton was appointed admr. of estate of Hu M.
Gault, deceased. Widow desires to serve as admr. along with
J. C. Gault. Hu A(M). Gault departed this life many years ago
intestate. He owned negroes.

Page 509 - Joel Broomfield vs James Cheshire and others. Joseph Broomfield
departed this life some years ago, having made a Will, in which
he desired the land to go to his children, being five in number.
James Cheshire and wife are the owners of 4/5 thereof, and that
Joel Broomfield is entitled to 1/5 thereof, of which he has not
received. Augustine Wilson, James B. Reagor and Henry Lynn are to
lay off support to Joel Broomfield his 1/5 share.

Page 509 - David G. Denson and others. Petition to sell slaves and land.
Clerk's report: That the widow of Jackson Nichols, William Floyd,
and J. F. Taylor filed, 1st all parties are before the Court and
2nd that it will be necessary to sell land. William Denson
departed this life some months ago in Bedford County, intestate,
leaving 87 acres of land and two slaves. David G. Denson admr.
of estate.

Page 509 - Hannah Harrison, John W. Greer and others. Petition to divide
slaves. John Harrison departed this life intestate some months
ago in Bedford County, and leaving as his children and widow,
and only heirs at law, Hannah Harrison, John W. Greer and wife
Julia A., Jeremiah Whitesell and wife Matilda J., Phoebe Delk,
Martha C. Harrison, Zachariah Harrison, and James C. Alexander
and wife Mary. Hannah Harrison gets the choice lot.

Page 512 - John S. Davis admr. and Nancy Streater. An agreement between
John Streater in his life time and Nancy Streater, that when
ever Nancy Streater should desire to go to house keeping of to
farming separate from John Streater, that she should receive
from the farm of John Streater a sufficient portion of the live
stock &c.

1852 September Term

Page 513 - Hazardy Oliver admrix and Thomas Oliver admr. Hazardy Oliver
admrix. and Thomas Oliver admr. of Wright Oliver, deceased.
Wright Oliver departed this life intestate, and left Hazardy
Oliver as his widow and Thomas, William, and Mary Oliver who has
since the death of her said father, intermarried with Joseph
Larue, and Joseph Harrison and James Oliver his children and
heirs at law, the last three of whom are minors, being in all
seven (7) heirs. Wright Oliver also left slaves.

Page 513 - William Word admr. of Julius Terry, deceased. Exparte -
Petition to sell part of Town Lot. Isaac Breen, William Brown
and J. P. Steele to lay off support to the widow and family.

Page 514 - L. W. Barrett, George W. Greer and Randolph Newsom laid off
support of widow and family of John Harrison, deceased.

Page 514 - George Cortner, G. W. Heard and John H. Scott laid off support
to widow and children of Garland Ayres, deceased.

Page 514 - William B. M. Brame, Lewis Tillman, Samuel Thompson, Alexander
Sanders, G. H. Stewart, and N. Thompson, 2nd. laid off support
of widow and family of John Streater, deceased.

Page 515 - A. B. Moon, William Brown and M. Blanton laid off support to
widow and family of William Allison, deceased.

Page 516 - Martha A. Gault and others vs Jonas Sutton. Petition to recall
letters &c.

Page 516 - John H. Oneal appointed Commissioner to sell the fencing now
remaining around the Court House in Shelbyville.

1852 October Term

Page 517 - John M. Warner admr. of estate of Eunice Warner, deceased.
John W. Rutledge and Samuel J. Warner and John F. Thompson,
securities.

Page 518 - Anthony Thomas admr. of estate of Samuel G. Knight, deceased.
R. L. Thomas and John W. Frizzell, securities.

Page 518 - John J. Mankin and William H. Mankin admrs. of estate of James
Mankin, deceased. Presley Jones and William Elmore, securities.

Page 518 - John W. Frizzell admr. of estate of Green B. Majors, deceased.
R. L. Thomas and William Linch, securities.

Page 518 - Joseph Hiles admr. of estate of Alfred Hyles, deceased.

Page 523 - William W. Miller, Nehemiah Sugg and John Thomas laid off support
for widow and family of Samuel Knight, deceased.

Page 523 - James R. McKinley and J. J. Cooper laid off support to Lydia
Damron and one of the children of J. M. Spence.

Page 523 - Joseph Anderson, William Wortham and Robert Ray laid off support
to widow of Elias Jones, deceased.

Page 524 - John J. Mankin admr. of Abraham Power, deceased.

Page 524 - John W. Rutledge guardian of Mary E. Rutledge.

Page 524 - John F. Thompson admr. of Henry Earnhart, deceased.

Page 524 - William M. Smith and Eliza Elliott admrs. of estate of Richard
N. Elliott, deceased.

Page 525 - L. M. Ransom guardian of his minor children.

Page 525 - Robert Buchanan and William M. Hord admrs. of Edwin B. Hord,
deceased.

Page 525 - John Q. Davidson admr. of Edmund Hord, deceased.

Page 525 - George M. Ray admr. of Joseph R. Ray, deceased.

Page 525 - James C. Snell admr. of Asahel C. Snell, deceased.

Page 526 - Emeline Lamb guardian of Giles Jefferson Lamb.

Page 526 - Alfred Campbell guardian of John H. Heaslett and Sarah Emily
Heaslett.

Page 526 - James T. Snoddy guardian of Martin V. Heaslett.

Page 526 - Leonard Heaslett guardian of William Penn Heaslett.

Page 526 - William T. Tune guardian of Edmund Whitman, deceased.

Page 526 - John Oneal and David C. Jones admrs. of Elias Jones, deceased.

Page 526 - William Young admr. of Robert B. Vance, deceased.

Page 527 - John H. Gambill admr. of Judith W. Gambill, deceased. John
Stephenson and James C. Gambill, securities.

Page 527 - James B. Dixon admr. of Clement C. Dixon, deceased. James Dixon,
security.

Page 527 - John S. Davis admr of John Streater, deceased. John Streater is
dead and left a widow Susan Streater and children, John, Mildred
and Casander Streater and that he was owner of slaves to be
divided.

1852 October Term

Page 528 - Eliza J. Ogilvie and others, widow &c. Petition for dower.
R. C. Ogilvie is dead, died intestate and the owner of several
tracts of land. He left a widow Eliza J. Ogilvie and other heirs
Augustine Wilson (being related), Alex. B. Moore and William
Collins to lay out her dower.

Page 528 - Susan Streater and others. Petition for dower.

Page 529 - William Young admr. of Robert B. Vance, deceased. Exparte -
Petition. Robert B. Vance is dead and left a widow and one
child surviving him, as his only heirs at law. William Young
appointed admr. Vance died the owner of two slaves. It is
necessary to sell slaves.

Page 529 - J. C. Gault and Martha A. Gault admrs. Petition to sell slaves.
Slaves sold.

Page 530 - Hazardy Oliver admrix. of Thomas Oliver, deceased. The sale of
slaves.

Page 531 - Power of Attorney, 20 September 1852, executed by Lucy Moseley to
Absalom Moseley and Benjamin Moseley.

Page 531 - Power of Attorney, 27 September 1852, executed by Margaret M.
Arnold to Oliver P. Arnold.

Page 531 - Power of Attorney, 27 September 1852, executed by Preston Frazer
to William P. Snell of Arkansas.

Page 532 - Francis M. Harrison vs Joseph Morton and Jesse Brown. Petition
for probate of Will.

Page 532 - Green T. Neeley, Jacob Moulder and Edward Stephenson laid off
support to Henry C. Earnhart, a minor heir of Henry Earnhart
who died intestate not leaving a widow. John H. Oneal guardian
of Emily Earnhart, Manerva Earnhart, and Henry C. Earnhart, minor
children of Henry Earnhart, deceased.

Page 533 - Mary Newsom guardian of Tarlton O. Newsom, James P. Newsom,
Virginia T. Newsom, and Nancy Newsom. Thomas Dean security.

Page 533 - Robert B. Davidson admr. of estate of Mary S. Campbell, deceased.

Page 533 - John F. Thompson, M. Earnhart and others. Exparte - Petition to
sell land.

Page 533 - Clement Cannon admr. of estate of Mary Locke, deceased. Thomas B.
Cannon and Robert Cannon, securities.

Page 533 - Orphan boy by name of Isaac Williams, age 15 years, was bound to
E. D. Dromgoole until he arrives at age 21, to teach him to read,
write, and cipher.

Page 536 - The widow of James P. Couch, deceased, relinguishes her right
to admr. upon her husband's estate. Blount G. Green appointed
admr. John F. McCutchen, Robert C. Jennings and Andrew Vannoy
laid off support to Margaret Couch, widow of James P. Couch, and
her family.

Page 537 - James R. Reagor admr. of estate of Henry W. Kerby, deceased. W. W.
Stanfield and John Stanfield, securities.

Page 538 - William B. M. Brame, Lewis Tillman and Newsum Thompson, 2nd, laid
off support to Susan Streater and family, widow and heirs of John
Streater, deceased. Also, allotted Nancy Streater (Miss) her
part of estate. John S. Davis, admr.

Page 538 - J. H. Scott, George Cortner and G. W. Heard laid off support to
Susan Ayres, widow of Garland Ayres, deceased.

Page 538 - Elijah Chappel, aged 14 years, and James Chappel, aged 7 years,
orphans, was bound unto C. R. P. King until they each arrive at
the age of 21 years. King is to teach them to read, write and
cipher.

Page 539 - A. L. Landis and John Harrison appointed to aid the exrs. to lay
off support for widow of A. Shofner, deceased.

Page 539 - Joshua Crowel guardian of Mary E. Crowel.

Page 539 - Juliett Caruthers and John F. Caruthers guardians guardian of
James, Sarah E., Eliza A., and William Caruthers, minors of
Archabald Caruthers, deceased.

Page 539 - Presley Prince admr. of Daniel Crisco, deceased, with Sophia
Crisco. G. M. Ray and William Prince, securities.

Page 542 - William T. Tune admr. of Jane Harris, deceased.

Page 542 - John B. Wilhoite admr. of Richard J. Warner, deceased. Richard
Warner and John M. Warner, securities.

Page 542 - Zachariah Harrison admr. of Jeremiah Whitesell, deceased. Hannah
Harrison, Matilda J. Whitesell and John W. Greer, securities.

Page 542 - J. A. Blakemore admr. of Daniel L. Barringer, deceased.

Page 543 - Fielding B. Lipford admr. of estate of Anthony P. Lipford, deceased.
G. M. Ray and Thomas Holt, securities.

Page 543 - Daniel Dean, William Russell and Robert Daniel laid off support
for Sophia Crisco.

Page 543 - John P. Hainey, Joseph Adams and James Coats laid off support to
Matilda J. Whitesell, widow of Jeremiah Whitesell, deceased.

Page 543 - Charles T. Philpott admr. of estate of Nancy D. _____, deceased.
Alfred Campbell and John C. Hix, securities.

Page 543 - John F. Watson admr. of estate of George W. Stewart, deceased.
Joshua Coleman, security.

Page 543 - John B. Wilhoite admr. of Purdy V. Warner, deceased. Richard
Warner and John M. Warner, securities.

Page 544 - John H. Gambill guardian of James, Lydia, Betsey Ann, William and
Preston Gambill.

Page 544 - Richard Warner guardian of Thomas Warner. John M. Warner and
John B. Wilhoite, securities.

Page 544 - William H. Stanfield guardian of Charles W. Kirby, minor heir
of Henry W. Kirby, deceased. John Stanfield and J. B. Reagor,
securities.

Page 544 - Michael Crowell guardian of Sarah R. Crowell. Jacob M. Parsons,
security.

Page 544 - Augustine Wilson guardian of Sarah E. and Mary T. Ogilvie.
Meredith Blanton, security.

Page 544 - Gwynn Foster with James Foster and R. H. Stem as securities,
entered into Bond. Gwynn Foster appointed commissioner to sell
land belonging to the Firm of Gwynn Foster & R. C. Ogilvie.
Gwynn Foster admr. of heirs of R. C. Ogilvie, deceased.

Page 545 - Committee appointed, Richard Warner, Edward Cooper, George W.
Brown, John M. Warner and John W. Rutledge, to sell land of heirs
and divises of John Warner, deceased.

Page 546 - John M. Warner, Samuel J. Warner and others and John M. Warner,
A. A. Robinson and others. Petition to sell land.
John Warner departed this life in 1834, left widow Eunice Warner,
8 children: Huldah B. Wilhoite, Anna A. Wilhoite now Anna A.
Robinson, William D. Warner, John M. Warner, Samuel J. Warner,
Mary Eunice Warner who is now Mary Eunice Rutledge, Purdy V.
Warner and Richard J. Warner, deceased, died before Eunice
Warner, never having been married, and that William D. Warner
also died before Eunice Warner, having one child Thomas Warner.
And that Huldah B. Wilhoite also died before Eunice Warner leav-
ing as her only children, Richard, Huldah, John and Narcissa and
that John has since died without being married and that the other
three survive, and the Court also being satisfied that William D.
Warner sold all of his interest in said real estate under John
Warner's Will to Eunice Warner who sold to John M. Rutledge,

Page 546 - (continued) And that Eunice Warner is now dead. The land will have to be sold and equally divided between them.

Page 548 - Abram Whinery guardian of Mary C. Biggs. Mary Biggs is dead and that Mary C. Biggs is her only child. That Abram Whinery appointed guardian in the State of Arkansas. Henry Dean is guardian of Mary Biggs formerly Mary Noblett, pay over to Henry Whinery, as the guardian of Mary C. Biggs, all of the fund in his hands belonging to his former ward.

Page 549 - John F. Watson admr. of George W. Stewart, deceased. Petition to sell land. George W. Stewart is dead. He died intestate and the owner of a slave. John F. Watson admr. of estate.

Page 549 - John F. Thompson and others. Petition to sell land. Land of Henry Earnhart, deceased. Lands on waters of Sinking Creek. Petitioners, Emily Earnhart, Manerva Earnhart, and Henry C. Earnhart has interest in land.

Page 551 - Ellen Gamel relinquished her right as exrix. of the estate of her deceased husband, William Gamel.

Page 551 - William Trice, Hugh Hurst and John W. Wiggins laid off support to widow of Daniel L. Barringer, deceased.

Page 551 - William Word, admr. of Julius Terry, deceased. Petition to sell land. Candis Terry the widow and only heir at law of Julius Terry, deceased.

Page 551 - John A. Moore admr. of estate of Eleanor Moore, deceased.

Page 551 - Gwynn Foster, Leonard Bullock admrs. Petition to sell land. Gwynn Foster and R. C. Ogilvie, together, purchased of George L(T). Landis, a tract of land, 84½ acres. Need to sell land to pay debt.

Page 551 - Elizabeth Cooper, widow of James Cooper, deceased. He left slaves to her and 8 of his children, and Elizabeth being now dead and the slaves having now come into the possession of the petitioners as such executor.

Page 553 - James B. Reagor admr. and Charles Kirby &c. Petition to sell land. Henry Kirby is dead. That he held James B. Reagor's Bond for titles for tract of land. Henry Kirby left only one child, Charles Kirby with William Stanfield as his guardian. Land to be sold.

Page 553 - Hazardy Oliver admrix. and Thomas Oliver admr. Petition to sell slave, belonging to the estate of Wright Oliver, deceased. Negro boy Jesse sold to Jo Thompson.

1852 November Term

Page 555 - W. W. Gill, Joseph Morton and James E. Bradshaw laid off support
to widow and family of William Gammill, deceased.

Page --- - Page following 557 with no number.
December the 14th 1850. This day Doctor Adcock, a citizen of the
23rd District of Bedford County, appeared before me and desired to
record the mark of his geese, which he says, is the right toe on
the right foot cut close off to the foot.
Andrew Vannoy, Clerk
Bedford County Court.

BEDFORD COUNTY COURT MINUTES, BOOK 1852 - 1855

1852 December Term

Page 1 - James F. Shearin admr. of estate of William Hammill, deceased.
(could be Gammill)

Page 1 - Andrew Vannoy, John F. McCutchen and Robert C. Jennings laid off
support to Margaret Couch, widow of James P. Couch, deceased, and
her family.

Page 3 - William Campbell admr. of estate of Eve Burrow, deceased.

Page 4 - William Campbell admr. of estate with Will annexed of Ephraim Burrow,
deceased.

Page 4 - William H. Dyer admr. of estate of Martha Dyer, deceased.

Page 4 - Robert Pate admr. of estate of H. A. Pate, deceased.

Page 4 - Isaac W. McGown admr. of estate of John McGown, deceased.

Page 4 - James R. Russ admr. of Thomas J. Russ, deceased, estate.

Page 4 - Christian Freeman admr. of estate of Russell Freeman, deceased.

Page 5 - James D. Neill guardian of Samuel M. and Mary M. Harper, minor
heirs of William C. Harper, deceased.

Page 5 - John M. Gibson guardian of Jane England, minor heir of Jonathan
England, deceased.

Page 5 - Joseph M. Rayburn guardian of John, Nancy, Isaac M., Pamelia A.,
Martha N., and Rebecca T. Rayburn.

Page 5 - Joshua Coleman guardian of Ridley Bearden, Harrison _. Bearden,
Lawson H. W. Bearden, and Sarah C. Bearden.

1852 December Term

Page 6 - W. J. Hill guardian of William and James Hill, minor heirs of John Hill, deceased. Isaac B. Webb and F. P. McElwrath, securities.

Page 6 - William G. Thompson be allowed $6.00 for services as Common School Commissioner in the Richmond Township from 20 Dec 1851.

Page 6 - Alexander Ray be allowed $8.00 for services as Common School Commissioner in the Richmond Township for 8 days from 1852.

Page 6 - H. C. Holt and W. W. Gill be allowed $12.00 each as Common School Commissioners in Township 4, Range 4.

Page 6 - Mrs. Alley Trollinger be allowed $30.00 for support.

Page 6 - Jackson Landers be allowed $30.00 for support.

Page 7 - George W. Parsons and John F. Thompson and Price C. Steele be allowed $6.00 each for 6 day as Common School Commissioners in Range 4, Section 7.

Page 7 - Z. Harrison reported list of estate of Jeremiah Whitesell, deceased. Joseph Adams, James Coats and John P. Hainey laid off support to Matilda J. Whitesell, widow of Jeremiah Whitesell, and her family.

Page 7 - John F. Thompson and others. Exparte - Petition to sell land. Petitioners, John F. Thompson, Michael Earnhart, Emily Earnhart, Minerva Earnhart, and Henry C. Earnhart.

Page 9 - John F. Caruthers, Sarah C. Caruthers and others. Petition to divide slaves. Petitioners, John F. Carithers, Sarah E. Caruthers, James, Eliza A. and William Caruthers, the last being minors who petition by their guardian Juliett and John F. Caruthers. John F. Caruthers has attained the age of 21 years and desires his share.

Page 10 - Price C. Steele Exr. of James Cooper, deceased. Slaves sold.

Page 11 - James B. Reagor admr. and Charles W. Kerby by his guardian William Stanfield. Petition to sell land. 27 Nov 1852 sold to John Evans.

Page 12 - Elizabeth England, minor by her guardian John M. Harper. Elizabeth, a minor, residing in Smith County, Texas, heir of Samuel Harper, deceased, wants Thomas W. Harper admr. of Samuel Harper's estate to pay over to her guardian in Texas her portion of estate.

Page 12 - Richard Warner Exr. of John Warner, deceased. Petition to sell 22 slaves.

Page 13 - J. F. Watson admr. of George Stewart, deceased. Petition to sell slaves. On 13 Nov 1852 at Coldwell's Store, sale of slave William to Elisha Wammack.

1852 December Term

Page 14 - Elizabeth England, minor by her guardian John M. Harper. Elizabeth
is minor of Samuel Harper, deceased and who resides in Smith County,
Texas. She is to receive her share of the estate.

Page 15 - James B. Reagor, admr. of John Lacy, deceased. Petition to sell
slaves. John Lacy died intestate and was the owner of a slave and
that Talitha Lacy had a life estate in said slave who is also dead.
Admr. stated that it is necessary to sell slave.

Page 15 - Eliza Jane Ogilvie and others. Petition for dower. Jury to lay
off to Eliza Jane Ogilvie her dower out of the real estate of
Richard C. Ogilvie, her deceased husband, to be injoyed at the
death of Nancy Ogilvie in Bedford County, on waters of Clem's
Creek, a branch of the North Fork of Duck River.

Page 16 - Jordan C. Holt admr. of John Wilhoite, deceased, and W. J. Stegall
and wife Hannah M. formerly Hannah M. Wilhoite and Richard N.
Wilhoite, John Wilhoite, Jr., Narcissa Wilhoite, and Huldah Wilhoite
by their guardian Richard Warner. Petition to divide slaves, 18.

1853 January Term

Page 21 - Inventory of estate of Green B. Majors, deceased.

Page 21 - Robert H. Temple admr. of estate of John S. Frazer, deceased.

Page 22 - John S. Brown admr. of estate of Janet Ray, deceased. James M. Ray,
F. F. Fonville, John H. Gambill, and B. F. Greer, securities.

Page 22 - Zephanial Weaver admr. of estate of David Weavers, deceased.

Page 22 - William Campbell admr. of estate of Maddison L. Burrow, deceased.
John C. Hix and Benjamin F. Wiggins, securities.

Page 22 - Joseph Thompson admr. of estate of James Thompson, deceased. J. F.
Thompson, security.

Page 22 - John C. Hix admr. of estate of Sarah Allbright, deceased. William
C. Hix, security.

Page 22 - Jeremiah Culverhouse guardian of Elizabeth and Jane Culverhouse,
minor heirs of Jesse Culverhouse, deceased. James Foster, security.

Page 23 - Susan Burt guardian of Lucy Burt and Salometh Burt, minor children
of said Susan Burt. John S. Davis and Thomas S. Burt, securities.

Page 23 - James L. Armstrong guardian of Marianne A. Marshall, Sally D.
Marshall, Robert Marshall, James L. A. Marshall, Alexander M.
Marshall and Elijah J. Marshall.

Page 23 - B. B. Harper guardian of William and John England, minor heirs of
Jonathan England, deceased. J. H. Gambill, security.

1853 January Term

Page 23 - An orphan boy named William Henry Ward, age 10 years, bound to William F. Beck until he is 21 years of age. He is to learn the trade of saddler.

Page 24 - Jerome Albright, Hiram Neese and Jerrel Burrow laid off support for Margaret Burrow and her children.

Page 25 - William Campbell admr. of Maddison L. Burrow, deceased. Petition to sell slaves. There are six distributees of Maddison L. Burrow, deceased, of his estate. The estate only had one negro slave, Sarah, about 9 years old.

Page 25 - Herod F. Holt and Jordan C. Holt, exrs. of Joshua Holt, deceased. Joshua Holt died devised the slaves (8) to be equally divided amongst his children. Eleanor Holt is now dead, as well as two of the slaves. It is necessary to sell the slaves and divide the proceeds.

Page 26 - James Harris guardian of Ann Harris, a lunatic.

Page 26 - James M. Ray and others. Petition to sell land. Land cannot be divided. To be sold.

Page 27 - William Word and others. Petition to sell land and dower. Commissioners appointed to lay off Dower's part.

1853 February Term

Page 29 - Barnet Stephens guardian of William M., Pleasant A., Thomas F., and Sarah E. Stephens, his minor children.

Page 29 - Wesley S. Evans and Thomas J. Stanfield admrs. of estate of John Evans, deceased. A. W. Evans and J. J. Crunk, securities.

Page 29 - Newton K. Shofner resigned as guardian of Julia S., Eliza Jane, and Milley H. Webster, minor heirs of Henry Webster, deceased. Levi Turner appointed guardian. Gabriel Maupin and Gabriel Shofner, securities.

Page 29 - Joseph Hastings, D. D. Hix, and James B. Reagor laid off support for widow of John Evans, deceased.

Page 29 - John W. Norvell guardian of minor heirs of George W. Mullins, deceased.

Page 30 - Benjamin Merritt admr. of estate of Samuel McClure, deceased. William Thomas, security.

Page 30 - Howel M. Dawdy, J. P. of the 19th District, was empowered to examine Sarah Neill, wife of James D. Neill, and Martha Gibson wife of John M. Gibson, about their father Samuel Harper, deceased.

1853 February Term

Page 30 - Andrew Neill and wife and others. Petition to sell land. The
lands of Samuel Harper, deceased. James W. Wallace purchased the
interest of Thomas J. Bartley and wife Elizabeth and Edward N.
Harper, in the estate of Samuel Harper, deceased. James D. Neill
guardian of Samuel M. and Mary M. Harper who are minors, and
Benjamin B. Harper appointed guardian for William and John England
who are minors, and that John M. Gibson appointed guardian of Jane
England a minor, and John M. Harper guardian of Elizabeth England
a minor, the first two minors being entitled to one share and the
last four minors are entitled to one distributees' share.

Page 31 - This day, Mary Phillips wife of Miles Phillips, formerly Mary
Harper, appeared in Court and being examined privately and apart
from her husband the said Miles Phillips, giving her consent, that
the money arising from the sale of the land of Samuel Harper,
deceased, her father, might be paid over to her husband and that she
desires the money in the hands of Andrew Vannoy, the Commissioner,
should be paid over to her husband.

Page 31 - A. Ransom admr. and Commissioner on the estate of James H. Floyd,
deceased vs Robert S. Dwiggins. Court directed the sale of slaves
of estate of James H. Floyd, deceased.

Page 31 - W. M. Miller guardian of minor children of Benjamin Bowers, deceased.

Page 31 - Robert H. Majors guardian of minor heirs of Benjamin Bowers.

Page 32 - Davidson M. Smith admr. of estate of John Medearis, deceased.
Thomas McAdams and N. O. McAdams, securities.

Page 32 - William Morgan admr. of estate of Gabriel Barnes, deceased. R. H.
Sims and Robert H. Barnes, securities.

Page 32 - John E. Scruggs guardian of Eliza F. Dedman, minor heir of Philip
Dedman, Jr., deceased. Nehemiah Sugg and G. G. Osborne, securities.

Page 32 - John E. Scruggs guardian of William Waite, minor heir of William
Waite, deceased. Nehemiah Sugg and G. G. Osborne, securities.

Page 32 - Gabriel Maupin guardian of William C. Shofner, Nancy C. Shofner,
Mary Ann Shofner, and Sarah T. Shofner, minor heirs of Frederick
Shofner, deceased. Robert B. Maupin, security.

Page 32 - William Carlisle guardian of minor heirs of John Phillips, deceased.
Edmund Word and William O. Forbes, securities.

Page 33 - Jacob B. Delk guardian of Catharine, Mary Ann, Alexander, Barbara,
Martha Jane, and George W. Capley, minor heirs of George Capley,
deceased. Jacob M. Parsons, security.

Page 33 - Pierce Wilhoite admr. of estate of Hetty Wilhoite, deceased.
Thomas L. Word and John Wilhoite, securities.

Page 33 - Herod F. Holt, one of the executors of estate of Joshua Holt, deceased, entered into bond with Joshua Holt, Sr., and H. G. Holt, securities, to qualify as exr.

Page 33 - Leonard Bullock admr. of estate of R. C. Ogilvie, deceased.

Page 33 - Charles L. Philpot who was appointed admr. of Nancy Dixon, who was a citizen of Tennessee but not of Bedford County at the time of her death, that the letters of admr. be recalled.

Page 34 - G. D. Denson admr. Petition to sell slaves belonging to estate of William Denson, deceased. One sold to George Smith and one sold to Kiziah Taylor.

Page 35 - Settlement with John Claxton guardian of Mary E. Claxton &c.

Page 35 - Final settlement with William S. Eakin guardian of Sarah J. Spence, formerly Sarah Jane Eakin.

Page 35 - Settlement with Alexander Ray guardian of Barbara and Rhoda Davis.

Page 36 - William M. Hutson and Thomas Hutson and others. Petition to sell lands. 2 tracts. Barnet Stephens guardian of William M. Stephens, Sarah Stephens, Pleasant A. Stephens, and Jefferson G. Stephens, minors and are entitled to equal share of estate.

Page 37 - Howel M. Dawdy, Esq. to examine Sarah Neill and Martha Gibson, separate from their husbands, James D. Neill and John M. Gibson, relative to payment of money belonging to them in the hands of Andrew Vannoy, Commissioner, to pay their husbands, &c. Sarah Neill wife of James D. Neill formerly Sarah Harper and Martha Gibson wife of John M. Gibson formerly Martha Harper, they are willing for their husband to receive their share of money, that they are entitled to from the estate of Samuel Harper, deceased. 8 Feb 1853.

Page 38 - William Word admr. of Julius Terry and others. Petition to sell land or Town Lot. Sold on 25 Jan 1853 to John P. Steele, Esq.

Page 40 - Absalem Reavis guardian of William J. Johnson.

Page 40 - H. C. Hix guardian of minor heirs of Madison L. Burrow, deceased. William Campbell, security.

Page 40 - Thomas H. Coldwell guardian of minor heirs of James Couch, deceased. John C. Coldwell, security.

Page 40 - William Campbell admr. of Ephraim Burrow, deceased, also, Eve Burrow, deceased, report of inventory.

Page 41 - John, Robert, Ephraim, Lethe, and Madison L. Burrow, minor heirs of M. L. Burrow, deceased, by guardian J. C. Hix. Petition to

1853 February Term

Page 41 - (continued) sell land. Madison L. Burrow departed this life leaving a widow Margaret Burrow and his heirs, John, Robert, Ephraim,
Lethe, and Madison L. Burrow, his only children, all minors under
21 years. Madison L. Burrow died seized of about 70 acres in
District # 22. In 4 January 1853, widow Margaret Burrow relinguished
to her 5 children, her right and claim in the dower tract. The land
cannot be divided. To be sold.

Page 43 - H. F. Holt admr. of estate of Elinor Holt, deceased.

1853 March Term

Page 44 - Samuel Bobo, J.P. of 24th District, to examine Julia Ann Snoddy,
formerly Julia Ann Heaslett and wife of James T. Snoddy, separate
from her husband, her consent to hand over money from sale of the
lands of her father, William Heaslett, deceased, to her husband.

Page 44 - Samuel Bobo, J.P. of 24th District, to examine Mary C. Williams,
wife of James T. Williams and formerly Mary C. Hutson, her consent
for the money to be handed to her husband, upon sale of her father's
estate, Cutty B. Hutson, deceased.

Page 45 - James A. Heaslett and others. Petition to sell land. Lands of
William Heaslett, deceased, and divide among minor heirs.

Page 45 - John Pearson and wife Jane and Randolph Newsom guardian of the
minor heirs of Thomas Newsom, deceased. Exparte Petition. 7 Mar
1853, on report of Andrew Vannoy the Commissioner who sold the land.

Page 46 - J. W. MacCowen admr. of estate of John MacCowen, deceased. Richard
Nance, E. W. Hendrix and William Mallard laid off support to Sarah
MacCowen, widow of John MacCowen.

Page 46 - Milton A. Reagor guardian of Jane B. Reagor and Anthony W. Reagor,
separately, by Probate Court of Washington County, Arkansas.

Page 46 - James M. Ray. Exparte - Petition to sell land. 15 Feb 1853 day of
the sale. Thomas J. Williams purchaser.

Page 47 - John S. Brown admr. &c and others. Petition to sell slaves. Sale
on 15 Feb 1853. Slaves sold to John Cortner, C. W. Black, Samuel
Thompson, and Benjamin Moseley. Witnesses: James M. Ray and others.

Page 48 - Hardy Dunham, late of Bedford County, has departed this life. Court
ordered Howel M. Dawdy admr. of estate of Hardy Dunham.

Page 49 - Joseph Anderson, Robert Ray and C. L. Bates laid off L. Collins,
widow of Augustine Collins, deceased.

Page 49 - Benjamin Fugett and others. Petition to sell land Warrant. Warrant
No. 40291 was regularly issued to Nancy Fugett by the Government of

Page 49 - (continued) the United States of America on 25 June 1852 and since that time she has died and that petitioner legally entitled to said land warrant and that it will have to be sold for partition.

Page 49 - John T. Medearis guardian of Wiley W. Medearis.

Page 49 - Samuel Doak admr. of estate of John Bennett, deceased, late of Bedford County.

Page 49 - H. T. Ferguson admr. of estate of America Ferguson, late of Bedford County. H. C. Ferguson and A. D. Ferguson, securities.

Page 49 - John Noblett guardian of John and Mary Noblett, minor heirs of Thomas Noblett, deceased. J. E. Pearson, security.

Page 50 - William J. Barrett fuardian of Duncan L. Barrett, a minor heir of John Barrett, deceased, resigned as guardian and Court appointed Thompson Leroy W. Barrett as guardian.

Page 50 - James Vannatta guardian of James R. Nash, minor heir of John Nash, deceased.

Page 50 - Edwin W. Adams admr. of estate of Jane Russell, deceased, late of Bedford County. Jesse W. Brown and James Carlisle, securities.

Page 50 - William C. Stephenson admr. of estate of Augustine Collins, deceased. James Bigger and A. Adams, securities. Lively Collins, widow.

Page 50 - James Carlisle guardian of Benton Gabbert, minor heir of William Gabbert, deceased. James J. Newton and George G. Gabbert, securities.

Page 50 - George G. Gabbert guardian of Lucinda Gabbert, minor heir of William Gabbert, deceased. James Carlisle and Nelson Gabbert, securities.

Page 52 - Francis Stewart was bound to Jonathan C. Bates. Francis Stewart, age 13 years, to learn housewifery until 18 years of age.

Page 53 - George Huffman admr. of estate of Garland Ayers, deceased.

Page 53 - Mary C. Hudson (could be Hutson) formerly Mary C. Heaslett and wife of Thomas Hudson(Hutson). She being examined apart from her husband giving her consent for the money belonging to her, deriving from the sale of lands of her father William Heaslett, deceased, to be paid over to her husband.

Page 53 - E. J. Boardman is and has been a resident citizen of Bedford County for more than 12 (years) previous and that he is 21 years of age and honest and of good character, desires to obtain License to practice law.

1853 March Term

Page 53 - William M. Hutson and others. Petition to sell land. Land belonging to heirs of Cutty Hutson, deceased. Also, Barnett Stephens
admr. of Sarah Hutson, deceased.

Page 53 - Nelson Gabbert resigned as guardian of Benton and Lucinda Gabbert,
minor heirs of William Gabbert, deceased.

Page 54 - Samuel Bobo to examine Julia Ann Snoddy wife of James T. Snoddy and
Mary C. Williams wife of James T. Williams, apart from their hus-
bands. Julia Ann Snoddy formerly Julia Ann Heaslett, daughter of
William Heaslett, deceased. Mary C. Williams, formerly Mary C.
Hutson, daughter of Cutty B. Hutson, deceased.

Page 55 - State of Tennessee vs John and Robert Burrow and others. Petition
to sell land. Sale 3 Mar 1853. Sold to James D. Burrow, land in
District # 22 of Bedford County.

Page 55 - State of Tennessee vs John ONeal. John ONeal is indebted to the
State of Tennessee.

Page 56 - James Hastings and wife and others, Hiram Edde and others. Land sale
4 Mar 1853. 2 separate tracts.

Page 57 - James Edde, James Hastings and wife Ellen, Silas Pratt and wife
Patience and Hiram J. Edde. Hiram Edde, Jane Edde, Francis Edde,
minos Edde, Nancy Edde, Elizabeth Edde, and Candis Edde.
Hiram Edde purchased the land which is in Bedford County, which
in the Will of Joshua Holt or given to his daughter Candis Johnson
the wife of Hiram Edde during her lifetime, remainder to her children.

Page 59 - William Word admr. &c. vs Widow, heirs and creditors of Julius Terry,
deceased. Commissioners to sell the Town Lot or Lots, subject to
the widow's dower.

1853 April Term

Page 61 - Alfred Campbell guardian of John R. Heaslett, minor heir of William
Heaslett, deceased, resigned as guardian. Thomas Hutson appointed
guardian.

Page 61 - William H. Roane guardian of Spencer W. Roane and James H. Roane,
minor heirs of   (blank)   Roane, deceased.

Page 62 - John W. Wadley guardian of James Granville Wadley, minor heir of
George W. Wadley, deceased.

Page 62 - John S. Thompson guardian of Sarah J. Brown, minor heir of Ruffin
Brown, deceased. Samuel Rone and J. M. Hix, securities.

Page 62 - Thomas W. Coffey admr. of estate of Mary Dawdy, deceased. James W.
Coffey and William Wood, securities.

1853 April Term

Page 62 - Joannah Nash admr. of estate of Abner Nash, deceased. John W.
Cowan and Levi C. Johnson, her securities.

Page 63 - Benjamin Deckard admr. of estate of John Bradford, deceased.
Robert Matthews, security.

Page 64 - Nancy Farris be allowed $30.00 for taking care of 2 idoit children.

Page 64 - William Henley, a very aged and poor man, be allowed $15.00.

Page 65 - Ordered that George W. Ruth be allowed $61.62 for keeping in the
jail Peggy Perrimore, 155 dats. She is a free woman of color.

Page 65 - Thomas L. Thompson, a pauper, be allowed for support $30.00.

Page 65 - Joseph Anderson be allowed $10.00 for dressing and burying a dead
infant found is a sink hole in Robert Ray's field.

Page 70 - John Caruthers and others. Petition to divide slaves.

Page 70 - John S. Davis admr. of John Streater, deceased, and Susan Streater,
widow &c. Petition to divide slaves (21). And, Susan Streater and
others. Petition for dower. Dower on waters of Duck River.

Page 72 - Herod F. Holt exr. Petition to sell slaves. Slaves belonging to
the estate of Joshua Hold, deceased. Two slave sold to Joshua Holt, 4th,
one sold to Michael Holt, Sr., one sold to James Smith, and one
sold to James L. Phillips.

Page 73 - John M. Warner and others. Petition to sell land. Sale on 23 Nov
1852, 250 acres. John M. Warner purchased the land, it being land
of John Warner, deceased, devised to his children. Also, sold 100
acres of cedar land to L. T. Williams. The remainder was unable to
sell. Tract of land on south side of Duck River.

Page 75 - State of Tennessee vs Wiley Jarnagan. Case of Bastardy. Rhoda
Couch supported by her affidavit that Wiley Jarnagan was the father
of an illegitimate child of which she had been delivered in Bedford
County. Jarnagan cannot be found in Bedford County. They believe
Jarnagan went to Coffee County. Said Wiley Jarnagan with G. W.
Jarnagan intered into bond.

Page 78 - William M. Smith resigned as admr. of Richard Elliott, deceased.
William M. Low now admr.

Page 78 - James L. Woods guardian of Martha F. minor heir of George P. Muse,
deceased.

Page 79 - State of Tennessee, for the use of Mary Sharp vs John ONeal. Case
of Bastardy. Defendant denies being the father of the bastard
child of Mary Sharp.

1853 April Term

Page 79 - Mrs. Jane Pearson formerly Jane Newsom, was examined separately
from her husband John E. Pearson, she being the daughter of Thomas
Newsom, deceased.

Page 80 - William Word admr. of Juoius Terry, deceased, vs Candis Terry et al.
Petition to sell land. Sale of 2 April 1853. To sell all land
except dower tract.

Page 81 - The bridge across Flat Creek on the Fayetteville Road has been
built by R. S. Dwiggins, is now ready for public use. Cost $400.00.

1853 May Term

Page 83 - Daniel Dian, William Russell and R. C. Daniel to lay off support
to widow and family of Daniel Chrisco, deceased (Crisco). Presley
Prince admr. of the estate.

Page 83 - Pierce Wilhoite admr. of estate of Hetty Wilhoite, deceased. List
inventory.

Page 83 - An orphan child named Neoma Massey was bound to John Powell of
Bedford County to learn housewifery.

Page 83 - William Little admr. of estate of Martin Lamb, deceased. Edmund
Cooper and David A. Ozment, securities.

Page 84 - David A. Ozment and C. L. Batte admrs. of estate of Samuel G.
McGowen, deceased. C. L. Batte, William Little and John W. Mayfield,
securities.

Page 84 - John Bomar guardian of Thomas Sharp, minor heir of William Sharp,
deceased.

Page 84 - John F. Thompson guardian of Edward M. and Wilie F. Shearin, minor
heirs of Thomas Shearin, deceased. William Shearin and John W.
Mayfield, securities.

Page 84 - Thomas Shearin guardian of Hugh L. W. and Newton C. Shearin, minor
heirs of Thomas Shearin, deceased.

Page 84 - William Burns guardian of minor heir of Thomas P. Burns, deceased.
Andrew Vannoy and Jesse F. Vannoy, securities.

Page 84 - Phillip Hodge guardian of Margaret C. Fisher, minor heir of John
Fisher, deceased. Eli H. Stephens, security.

Page 85 - Robert H. Majors guardian of Harriett N. Clark, minor heir of
Newton Clark, deceased. William P. Majors, security.

Page 85 - Joseph Anderson, Charles L. Batte and Robert Ray laid off support
to Lively Collins, widow of Augustine Collins, deceased.

1853 May Term

Page 86 - John F. Caruthers and Sarah Caruthers and others. Petition to divide slaves (6). Sale at the house of Juliett M. Caruthers, of the estate of Archibald Caruthers, deceased. Sold 28 April 1853. James Caruthers, Sarah E. Caruthers, Eliza A. Caruthers, William Caruthers, and Juliett M. Caruthers guardian sold negro boy to John F. Anderson.

Page 86 - John Hart, Enoch Williams and John C. Coldwell to lay off support to Judah Hickman, widow of Joseph Hickman, deceased, support for herself and family.

Page 87 - Jennings Moore and others. Petition. R. C. Ogilvie conveyed the acre of ground to Jennings Moore, Alexander B. Moon, Briant Landers, Jo Brown, A. Wilson, R. W. Fain, and Green L. Poplin, as Trustees for the benefit of a Female School and Academy and no other purpose and that Green L. Poplin and R. W. Fain removed from the neighborhood and that they will have to be removed from their Trust and others be appointed to carry out said Trust. William Little and David A. Ozment appointed.

Page 87 - Elizabeth Houston, widow of William Houston, deceased, appeared and showed why the nuncupative Will of William Houston, deceased, should be recorded and filed.

Page 87 - Settlement with H. Clagett guardian of Z. W. C. Waters.

Page 90 - James _. Wilson, William M. Shaw and Valentine Lentz to lay off to Rebecca McGowen, widow of S. G. McGowen, deceased.

Page 90 - Ordered by Court that admrs. of Elias Jones, deceased, pay over to Jemima Jones, widow, $10.00, a portion of her support.

Page 90 - State of Tennessee vs John ONeal. Charge of Bastardy. To report to next Court.

Page 90 - William Word admr. and others. Petition to sell land. Land to be sold and report to next Court.

1853 June Term

Page 92 - Bryant House admr. of estate of Dudley P. T. House, deceased. Robert F. Arnold, security. NOTE: This was made void next day at Court.

Page 92 - George W. Heard admr. of estate of John Lawrence, deceased.

Page 92 - John F. Thompson resigned as guardian of Edward M. Shearin, heir of Thomas Shearin, deceased. William Shearin appointed guardian.

Page 93 - George W. Buchanan guardian of James Henry Reed. Robert H. Terry, security.

1853 June Term

Page 94 - Benjamin F. Greer admr. of estate of Matilda Blessing, deceased.

Page 94 - James S. Maupin guardian of his infant child, Jane B. Maupin.
Gabriel Maupin, security.

Page 94 - Allen Morris guardian of minor heirs of E. H. Hopkins, deceased.
Joseph Anderson, security.

Page 94 - Joseph Anderson guardian of Isabella W. Anderson. Allen Morris,
security.

Page 94 - Samuel McMahan, William Wood, Jacob Coffman, and Alex. Lee to lay
off to widow and family of Winston Taylor, deceased.

Page 95 - William D. Elkins vs Robert H. Majors guardian of children of
Benjamin F. Bowers. Ordered Majors to pay over to William D.
Elkins 1/6 part and cost of case, about Will of William P. Elkins.

Page 96 - W. G. Laughry and others. Petition to sell land. Report to next
Court.

Page 96 - Joannah Nash and others vs Thomas Nash and others. Petition to
sell lands. Lands of estate of George W. Nash, deceased, for his
children.

Page 96 - William G. Laughry and others. Petition to sell land. Clerk's
report. Deposition of Ro. L. Singleton, Bartlett Bird and L. P.
Fields. William G. Laughry, Nancy A. Keele and Robert Lambert are
legally entitled to the 270 acres of land, and William G. Laughry is
entitled to 3/5th of said land, Robert Lambert and Nancy A. Keele
entitled to 1/5th each. The land cannot be divided and recommended
that the land be sold.

Page 97 - C. P. Houston and others. Petition to sell slaves and dower.
William Houston, deceased, departed this life in Bedford County,
leaving petitioner Elizabeth, his widow and petitioner William
a minor, his only heir at law and that C. P. Houston is Executor of
his Last Will and Testament, also guardian of his only heir, William.
Widow, Elizabeth, has dissented from the Will of her late husband
and that she is entitled to dower out of the land and 1/3 part of
the slaves. Robert H. Majors, James Ogilvie and Augustine Wilson
are to allott to the widow 1/3 part of land and that Robert H.
Majors, James Ogilvie and Benjamin F. Whitworth to divide the slaves.
2/3rd goes to William Houston.

Page 98 - William Word admr. and others. Petition to sell land. 4th June
1853 offered for sale the parts of 2 Town Lotsand was purchased by
Jehu A. Blakemore.

Page 99 - John P. Steele admr. of estate of Joel Lawrence, deceased. Mary
Lawrence is widow and Alfred Mallard, Joseph M. Burnett and George
Gregory to lay off support to widow.

1853 June Term

Page 99 - J. A. Blakemore admr. with Will annexed, of John Whitesell, deceased.

Page 99 - Ellen Hastings formerly Ellen Edde, appeared in Court and was examined privately by the Court separate from her husband, James Hastings, touching her consent that the money due to her arising from the sale of the lands of Candis J. Edde, deceased, may be paid over to her husband.

Page 100 - Nicholas Burns and others vs Mary Staggs and others. Petition to sell land. Court ordered that Andrew Vannoy lend to James Story the share of Mrs. Mary Staggs (now Mary Mills) in the proceeds of the sale of land. Nicholas Burns is holding the money.

Page 101 - State of Tennessee for the use of Mary Sharp vs John Oneal. Bastardy. John Oneal denies being the father of the child. Mary Sharp to appeal to next Circuit Court.

Page 101 - State of Tennessee vs Wilie Jarnagan. Bastardy. Defendant cannot be found in Coffee County.

1853 July Term

Page 103 - William Little admr. of estate of Martin Lamb, deceased, with Will annexed.

Page 103 - George W. Parsons guardian of Phillip A. Parsons, minor heir of George W. Parsons, deceased. Thomas T. Parsons and Abram Claxton, securities.

Page 103 - L. W. Barrett admr. of estate of James Bird, deceased.

Page 103 - Hiram Harris of Marshall County, Tennessee guardian of L. J. Lents, B. T. M. Lents and John H. T. Lents, minor heirs of John L. Lents, deceased.

Page 103 - Elizabeth Lents admrix of John J. Lents, deceased.

Page 103 - William Mullins and Andrew E. Mullins admrs. of estate of Mathew Mullins, deceased.

Page 104 - On the petition of James Finey and Isaac Atkinson, citizens of the 9th Civil District, it is ordered that the line of said District and the 11th District be changed as follows, to wit, Beginning at the West Fork of Alexander's Creek at the widow Presgrove's, thence north with the old Nashville Road to the mouth of the lane north of Finney's dwelling house, thence east about 33 poles, thence north about 111 poles to said Atkinson's corner, thence west to the old Nashville Road.

Page 105 - Johana Nash, et als. Petition to sell land of Abram Nash, deceased. To Thomas Nash, Travis Nash, Augustine Nash, Benjamin Garret and

Page 105 - (continued) wife Emily, William Harville and wife Louisa, John McGimsey and wife Polly, all of whom are non-residents of Tennessee and also that Travis Nash and Newton Parsons and wife Louisa Parsons and William Nash son of George W. Nash, have duly summoned. John H. Oneal guardian to answer for them for _____ Nash.

Page 106 - A. B. Moon, William Collins and Jennings Moore to lay off support to Elizabeth Lents, widow of John J. Lents, deceased.

Page 106 - Appropriations. $1000.00 for building a bridge across Duck River at or near the ford known as Warner Ford. Commissioners: Green T. Neely, John A. Warner, James B. Jones, Benjamin Earnhart and John F. Thompson.

Page 106 - $400.00 to build a bridge across the Garrison Fork of Duck River at the mouth of Knobb Creek. A. Erwin, Archibald Murphy, John R. Eakin, Jonas Myers and John Q. Davidson appointed Commissioners.

Page 107 - Frances Black by her next friend C. W. Black. Frances Black has property of which was in the estate of Ephraim Burrow, Eve Burrow and Andrew J. Eaton has been be decree of the Chancery Court, entitled upon her that a Trustee had been appointed to manage said business before it can be paid over. Also, Court agrees that George W. Pratt is suitable Trustee and that Frances Black desires that he be appointed.

Page 107 - G. G. Osborne, Esquire Haggard and J. P. Townsen to lay off support to Jane Mullins, widow of Matthew Mullins, deceased.

Page 109 - William G. Laughry and others. Petition to sell land. William G. Laughry purchased the land.

Page 110 - Court ordered that Nancy A. Rowton receive her dower. William Koble (Coble) guardian of Nancy A. Keele and Robert Lambert having interest of land.

Page 111 - C. P. Houston and others. Petition for dower and division of slaves. Commissioners to lay off to widow Elizabeth Houston, widow of William Houston, deceased, her dower. She also is to have a tract and the mansion house and improvements. 28 June 1853. 16 slaves to be divided between Elizabeth Houston and son William. C. P. Houston guardian of William Houston.

Page 113 - Inventory of William Houston, deceased.

Page 115 - Mariah E. Phillips renewed guardianship of Mary C. H. Phillips, minor heir of B. Phillips, deceased. Charles L. Cannon, security.

Page 117 - Nicholas Burns, George W. King and others. Petition to sell land. Jehu Blagg and wife Judy Blagg are entitled to one share of the proceeds of land of William Staggs, deceased. They being residents of Ray County, State of Missouri and has executed Power of Attorney to Thomas Lents to receive money coming to them from estate of William Stagg, deceased, they have also executed a Deed to their share to Nicholas Burns.

Page 118 - Motion of James L. Scudder, Esq., that Dewitt C. Whitthorne is and has been a citizen of Bedford County for more than 12 months and has been born in said county and that he is now 21 years of age and desires to obtain a License to practice law.

Page 118 - Power of Attorney, __ day of July 1853, by John Jamison of Bedford County to Merritt Maupin.

Page 118 - Thomas Cook guardian of James J., Robert H., Nancy, Elizabeth and Catharine Cook, minor heirs of (blank)   .

Page 119 - Thomas Shearin admr. of estate of John K. Lowwell, deceased. J. M. Ledbetter and James F. Shearin and William Shearin, securities. Green T. Neeley, Jacob B. Delk and Samuel Card, Sr., are to lay off support to widow and family of John K. Lowwell, deceased.

Page 119 - Nuncupative Will by Josiah C. Gault, deceased, was produced for probate, and by the widow being made known, consents was admitted to probate. Lucy C. Little and Lurana J. Winsett are witnesses. William Little, executor. E. D. Winsett and R. A. Gault, securities.

Page 119 - William Little admr. of estate of Hugh M. Gault, deceased. E. D. Winsett and R. A. Gault, securities.

Page 119 - William Little exr. of estate of Martin Lamb, deceased, brought into Court a list of inventory.

Page 120 - Henry Brown admr. of estate of Solomon Brown, deceased. Spencer Brown and Edmund Cooper, security.

Page 120 - William Armstrong admr. of estate of Bethyra(?) Moore, deceased. William Wood and W. L. Brown, securities.

Page 120 - John W. Mayfield admr. of estate of Robert Ray, deceased. D. A. Ozment, W. M. Ray, William Shearin, and John F. Thompson, securities.

Page 120 - William M. Ray guardian of Martha M. Ray and Andrew J. Ray, minor heirs of Robert Ray, deceased.

Page 120 - William Shearin guardian of Thomas M. Ray, minor heir of Robert Ray, deceased.

1853 August Term

Page 121 - John Knott guardian of minor heirs of Wilson Steele, deceased.

Page 121 - Mary Ray guardian of Nancy Jane L., Marling C., America Rosanna, and John W. M. Ray, minor heirs of Robert Ray, deceased.

Page 121 - David R. Vance guardian of Virginia Vance and Robert Vance, minor heirs of Robert Vance, deceased.

Page 121 - Johanna Nash and others. Petition to sell land of Abner Nash, deceased. Abner Nash departed this life __ day of ___ 1853, leaving the parties mentioned in the petition as his heirs &c. He died seized of a tract of land in Civil District # 5, about 22 acres.

Page 122 - Jerome Albright and others. Petition to sell land. Report to next Court.

Page 123 - William Young admr. of Robert B. Vance, deceased. Petition to divide slaves. Robert B. Vance is dead and died intestate, leaving his widow Elizabeth Vance and two children, Virginia and Robert Vance surviving him. He also owned slaves.

Page 124 - Wiley F. Daniel admr. of estate of Richard W. Edmondson, deceased. Joseph Hastings, A. C. Wood and James W. Proby are to lay off support for widow and family of Richard W. Edmondson, deceased.

Page 124 - Ross D. Deery admr. of estate of Mary Lane, deceased. William B. M. Brame, security.

Page 125 - Wesley S. Evins admr. of estate of estate of William M. Evans, deceased. Robert H. Terry and McEmsley Arnold, securities.

Page 125 - Robert F. Arnold admr. of estate of D. P. T. House, deceased.

Page 125 - Henry Graham, now a citizen of Bedford County, produced in open Court, a copy of his Declaration which had been made in Chancery Court in Nashville, Tennessee, on 6th day of November 1850, declaring his intention to become a citizen of these United States and to renounce forever all allegiance and fidelity to her Majesty Queen Victoria, Queen of Great Britain and Ireland, or any other Sovereignty whatever. Properly certified under the Seal of said Chancery Court at Nashville, who solemnly swore that he would support the Constitution of the United States, and that he had absolutely and entirely renounced and abjoined all Allegiance and Fidelity to her Majesty Queen Victoria, Queen of Great Britain and Ireland, and to every other foreign Prince, Potentate, State or Sovereignty when or before he was a subject, whereupon it was ordered by the Court that these facts be so certified under the Seal of this Court.

1853 August Term

Page 126 - Mrs. Mary Streeter be released from paying tax on 7 slaves, situated in 21st District and they being listed in 7th District.

Page 126 - L. W. Barratt admr. of estate of Mary Brown, deceased.

Page 127 - State of Tennessee vs Wiley Jarnagan. Charge of Bastardy. Continued.

1853 September Term

Page 129 - Gabriel Shofner resigned as guardian of Mary M. and Virginia E. Webster. Plummer W. Shofner was appointed guardian.

Page 129 - Alfred H. Gambill guardian of his minor daughter Huldah M. Gambill.

Page 130 - William W. Gaunt admr. of estate of John A. Gaunt, deceased. Hugh C. Hurst and Nicholas Burns, securities.

Page 130 - Benjamin F. Duggan admr. of estate of Samuel Elliott, deceased. William C. Blanton, security.

Page 130 - Eliza C. Moore, widow of Henry Moore, deceased, relinguished her right to admr. upon the estate of her deceased husband, Jesse W. Brown was appointed admr. James H. Curtiss, security. John Armstrong, Thomas S. Mays and James Helton to lay off support to Eliza C. Moore.

Page 130 - William Word admr. of estate of Joseph J. Looney, deceased. John S. Brown and John Cortner, securities.

Page 131 - Robert Lacy, one of the executors of the Last Will of Elijah Lacy, deceased, which Will was proven, relinguished his right to execute said Will. Abram Reagor, the other executor was appointed exr.

Page 131 - James T. Williams admr. of estate of Susanna Hutson, deceased. William M. Hutson and Thomas Hutson, securities.

Page 131 - B. F. Russell admr of estate of William M. Russell, deceased. John S. Brown, security.

Page 131 - William M. Low resigned as admr. of estate of R. N. Elliott, deceased. David Elliott appointed admr.

Page 131 - Elijah Holt guardian of Jasper Holt, minor.

Page 132 - James H. Curtiss, Jr. guardian of Nancy R. Curtiss, his minor daughter.

Page 132 - David A. Ozment guardian of Asa G., Edwin E., and Eldridge L. G. McGowen, minor heirs of Samuel McGowen, deceased. Thomas D. Tarpley and Charles L. Batte, securities.

1853 September Term

Page 132 - Thomas D. Tarpley guardian of Henry E., Fluvanna C., and Samuel G. McGowen, minor heirs of Samuel G. McGowen, deceased.

Page 132 - Johanna Nash and others. Petition to sell land. Land sold 1 day of September 1853 to William C. Orr and David P. Orr. Abner Nash, deceased, one of the defendants and heirs at law.

Page 133 - Jerome Albright and others. Petition to sell land. Sale on 31 August 1853. Land on headwaters of W------ branch of Big Flat Creek. James J. Burrow purchaser.

Page 134 - Andrew E. Mullins and William Mullins admrs. of Mathew Mullins, deceased. Petition to sell slaves. Mathew Mullins died intestate and left his widow and 8 heirs or distributees surviving him and that he left 6 slaves.

Page 135 - Thomas J. Stanfield, Wesley Evans and others. Petition to sell land. Land belonging to Charles Kirby ordered by the Court to be sold. Charles Kirby being only child of Henry Kirby, deceased. 27 Nov 1852 the land was sold by William Stanfield and John Evans became the purchaser. Now, John Evans is dead, having died intestate that he left surviving him, Nancy Evans his widow, James R., Lucy A., Martha, Elizabeth, Susan T., Mary, Caroline, Clementine, Thomas, and Alvis K. Evans, his only children and heirs at law. Thomas J. Stanfield and Wesley Evans admrs. of the estate. Land to be sold to pay debts.

Page 136 - William Tatum and wife Mary Petition for inquest of lunacy as to Thomas Statham. Court states that Thomas Statham, a resident of Bedford County, and that William Tatum and wife are merely related to him and as such are merely interested as to his mental capacity. A Committee was appointed to examine him and see if he is capable of attending to his own affairs with safety to himself and his family. Report from Court found Thomas Statham mentally and physically incapable of managing his own affairs &c. Court ordered Thomas Statham placed under the guardianship and control of A. M. McElroy.

Page 137 - William G. Laughry and others. Petition to sell land. Robert A. Lambert sold to Edmund Cooper the said funds in hands of John H. Oneal arising from the sale of the Rowton lands.

Page 138 - Susan Statham. Petition to appoint Trustee. Ann Phillips bequeathed to her daughter Susan Statham for and during her natural life and at her death to be equally divided amongst the heirs of her body, lawfully begotten, the 7 slaves, and that her husband Thomas Statham is mentally and physicially incapable of taking care of said property and managing it. Susan Statham desires the Court to appoint A. M. McElroy her Trustee to manage and control the said slaves for her use and support.

80

1853 September Term

Page 138 - D. A. Ozment and C. L. Batte, admrs of S. G. McGowen, deceased.
Petition to sell slaves. Samuel G. McGowen died intestate and the
owner of slaves (2), and that David A. Ozment and C. L. Batte
were appointed admrs. of said estate. A. M. McElroy Trustee for
Susan Statham, with money. W. H. Nailor and Thomas P. Powell,
securities.

Page 139 - William Wood resigned as guardian of Nancy Ray, minor heir of
John Ray, deceased. Nelson Gabbert was appointed guardian.

Page 139 - Neely Coble guardian of his minor daughter.

Page 139 - William Shearin admr. of Thomas McGuyer, deceased.

Page 140 - Margaret Hazelwood formerly Margaret Ray, was privately examined
by the Court from her husband William Hazelwood, touching on money
due her from sale of the lands of her Grandmother Gennet Ray,
deceased, to be paid over to her husband.

Page 140 - Rebecca J. McGowen and others. Petition for dower. Samuel G.
McGowen is dead and died intestate, seized of land that he left
Rebecca J. McGowen his widow and the other parties as his only
heirs at law. Rebecca J. McGowen is entitled to the dower, 1/3
part.

Page 141 - Mary Ray and others. Petition for dower. Robert Ray died intestate and that he left Mary Ray his widow and other children. He
died seized of several tracts of land. Mary Ray is entitled to her
dower.

Page 141 - William Turner and others. Petition to sell land Warrants. James
Beavers, on 18 August 1851, paid by U. S. of America Bounty Land
Warrant No. 12171 for 80 acres for his service as a private in
Captain Williamson's Company Tennessee Militia, War of 1812 that
since the issuance of said land Warrant, James Beavers has departed this life and that by Deed executed on 19 August 1851 conveyed
said land Warrant to William Turner and wife Ann and Solomon
Brintlet and wife Sukey have filed their petition in this Court,
they desire that the land be sold. Rhoda Beavers be appointed
Commissioner to sell land Warrant No. 12171 and she assign and
transfer according to law.

Page 142 - John F. Thompson and Jesse M. Ledbetter and Joseph Anderson to lay
off support to widow and family of Robert Ray, deceased.

Page 144 - James Garrett guardian of minor heirs of R. C. Garrett, deceased.

Page 144 - Thomas Holland admr. of estate of Thomas Holland, Sr., deceased.

Page 144 - Alexander Eakin exr. of the Will of Mary Jane Eakin, deceased.

1853 September Term

Page 145 - John P. Haney, John W. Greer and Stephen Freeman to lay off
support to Rozella Russell, out of the estate of her deceased
husband William M. Freeman.

Page 145 - Mary A. A. A. McCuistion, minor who petitions by her guardian
John H. Oneal vs William Crawford and others. Petition to sell
land. Defendants, Charles Crawford and Samuel Jones are non-residents. Complainant wants land sold and invested in other property.

Page 145 - Pearce Wilhoite and others. Petition to sell land. 16 acres.

Page 146 - Elizabeth Catharine Moor and others. Petition to sell land.
Henry Moor departed this life intestate in Bedford County and
that during his life time executed a Trust Deed on his land
consisting about 115 acres in Bedford County on which he resided
at the time of his death, to James H. Curtiss, Jr. The lands to
be sold to pay debts of Henry Moor, deceased. Elizabeth Catharine
Moor, widow of Henry Moor, deceased, is entitled to dower.

Page 146 - William M. Hutson and other heirs at law of Cutty B. Hutson, deceased
Complainants are the only heirs at law of Cutty B. Butson, deceased,
and Sarah Hutson, widow of Cutty B. Hutson, is now deceased. Desire
land to be sold.

Page 146 - State of Tennessee vs Willie Jarnagan. Bastardy. Jarnagan is in
Coffee County, Tennessee.

1853 October Term

Page 150 - William Collins, Jennings Moore and Alexander B. Moon to lay off
support to widow and family of John F. Lentz, deceased.

Page 150 - Jordan C. Holt, Jr. guardian of Izadora A. Holt, minor heir of
Jordan C. Holt, Sr., deceased.

Page 150 - Benjamin Moseley guardian of Mahulda Ann Holt and Moriah Holt,
minor heirs of Jordan C. Holt, deceased.

Page 150 - James H. Elmore guardian of his wife Nancy Tilman Elmore, a minor
heir who has funds in the hands of a Commissioner.

Page 150 - David R. Vance admr. of estate of John M. Green, deceased. Willis
Green and Hosea Green, securities. C. B. King, Thomas House and
Elijah Holt to lay off support to widow and family of John M.
Green, deceased.

Page 151 - George W. Cunningham admr. of estate of James Meadows, deceased.

Page 151 - Andrew Reed admr. of estate of Malinda Reed, his deceased wife.
Wilson C. Reed, security.

Page 151 - Claiborne W. Coats admr. of Henry C. Coats, deceased. James Coats and J. N. Reed, securities.

Page 151 - John R. Coffey admr. of estate of Rice Coffey, deceased. Henry B. Coffey and N. C. Harris, securities.

Page 151 - Miles Phillips and Joseph Bartley admrs. of estate of James D. Neill, deceased. B. B. Harper and J. M. Gibson, securities. Michael Moore, J. W. C. Cunningham and James Harrison to lay off support to Sarah Neill, widow of James D. Neill, deceased.

Page 152 - Thomas G. W. Wright guardian of Margaret J. Ferrell and Martha A. Ferrell, minor heirs of Richard Ferrell, deceased. David R. Vance and John Q. Davidson, securities.

Page 152 - Margaret Hall admr. of estate of Joshua Hall, deceased. Edmund Cooper and Thomas Kimmons, securities.

Page 153 - Levi Underwood and wife, aged, poor people be allowed $25.00.

Page 153 - Thomas Daniel be allowed $300.00 for extra work on Shofner Bridge.

Page 153 - Sarah Burditt guardian of Sarah K. Burditt.

Page 153 - John Thomas Cunningham, a minor age 7 years, was bound to George W. Cunningham until he arrives at the age of 21 years, to learn the art of farming.

Page 154 - John R. Coffee admr. of Rice Coffee. Petition to sell slaves. Rice Coffee departed this life leaving 13 or maybe 14 heirs and that he left them 13 negro slaves. The slaves will need to be sold to divide proceeds among the heirs.

Page 154 - William M. Hutson and others. Petition to sell land.

Page 154 - This day the petition of the citizens of the Town of Wartrace Depot in Bedford County, was filed in Court which petition is in the words and figures following, to wit, -
State of Tennessee, Bedford County. To the Worshipful County Court of Bedford County, The undersigned petitioners of the Town of Wartrace Depot in said County, petition your worship to grant us the privilege of encorporating said Village, running one quarter of a mile in every direction from the center of said Depot ground so as to elect officers to carry into effect the laws provided in such cases, and for the benefit of the good citizens of said Village, for which your petitioners will we pray, this the 3rd day of October 1853.

Daniel Stephens	T. A. Prince	R. P. Ganaway	Joseph Sherwood
Robert Buchanan	R. E. Coffee	T. P. Ganaway	Robert Erwin
John Stephens	T. C. Mills	John A. Ganaway	M. Payne
N. C. Harris	Wm. H. Sims	B. Z. Ganaway	A. T. Garrett
W. H. Clark	C. M. Norville	John R. Coffee	A. M. Keller

1853 October Term

Page 154 - (continued)
      W. B. Norville   J. D. Payne   W. T. Green   J. W. Tilford
      G. W. Martin   A. E. Mullins   Willis Pruett
      Drawn off for Registration October 12th, 1853.
      On motion it was ordered by said Court that said Town be incor-
      porated as a Town of Wartrace Depot, with all the privileges and
      powers and liabilities prescribed by the Act of General Assembly
      of the State of Tennessee, Chapter No. 17, passed January 7th
      1850 and that the Corporation of said Town extend one quarter of
      a mile in every direction from the center of the Depot grounds.
      And is was ordered by the Court that said petition be spread
      upon the Minutes of the Court, and that a copy of this entry
      properly certified be given for registration and that the same
      be registered in the Register's Office in Bedford County, twelve
      acting Justices being present and voting in the affirmative.
                      Signed: P. C. Steele
                           Jos. Hastings
                           Wm. Galbreath

Page 156 - Mary A. A. A. McCuistion by her guardian John H. Oneal vs William
      Crawford and others. Petition to sell land. The residence of
      John Harrison is unknown. Notice of sale in newspapers.

Page 156 - By petition of Samuel McDowell and it appearing to the Court that
      the gates erected by General Robert Cannon on and across the road
      passing said Cannon's land and to said McDowell's Mills, under and
      by authority of this Court, are not such gates as are required by
      law. It is ordered by the Court that said gates shall be opened
      and remain open until the said Cannon shall erect such gates as
      are required by law, or until the further order of this Court.

Page 156 - William J. Whitthorne is and has been a citizen of Bedford County
      for a number of years and that he is over the age of 21 years, of
      good character &c, desires to obtain a License to practice Law.

Page 156 - Polly Nance is in a state of mental derangement, that she is a
      citizen of Bedford County and that she is a pauper and it is there-
      fore ordered by the Court that the Clerk to certify the same to
      the managers of the Lunatic Assylum at Nashville, Tennessee in
      order that she be admitted into said Assylum, under the Acts of
      the General Assembly of the State of Tennessee.

Page 157 - State of Tennessee vs Willie Jarnagan. Case of Bastardy. Willie
      Jarnagan has failed to answer or appear in Court.

Page 157 - State of Tennessee vs G. W. Jarnagan. Bastardy. Put into hands
      of Sheriff of Bedford County.

Page 158 - David R. Vance admr. &c and Isaac Jason Green and Margaret Ann
      Green. Petition to sell land. John M. Green departed this life
      intestate, seized of land. Isaac Jason and Margaret Ann Green,

1853 October Term

Page 158 - (continued) his only heirs at law. John A. Green was considerably
in debt. Report to next Court.

Page 158 - Thomas J. Stanfield and Wesley Evans and others. Petition to sell
land. Land of John Evans, deceased. W. W. Stanfield purchaser.

1853 November Term

Page 160 - James W. Woodfin admr. of estate of James Hale, deceased, with D. J.
Hale and J. W. Woodfin. Thomas Warren and R. L. Thomas, securities.
James Scruggs, Thomas Warren and James Frizzell to lay off support
to Susan Hale, widow of James Hale, deceased.

Page 160 - Elizabeth Watkins guardian of William S. Watkins, her minor son.
William Burns and Jesse F. Vannoy, securities.

Page 161 - John Thomas guardian of minor heirs of Mary McClure, deceased.

Page 161 - R. S. Clark guardian of Sophronia Meadows, a minor heir of Pumphrey
Meadows, deceased.

Page 161 - J. L. Couch guardian of Pumphrey Meadows, a minor heir of Pumphrey
Meadows, deceased.

Page 161 - John Read guardian of Cyntha Ann Read, a minor heir of James M.
Read, deceased. Joseph Hastings, security.

Page 161 - James Y. West guardian of Isaac A. Thorneberry.

Page 161 - Levi Thronsberry guardian of Sarah E., Benjamin L., James K.,
Joel M., Andrew J., and Tabitha F. Thornsberry, with William Brown
and James Y. West.

Page 161 - Samuel Doak guardian of William E. and David C. Delk.

Page 162 - H. H. Holt admr. of John T. Muse.

Page 162 - Thomas Lipscomb admr. of Michael Meadows, deceased.

Page 162 - G. E. Bowden guardian of James P., Nancy, Elenus, Daniel W.,
William and Priscilla Parker, minor heirs of Charles Parker,
deceased. W. G. Knight and A. (Widow Nancy, remarried Carter
Blanton and died by 1857).

Page 162 - James W. Oakley guardian of Nancy Ann Hester.

Page 162 - H. P. McGuyer admr. of Samuel McDowel, deceased. John McGuyer,
security.

Page 163 - Benjamin F. Greer admr. of estate of George W. Fogleman, deceased.

Page 163 - Augustus Cannon admr. of estate of Minos Cannon, deceased. Clement Cannon and W. W. Gill, securities.

Page 163 - Bennet Rogers admr. of estate of Levi Rogers, deceased. Elijah Couch, J. W. Proby and James McGill to lay off support to widow and family of Levi Rogers, deceased.

Page 163 - B. F. Russell admr. of estate of William M. Russell, deceased.

Page 165 - John R. Coffee admr. &c. Petition to sell 3 slaves.

Page 166 - John R. Coffee, H. H. Coffee, B. B. Coffee and Mary G. Kindle vs Henry C. Yell and others. Henry C. Yell, Sarah J. Robinson wife of (blank) Robinson, Mary Elenor, Nancy Elizabeth and Archibald Yell, the last five are minors and are all non-residents of State of Tennessee, and reside in the State of Arkansas, and are the children of Martha Yell who was a child of Rice Coffee, deceased.

Page 167 - Eliza Catharine Moore, widow and others. Heirs of Henry Moore, deceased and Jesse W. Brown admr. of Moore and James H. Curtiss, Jr. Exparte - Sale of land in Bedford County on waters of Sinking Creek. James H. Curtiss purchaser.

Page 168 - William M. Hutson and others. Petition to sell dower of Susannah Hutson, deceased. On 28 October 1853, sold dower tract to William M. Hutson. Other petitioners are Thomas Hutson, James L. Williams and wife Mary C. Williams, William M. Stephens, Sarah Stephens, Pleasant A. Stephens, and Jefferson G. Stephens. Land belonged to Susanna Hutson, deceased. It being land of her husband, Cutty B. Hutson, deceased.

Page 170 - James A. McL(Lean or McLure) and others. Petition to sell land.

Page 170 - David G. Denson and others. Petition to sell land. Land belonging to heirs of William Denson. Sale on 15 October 1853. Sold to Albert T(P). Knott. Land in Bedford County.

Page 172 - Mary Lawwell and others. Petition for Dower. John K. Lawwell is dead and that he left surviving him petitioners, Henry, Ethan, Elizabeth, William, and Bennice Lawwell, his children and only heirs at law. Thomas Shearin admr. Mary Lawwell, his widow, is entitled to Dower which has not been allotted to her. Ordered to be done by Augustus Wilson, John F. Thompson and Green T. Neely, Commissioners.

Page 172 - James A. McL(Lean or Lun) and others. Petition to sell land. Heirs of Mary McL(Lean). To report to next Court.

Page 172 - Alexander Ray and others. Petition to sell land. 7 Nov 1853, Willis W. Wilhoite produced written transfer and payment of William Hazelwood and wife Margaret of all interest that they have in the

Page]72 - (continued) funds in the hands of John H. Oneal, clerk, arising from the sale of the lands belonging to the estate of James Ray, deceased, they having]/6 part of 1/6 share.

Page 173 - John McGuire guardian &c. Petition to divide slaves. William McGuire, Benjamin McGuire and John McGuire are jointly the owners of slaves (3), which are under the control of John McGuire as their guardian and that William McGuire has arrived at the age of 21 years and desires his share of the estate. Slaves to be sold, cannot be divided.

Page 173 - Rebecca J. McGowen and others. Petition for Dower. Rebecca J. McGowen widow of Samuel G. McGowen, deceased, desires her dower and includes the mansion house and all improvements &c. Land on Shelbyville-Columbia Road.

Page 174 - Thomas Lipscomb admr. Petition to sell slaves. Michael Meadows is dead, the he devised the slaves in petition to Jane Meadows during her natural life, who is now dead, and at her death to his children, that he appointed (blank) Harris and James Meadows as executors, and they are both dead. Thomas Lipscomb has been appointed admr. of the estate of Michael Meadows, deceased, and that he possessed the slaves (about 20). Slaves to be sold.

Page 175 - Johannah Nash and others. Petition to sell land. Lafayette Nash by his Attorney, produced him in open court, a transfer from Travis C. Nash to him of all rights, title &c which Travis C. Nash has in the funds now in the hands of the Clerk, arising from the sale of the lands belonging to Abner Nash, deceased. "For and in consideration of the natural love and affection which I have towards my brother Lafayette Nash, I transfer &c from the sale of the lands belonging to the heirs of Abner Nash, deceased, my interest in the same being the 1/11th part of the same.This 3 Nov 1853. Signed, T. C. Nash".

Page 176 - J. C. Hix and D. D. Hix, Commissioners and Executors vs Herrod F. Holt and John J. Hurst. Motion for judgement on note.

Page 177 - Mary Ray et als. Petition for Dower. Mary Ray, widow of Robert Ray, deceased.

Page 178 - This day the Plat and Certificate of the Corporation Limits of the Town of Wartrace was produced to the Court. (Plat on page 178)

Page 179 - Mary A. A. A. McCuistion, a minor who petitions by her guardian John H. Oneal vs Charles Crawford, William Crawford, Sarah Crawford, Samuel Jakes, and Jno. Harrison. The lands in the petition should be sold.

Page 180 - Elizabeth Lentz and others. Petition for Dower. John J. Lentz died intestate, seized and possessed of land, leaving Elizabeth, his widow and the said L. J., B. F. M., and John H. T. Lentz, his children and his only heirs, whose guardian Hiram Harris, and that the widow

1853 November Term

Page 180 - (continued) Elizabeth has not received her dower. A. B. Moon, John L. Thompson and A. Wilson to lay off her dower lands.

Page 180 - Hannah Harrison and others. Petition for dower. John Harrison died intestate and seized of land, leaving the said Hannah his widow and his heirs. Hannah has not received her dower. Randolph Newsom, George W. Greer and Leroy W. Barrett to lay her dower.

Page 180 - State of Tennessee vs William R. Manly. Bastardy. William R. Manly was called into Court and answer the warrant of State of Tennessee and charge against him for Bastardy. He defaulted.

Page 180 - Hannah Harrison and others. Petition to sell land. Land of John Harrison, deceased. Zachariah Harrison is entitled to an interest of 1/3, Elisha Reed and wife Martha C. entitled to 1/3, Matilda J. Whitesell 1/6, and William C. and D. C. Delk 1/6 and Hannah Harrison is entitled to dower out of the land.

1853 December Term

Page 184 - Zachariah Davis, Thomas Pickle and James W. Coffey to lay off support to widow and family of Joseph J. Looney, deceased.

Page 185 - James W. Proby, James McGill and J. L. Couch to lay off support to Elizabeth Rogers, widow of Levi Rogers, deceased.

Page 185 - Alfred Ransom admr. and others. Exparte - Mrs. Martha L. Vernon was privately examined apart from her husband William T. Vernon. She stated he had the right to control her own property and money, the same belonging to the estate of James H. Floyd, deceased. Dec 5,1853

Page 185 - Thomas L.Mays, John Armstrong and James Helton to lay off support to Catharine Moore, widow of Henry Moore, deceased.

Page 185 - Michael Moore, J. W. C. Cunningham and James H. Harrison to lay off support to Sarah Neill, widow of James D. Neill, deceased, and her family.

Page 186 - Hiram Edde admr. of Candis Edde, deceased. Pierce Wilhoite, security

Page 186 - J. M. Gibson guardian of Samuel Miles Harper and Mary Matilda Harper

Page 186 - William Oliver guardian of Joseph Oliver, minor heir of Wright Olive Passada Oliver, security.

Page 186 - Passada Oliver guardian of Henry H. Oliver and James B. Oliver, mino children of Wright Oliver, deceased. William Oliver, security.

Page 186 - M. T. Williams guardian of John M. Williams and T. W. Williams. John Jordan, security.

1853 December Term

Page 187 - John Jordan executor of James E. Williams, deceased. William H. Hight
         and John W. Simpson, security.

Page 187 - William D. Elkins guardian of David Elkins, a lunatic. Robert Denniston
         security.

Page 187 - James W. Buchanan guardian of John Brown, Mary Elizabeth, William
         Crawford, Eleanor Francis and Sarah Lema West, minor children of Isaac
         M. West. George W. Buchanan, security.

Page 187 - Thomas Hutson guardian of John H. Heazlette. William M. Hutson, J. F.
         Watson and Wilson D. Blankenship, securities.

Page 187 - J. C. Hix admr. of estate of Sarah Albright, deceased.

Page 187 - Thomas P. Powell, Justice of the Peace of Bedford County, resigned.

Page 188 - Richard Warner, Commissioner vs Eli H. Stephens and J. M. L. Stephens.
         Judgement by motion. Defendants had not paid for purchase of a slave.

Page 188 - Guynn Foster, Leonard Bullock admrs. and others. Petition to sell land.
         Eliza Jane Ogilvie purchaser.

Page 189 - Martha E. Crutcher and others. Petition for sale of slaves. Martha E.
         Crutcher, widow of S. F. Crutcher; George W. Buchanan and wife Virginia
         L. Buchanan and Robert White a minor under 21 years who petition by his
         regular guardian William H. Crutcher, from which the Court is satisfied
         that Susan White departed this life intestate in Williamson County,
         Tennessee and that Martha E. White who afterwards intermarried with
         Sterling F. Crutcher was appointed admris. of estate, and negro slaves.
         Slaves to be sold.

Page 190 - David R. Vance admr. &c and others. Petition to sell land. John McGrew,
         deceased, left minor children. The tracts of land should be sold and
         proceeds go to his minor children.

Page 191 - D. D. and J. C. Hix vs S. Doak, Samuel G. Hays and Jo Thompson. Judge-
         ment.

Page 191 - David Elkins, a lunatic, by his next friend Mary S. Elkins vs William
         D. Elkins, guardian. Petition for removal of guardianship. So ordered.

Page 192 - State of Tennessee vs William R. Manley. Bastardy. Recover of Sarah
         E. Loyd failed to appear &c.

Page 192 - Catharine Dougal, widow of John Dougal, deceased, appointed exrix.

Page 192 - Pierce Wilhoite and others. Petition to sell land. Commissioners sold
         land 22 Nov 1853. Pierce Wilhoite purchaser.

Page 193 - Passady Oliver and Thomas Oliver, admrix. and admr. Petition to sell
         slaves. NOTE: Pasady Oliver is some times called Hazardy.

1853 December Term

Page 193 - (continued) Negroes bought by William Oliver and Joseph M. Larue, estate of widow, and heirs of Wright Oliver, deceased.

Page 193 - Elizabeth Lentz and others. Petition for dower. Plat on page 194. Assigned to Elizabeth Lentz widow of John J. Lentz, deceased, including the mansion house and improvements. 24 Nov 1853. Elizabeth Lentz for and during her natural life.

Page 195 - Hannah Harrison and others. Petition for dower &c. Hannah Harrison widow of John Harrison, her deceased husband, the following tract of land includes the mansion house and improvements. The report not being excepted to in all things confirmed and is ordered by the Court that all the right title claim and interest which Zachariah Harrison, Elisha Reed and wife Martha C., Matilda J. Whitesell, David C. Delk and William C. Delk have and to the tract of land report be devested out of them and vested in Hannah Harrison during her natural life.

Page 195 - Hannah Harrison and others. Petition to sell land. The land that the above had interest in, is to be sold. 90 acres. Elisha Reed purchased

Page 197 - Price C. Steele, Commissioner vs Samuel Doak, Joseph Thompson and J. . Blakeman. Judgement.

Page 198 - Thomas Lipscomb admr. with Will annexed of Michael Meadows, deceased. Petition to sell slaves. 21 slaves sold.

Page 199 - D. L. Evans, William Galbreath and Thomas Lipscomb to lay off support to widow and family of George W. Fogleman, deceased, her deceased husband. Report to next Court.

Page 199 - P. C. Steele admr. of estate of Alesey Stewart, deceased. William Brown, security.

1854 January Term

Page 200 - John Stammers guardian of Susanna Stammers. Joseph Anderson and John C. Wilson, securities.

Page 200 - William A. Loyd guardian of William T. Miles and Henrietta Miles.

Page 200 - Wilkins Blanton admr. of William S. Pollock. Samuel Bobo, security.

Page 200 - John H. Floyd guardian of John Floyd, William Floyd and James Floyd, minor heirs of Jas. H. Floyd, deceased. William Floyd and E. D. Winsett, securities.

Page 201 - John B. Winn guardian of Mary G. and Sarah J. Taylor. E. P. Winn and L. A. Winn, securities. (James Foster had resigned as their guardian

Page 201 - David T. Chambers guardian of Robert Brown and Eliza Jane Brown. John W. Mayfield and D. A. Ozment, securities.

Page 201 - Commissioners to lay off support to Manerva Williams, widow of James E. Williams, deceased.

Page 201 - David T. Chambers and others. Petition to divide slaves. Petitioners Robert and Eliza Jane Brown are the only children and heirs of Solomon Brown and that David T. Chambers intermarried with Evaline Brown the widow of Solomon Brown in the month of April]853 and that Solomon Brown departed this life some 2 years since intestate in the State of Missouri. Solomon Brown was the owner of about 10 slaves.

Page 203 - George W. Spruce and wife Elizabeth and others. Petition for dower. Richard Musgrave is dead, that he died intestate in Bedford County and was the owner of a tract of land described in the petition, that he left to his widow Elizabeth, the petitioner who has since intermarried with George W. Spruce and petitioners William E., James R. and Nancy R. his only children and heirs. The widow had not received her dower. Court ordered Commissioners to lay off to widow Elizabeth 1/3 of said estate including the dwelling house.

Page 204 - John R. Coffey and others vs Henry C. Yell and others. Petition of division of land. Rice Coffey died seized and possessed of a tract of land in Civil District # 3, about 250 acres. He left as his children, Henry B. Coffey, John R. Coffey, B. B. Coffey, Mary Kindle and A. H. Coffey who are living and that his daughter Martha Yell died leaving as her children Jane Robinson wife of (blank) Robinson, Henry C. Yell, Mary E., Nancy E., and Archibald Yell, who are entitled to the share of their mother, making in all 6 shares. Land to be divided.

Page 204 - John R. Coffee, Henry B. Coffee, Alexander Hamilton Coffee, B. B. Coffee and Mary Kindle and others vs (blank) . Petition to divide land.

Page 205 - Minos Cannon elected Constable in 7th District.

Page 207 - Malinda Puckett wife of Caswell Puckett was examined privately from her husband, by the Court, that the money arising from sale of the negroes belonging to James Cooper, deceased, to be paid over to her husband.

Page 208 - Thomas Lipscomb admr. of Michael Meadows, deceased. Petition to sell slaves. Upon application of Willis W. Wilhoite produced a regular transfer made by Wiley Daniel and Jane Daniel his wife by their Attorney Nathan Ragan also as Power of Attorney, duly executed in the County of Arkansas, State of Arkansas by Wiley Daniel and wife Jane Daniel authorized Nathan Ragan to sell and transfer all rights and interests which Wiley Daniel and wife Jane Daniel have in and to the estate of Michael Meadows, deceased, in the hands of Thomas Lipscomb, administered by which transfer Wiley Daniel and wife Jane Daniel have sold all their interest in said estate to Willis W. Wilhoite.

Page 208 - Mary A. A. A. McCuistion, a minor who petitioned by her guardian John H. Oneal. Commissioners to sell lands. Those who had interest in the

1854 January Term

Page 208 - (continued) land are, Mary A. A. A. McCuistion, William Crawford, Charles Crawford, Sarah Crawford, Samuel Jones and John Harrison. The land is in Bedford County on waters of Big Flat Creek in District # 2 about 103 acres. Jesse C. Coleman purchaser.

Page 210 - Jane Mullins and others. Petition for dower. Matthew Mullins is dead and that he died intestate in Bedford County, seized of a tract of land and that Jane Mullins is his widow and James Mullins, John Mullins, William Mullins, Andy Mullins, Sally Chandler, Frank King and wife Polly, Henry Stephens and wife Nancy, and Jane, Nancy A., and Mathew McKelby only children of Susan McKilby(?), deceased, are his only children and heirs at law and William Mullins and Andy Mullins are his admrs. on the said estate. They were not notified that Jane Mullins not received her dower, which is 1/3 of the real estate.

Page 210 - L. A. Wynn and others. Petition to divide land. John Taylor is dead and he left surviving him, a widow who has since intermarried with L. A. Wynn, and Mary G. and Sarah E. Taylor being minors by their guardian J. B. Wynn his duly children and heirs, and John Taylor was the owner of the 2 tracts of land and the petitioners desires to have the land divided.

Page 211 - D. A. Ozment and C. L. Batt, admrs. of S. G. Gowen, deceased. Petition to sell slaves. One bought by Joseph Lindsey and one to Rebeccah McGee

Page 211 - This day personally appeared in open Court, N. O. McAdams and John M. Smith, respectable citizens of said Court and being duly sworn according to law declared that John Medearis was a Revolutionary Pensioner of the United States at the rate of $480.00 per annum, that he died on the 3 day of March 1834, leaving no widow and but one child now living, to Polly Smith. The Court is perfectly satisfied as to the death of John Medearis on the 31st March]834.

Page 212 - Martha E. Crutcher, George W. Buchanan and wife Virginia L. and Robert White, the last of whom is a minor and petitions by his guardian Will H. Crutcher. Petition to sale slaves. Slaves to be sold.

Page 213 - James A. McLure(?) and others. Petition to sell land. Lewis Lynch the purchaser.

1854 February Term

Page 215 - Thomas B. Jeffries guardian of Drury Y. Jeffries, James D. Jeffries, Mary J. Jeffries and Virginia E. Jeffries, his minor children. Wilson and Meredith Blanton, securities.

Page 215 - Wynn Bearden admr. of estate of John W. Bearden, deceased.

Page 215 - George D. Stevenson admr. of estate of Robert R. Stephenson, deceased G. D. Stephenson, security.

Page 215 - Joseph P. Thompson admr. of estate of Prudence Thompson, deceased. Minos F. Thompson, security.

Page 215 - James T. Williams admr. of estate of Mary C. Williams, deceased. J. J. Crunk and Wilson Garrett security.

Page 215 - Joseph N. Card guardian of Mary F., Tappenas Lipscomb, minor children of John Lipscomb, deceased.

Page 216 - Power of Attorney, dated Feb 16, 1854, executed by H. L. Davidson to D. M. Shofner and M. D. Brittain.

Page 2]6 - Power of Attorney, dated Jan 30, 1854, executed by James Morgan to Gideon P. Baskette.

Page 216 - Power of Attorney, dated Feb 6, 1854, executed by J. M. Henson to William E. Erwin.

Page 216 - Power of Attorney, dated Feb 6, 1854, executed by James Sewell to Levi Sewell.

Page 216 - Wiley F. Daniel admr. of estate of Richard W. Edmondson, deceased.

Page 216 - John Jordan executor of estate of James E. Williams, deceased.

Page 216 - Bennett Rogers admr. of estate of Levi Rogers, deceased.

Page 216 - Charles Williams, Norman Finney and Joshua C. Coleman to lay off support to Nancy E. Bearden, widow of John W. Bearden, deceased.

Page 216 - J. G. Neeley, Absalom Reeves and Michael Dixon, Common School Commissioners in Sulphur Spring Township, made their report.

Page 217 - Orphan boy, William Henry Word, age 12 years, bound to John Wilhoite, to learn farming, until age of 21 years.

Page 218 - John R. Coffey and others. Exparte - To divide land.

Page 218 - Nancy E. Bearden and others. Petition for dower. Nancy E. Bearden, widow of J. W. Bearden, deceased, is entitled to dower in a tract of land. Augustine Wilson, County surveyor, Mathew Cunningham and Samuel Gordon to lay off dower which is 1/3 of said tract.

Page 218 - David T. Chambers and others. Petition to divide slaves. Slaves belonging to the estate of Solomon Brown, now dead, divided among his 2 heirs after setting a part to David T. Chambers and wife Evaline, 1/3 of slaves. The 2 heirs are: Robert and Eliza Jane Brown, minor heirs.

Page 220 - Guynn Foster, Leonard Bullock and others. Petition to sell land. Firm of Foster & Ogilvie, surviving parties of the firm.

Page 220 - L. A. Wynn and wife and others. Petition to sell land. 2 tracts are to be sold.

1854 February Term

Page 221 - John Taylor departed this life some years ago intestate, seized and
possessed of the tracts of land and descended to his only heirs at
law. Land cannot be equally divided. Land to be sold.

Page 222 - Court states that there was an error made by the Clerk of the County
Court with Henry Brown as admr. of Solomon Brown against Mrs. Evaline
Chambers. Court ordered the Clerk to reinstate said account and allow
the credit to Mrs. E. Chambers, against the guardian of the children
instead of against the sdmr. of the estate.

Page 223 - David R. Vance, admr. and others, heirs of John M. Green. Petition
to sell land. David R. Vance was appointed in December Term 1853 to
sell land, the same at the late residence of John M. Green on 5 Jan
1854. Wiley Riggins being the purchaser and Brandon King, security.

Page 223 - Moriah E. Phillips. Exparte - Petition. Moriah E. Phillips is guard
ian of her daughter Mary Catharine Hooser Phillips, did sell in State
of Mississippi in year of 1853, three negro slaves belonging to her
daughter. One sold to Henry C. Horton, one sold to B. W. Morris, and
one sold to Fanning Jones.

1854 March Term

Page 225 - Elizabeth Watkins reappointed guardian of William S. Watkins, minor
heir of William S. Watkins, deceased. Jesse F. Vannoy and William
Burns, securities.

Page 225 - John H. Warner admr. of estate of William D. Warner, deceased. Richard
Warner, security.

Page 225 - John H. Warner admr. of estate of Hulda Wilhoite, deceased. Richard
Warner, security.

Page 225 - Sarah Burditt former guardian of Sarah J. Burditt resigned her guardianship and Court approved.

Page 226 - William M. Hutson and others. Petition to sell land. Last install-
ment for sale of land to pay over to James T. Williams admr. of his
wife Mary C. Williams formerly Mary C. Hutson who has departed this
life and that he take the receipt of all persons entitled to said
fund. Also, that Clerk and Master and Commissioner in the other case
of the sale of the dower interest, after the death of Susanna Hutson
who has departed this life in which William M. Hutson and others are
parties, pay over to James T. Williams admr. of his wife Mary C. Will
iams formerly Mary C. Hutson, all her interest in the money arising
from sale of dower interest of Susanna Hutson, deceased.

Page 226 - Michael B. Thompson guardian for Jane Robinson, a minor heir of R. J.
Robinson, deceased. John F. Thompson and Thomas Thompson, securities.

Page 226 - William M. Burditt guardian of Sarah J. Burditt, minor heir of William
Burditt, deceased. Nathan Ivey and Joel H. Burditt, securities.

1854 March Term

Page 226 - Power of Attorney, 24 September 1853, executed by James Puryear to John Puryear.

Page 226 - Power of Attorney, 6 March 1854, executed by Ozni W. Bradshaw to M. M. Bigham.

Page 227 - G. G. Osborne guardian of Elizabeth J., John R., and Bartlett Bird, minor children of Sparrell Bird. Winn Thomas and John E. Scruggs.

Page 227 - John E. Pearson and wife Jane, and Randolph Newsom, guardian of minor heirs of Thomas Newsom, deceased. Partition to sell land, about 50 acres.

Page 228 - James A. Heaslett and others. Petition to sell land. Land sold to Samuel Bobo. Lands that belonged to the estate of William Heaslett, deceased. Samuel Bobo purchased said land.

Page 228 - James A. Heaslett and others. Petition to sell land. James T. Snoddy has paid for the land. Land did belong to William Heaslett, deceased. 90 acres and 135 poles.

Page 229 - James A. Heaslett and others. Petition to sell land. Land that belonged to William Heaslett, deceased. Alfred Campbell purchaser. 80 poles.

Page 230 - Jeremiah Holt, Common School Commissioner for Thompson Creek Township, made a report.

Page 230 - Elizabeth Lentz admrix. of estate of John J. Lents, deceased. Report of additional sale list.

Page 230 - Richard Anderson admr. of the estate of John Dougal, deceased, reported on inventory.

Page 230 - Charles Williams, Norman Finny and Joshua C. Coleman to lay off support to Nancy E. Bearden, widow of John W. Bearden, deceased.

Page 230 - Mary Lawwell's Dower plat, on page 230, widow of John K. Lawwell, deceased. 58 acres.

Page 231 - Jefferson J. Long admr. of estate of M. P. Locke, deceased. T. B. Jeffress, security.

Page 231 - Power of Attorney, March 6, 1854, executed by Joseph Parker to Isaah Parker.

Page 231 - Wiley F. Parker be released from paying Poll Tax for]853 and 54 on account of inability to labour and bodily infirmity.

Page 231 - John W. Allison guardian of Jane Robinson, resigned guardianship.

Page 231 - David Elkins vs William D. Elkins. Case continued.

1854 March Term

Page 232 - George G. Gabbert did not renew his guardianship bond for Martha
and Amanda Gabbert. James S. Newton appointed guardian. They were
the minor heirs of William Gabbert, deceased.

1854 April Term

Page 251 - William Campbell admr. of estate of Jesse Burrow, deceased.

Page 251 - Preston Frazier guardian of John S. Frazier.

Page 251 - Robert H. Barnes guardian of E. T. and D. M. and Lucy J. M. Barnes,
minor heirs of Susana and Daniel T. Barnes.

Page 251 - Milton R. Rushing executor of Hawkins Womack's Will.

Page 251 - James Carlisle guardian of Lucinda Gabbert, one of the minor heirs of
William Gabbert, deceased.

Page 251 - William Gabbert guardian of Jordan Gabbert, one of the minor heirs of
William Gabbert, deceased.

Page 252 - Pierce Wilhoite guardian of John and William Wilhoite, minor children
of Hetty Wilhoite, deceased.

Page 252 - Francis H. Keller guardian of minor heirs of Daniel Cortner, deceased
Williamson Haggart, security.

Page 252 - William C. King and Josiah R. King and others. Petition to sell land
Lands left to Jane Mullins, widow of Mathew Mullins, deceased. About
45 acres. Plat on page 253.

Page 254 - State of Tennessee vs Gilbert E. Holder. Indictment for lewdness.
Acquitted. Cost $14.58½.

Page 254 - To M. L. Rozar be allowed $5.00 for making a coffin for Ellen Harris,
a pauper.

Page 254 - Thomas L. Thompson, a pauper, be allowed $30.00.

Page 255 - Freeman & Trice be allowed $8.50 for shrouding and burial cloths for
James Calton.

Page 255 - Freeman & Trice be allowed $8.25 for shrouding and burial cloths for
Henry Carlton.

Page 255 - Freeman & Trice be allowed $11.10 for shrouding and burial cloths for
Lean Carlton.

Page 255 - Freeman & Trice be allowed $6.50 for shrouding and burial cloths for
Susan Henceley.

Page 256 - Plat of estate of Rice Coffee, deceased.

1854 April Term

Page 258 - John R. Coffee admr. and others. Petition for division of land.
A. H. Coffee gets Lot # 1, Henry B. Coffee gets Lot # 2, John R.
Coffee gets Lot # 3, Mrs. Mary Kindle gets Lot # 4, Benjamin B.
Coffee gets Lot # 5, the heirs of Martha Yell, deceased, gets Lot #
6. Lot # 6 vested in Jane Robinson wife of M. Robinson, Henry C.
Yell, Mary E. Yell, Nancy E. Yell and Archibald Yell, children of
Martha Yell formerly Martha Coffee.

Page 260 - James M. Ray and others. Petition to sell land. Court ordered C &
M to pay over to James M. Ray, Alexander Ray, Mary Fonville, William
Robinson and wife Jinsey and Samuel Thompson, assignees of A. R. Trice
each 1/6 of fund and that he pay to the heirs at law of John Ray,
deceased, 1/6th, which last 1/6th is to be subdivided and paid as
follows, to wit, To John Ray, W. W. Wilhoite a assignee of William
Hazlewood and wife Margaret and M. Anderson and Nancy his wife formerly Nancy Ray, Rosana Ray, and son John Ray, widow and child of
Lewis Ray, deceased, Stephen Freeman, John Cortner surviving husband
of Mary Cortner, deceased formerly Mary Ray and Peter Cortner surviving
husband of Sarah Cortner formerly Sarah Ray. Each 1/7th part of said
1/6th. And it appearing that the Court that Peter Cortner, John Cortner,
and Stephen Freeman were "tenants by the courtesy" of the interest of
their deceased wives in said land.

Page 26] - W. C. and J. R. King and others. Petition to sell land. Lands of
Daniel C. King, deceased. Depositions of C. P. King and G. W. Harris
stated that together with the widow Sarah A. W. King and W. C. and
J. R. King are all heirs at law of Daniel C. King, deceased. The widow
is entitled to her dower. Land cannot be divided. Land to be sold.
Sarah A. W. King made a Deed of Release that for the natural love and
affection which she bears to her said children, W. C. and J. R. King.

Page 262 - State of Tennessee, for the use of Lucy Ann Williams vs James D.
Payne. Bastardy. Lucy Ann Williams delivered on the __ day of]852
in Bedford County, an illigitimate child. The Defendant has failed
to deny on oath that he is the father. Report to next Court.

Page 262 - William Kingree vs Daniel McLaughlin. William Kingree states hat in
July Term]850, Daniel McLaughlin was appointed admr. of the estate
of Richard Burgess, deceased, that there is considerable amount of money
due him as admr. but your Petitioner does not know whether any money has
come to his hands as such. McLaughlin is insolvent.

Page 264 - William M. Goggins. Exparte - Petition. James D. Burrow purchased a
tract of land, in the case of John Burrow and others, minor heirs of
Madison L. Burrow, deceased, for the sale of land. A note was executed
with Banks D. Burrow and J. J. Burrow, securities. James D. Burrow
has conveyed to William M. Goggins and that he would be put in his place
to pay off notes.

Page 264 - Nancy C. Anderson formerly Nancy C. Ray, came into Court and was examined apart from her husband A. M. Anderson. He is to get her money.

1854 April Term

Page 265 - N. P. Modrell renewed his guardianship of minor heirs of Mary
Harris, deceased.

1854 May Term

Page 268 - Alexander Ray guardian of Rhoda Davis and Barbara Davis, minor
heirs of William Davis, deceased. James H. Harrison and Thomas S.
Mays, securities.

Page 268 - David G. Deason guardian of Rebecca A., Nancy Ann, and David D.
Word, minor heirs of Elizabeth Word, deceased. David A. Ozment and
William G. Hight, securities.

Page 268 - Peter Cortner guardian of his minor daughter Mary C. Cortner. T. S.
Mays and James H. Harrison, securities.

Page 268 - George W. Cunningham has failed to renew his bond for guardianship
of William Cortner, minor heir of Levi Cortner, deceased, therefore
Cunningham was removed. Smith Arnold appointed guardian. Isham
Reavis his security.

Page 269 - William G. Wood admr. of estate of Thomas Hensley, deceased. James L.
Woods and Josiah H. Maupin, securities.

Page 269 - E. M. B. Norville guardian for David Norville, John Norville, William
Norville, James Norville, Samuel Norville, Mary Norville, and Louisa
Norville.

Page 269 - Elizabeth Maupin guardian of Sarah L., Mary A., Thompson P., and
Betty B. Maupin, her minor children. Josiah H. Maupin, security.

Page 270 - William Kingree petition to be released from securityship. 1 May
1854, he was security for Daniel McLaughlin when D. McLaughlin was
appointed admr. of Richard Burgess, deceased. William H. Wisener
became security.

Page 270 - George Cortner admr. of estate of Matthias Cortner, deceased. Francis
H. Keller and Thomas C. Whiteside, securities.

Page 270 - Thomas H. Buckingham admr. of estate of Thomas McFarling, deceased.
Robert H. Terry and William McGill, securities.

Page 270 - Samuel D. Morgan and others. Petition to divide slaves. In March
Term 1852 this Court, that Robert H. Barnes guardian of Granville,
Edward, Daniel and Lucy Barnes was ordered to pay William M. Morgan,
guardian of Samuel D. and Susan Morgan, $25.00, when he had been
ordered to pay $30.00.

Page 271 - John, Robert, Lethe, and Madison L. Burrow, minors &c. by their
guardian John C. Hix. Petition to sell land. To collect money
for land that was sold.

1854 May Term

Page 271 - A. M. Tillman to obtain license to practice law.

Page 271 - James L. Woods, G. G. Osborne and Daniel Stephens to lay off support to Sarah B. Hensley, widow of Thomas Hensley, deceased.

Page 273 - George W. Ruth be allowed $36.75 for keeping and boarding Peggy Perryman, a woman of color.

Page 273 - Permelia Tucker and others. Petition to sell land. On 11 Feb 1854, sale of land. William J. Whitthorne purchaser.

Page 274 - L. A. Wynn and others. Petition to sell land. On 3 March 1854, sale of land and to report to next term of Court.

Page 274 - William G. Woods and others. Petition to sell land. William G. Wood and Thomas Hensley purchased land. Land belonged to Thomas Hensley, deceased, lately, intestate in Bedford County. It appears to the Court that Thomas Hensley, deceased, left only one child, Jane, and his widow. Widow wants dower reserved.

Page 276 - George Cortner admr. of Mathias Cortner, deceased. Petition to sell slaves. George Cortner admr. of Mathias Cortner, deceased. Mathias Cortner departed this life intestate in Bedford County. He died seized of 16 slaves. They are to be sold.

Page 278 - G. G. Osborne, James Myers and Joseph Couch to lay off support to widow and family of Mathias Cortner, deceased.

Page 278 - David S. Elkins, a lunatic &c. vs William D. Elkins. Petition to remove William D. Elkins as guardian of David S. Elkins because from time to time he has failed to provide David S. Elkins with clothing and mistreating him.

Page 279 - Col. Matt Martin to practice law.

1854 June Term

Page 280 - William G. Wood admr. and others. Petition to sell land. Gabriel Maupin purchaser.

Page 281 - Power of Attorney, dated 5 June 1854, executed by John Rippy to John J. Barnes.

Page 282 - John Stone admr. of estate of Thomas Stone, deceased. Lemuel Broadaway and Isaac Williams, securities.

Page 282 - James W. McCrory admr. of estate of Jarrett Linch, deceased. Gray Linch his security.

Page 282 - Stephen Hart guardian of Elizabeth Virginia Beaty, resigned as guardian William Galbreath was appointed guardian.

1854 June Term

Page 282 - Joseph Anderson, Jesse M. Ledbetter and Larkin B. Orr was elected School Commissioners in the North Fork Township.

Page 282 - William B. Holt, School Commissioner in Thompson Creek Township.

Page 282 - Jabal Ray be allowed $10.00 as School Commissioner in Thompson Creek Township.

Page 283 - Robert B. Davidson was appointed guardian of William B. Gregory and James W. Gregory, minor children of Rachel L. Gregory, deceased.

Page 283 - Deed of Trust - dated __ day of May 1854, executed by A. E. Morgan to George W. Thompson.

Page 283 - State of Tennessee, Bedford County, April 26, 1854. Commissioners to assign dower to Nancy E. Bearden, widow of John W. Bearden, deceased, husband, the following tract including the mansion house and inprovements. 14 24/160 acres.

Page 283 - E. M. B. Norville vs John W. White. E. M. B. Norville appointed guardian for David R. Norville, Mary Norville, William Norville and Louisa Norville, minor children of Felix B. Norville.

Page 284 - J. M. McCrory guardian of Sarah Springer and John Springer, minor heir of Dennis Springer, deceased.

Page 284 - William Campbell guardian of Francis Conwell, minor heir of Jane Conwell.

Page 284 - Alfred S. Huffman guardian of Daniel and Sarah A. Huffman, his minor children.

Page 284 - George W. Greer (spelled in book Grear) guardian of Victoria E., Sally Effy, Rebecca, and Joel P. Scales.

Page 284 - Orville Hensley guardian of Mary Eleanor, John Thomas and Clara Jane Mason.

Page 284 - Thomas Thompson guardian of Martha Ann, Margaret C., Jacob F., George W., John and Sarah Parsons, minor heirs of Michael Parsons, deceased.

Page 284 - John Jackes (Jakes) guardian of Nancy Ann Keel.

Page 285 - George W. Parsons and others. Petition to sell land and slaves. Property of George Parsons, deceased.

Page 285 - H. H. Nease vs Jordan C. Holt. Case continued to next Court.

Page 285 - James M. Johnson and Susan Newsom appeared in Court and desired to be released from all liability or obligation od an indenture bond

1854 June Term

Page 285 - (continued) executed by them in Court at May Term 1852 of this Court binding George W. H. Newsom, son of said Susan Newsom an apprentice of James M. Johnson &c. Released granted.

Page 285 - George W. Parsons admr. and others. Petition to sell land and slaves. Clerk's report. Margarett Parsons departed this life intestate in Bedford County on or about the __ day of ____ 1854, seized and possessed of among other things mentioned in petition, that the petitioners are the only heirs at law of said Margaret Parsons, as well as the only heirs at law of George Parson, deceased and that the property will have to be sold.

Page 286 - William C. King and others. Petition to sell land. To sell land and report to next Court.

Page 287 - John McGuire guardian &c. Petition to divide slaves. Report: Ones to be allotted slaves: William McGuire, Benjamin McGuire, and John McGuire. John McGuire is guardian of John McGuire, Jr.

Page 288 - George Cortner admr. of Matthias Cortner, deceased. Petition to sell 11 slaves. Slaves to be sold to: Wiley Riggins, George Cortner, Milly Cortner, John Huffman, George Cortner, William P. Greene, Milly Cortner, James C. Word, George Cortner, Sarah Troxler, and William Russell and others.

Page 289 - Mary Blanton and others. Petition to sell land and slaves. Charles H. Parker died intestate in Bedford County, seized and possessed of land. Nancy, the widow, is entitled to dower. Hezekiah Ray, H. C. Ferguson and A. Wilson to lay off to Nancy her dower of 1/3 of land including dwelling house in which the said Charles H. Parker resided at the time of his death. Plat showing the division of land.

Page 289 - Samuel K. Whitson admr. of estate of William H. Trigg, deceased.

Page 289 - E. M. B. Norville vs John W. White. Report to next Court.

Page 290 - John B. Bates, Warner Wallace and James M. Johnson to lay off support to Mary Ann Trigg, widow of William H. Trigg, deceased.

Page 290 - W. W. Miller, R. S. Thomas and A. D. Fugitt to lay off support to Sarah Linch, widow of Jarrett Linch, deceased.

Page 290 - Edmund Cooper assigned his name as security to Execution Bond of H. F. Holt.

1854 July Term

Page 291 - William G. Thompson and Alexander Ray and Stephen Freeman are elected Commissioners for School in Richmond Township.

Page 291 - Alexander Sanders, John M. Warner and L. Temple elected School Commrs. for Powel's Creek and Elbethel Township.

1854 July Term

Page 291 - John Oneal, G. T. Neeley and Alexander Dysart elected School Commrs. for Sinking Creek Township.

Page 292 - John T. N. Card guardian of Margaret E. Card and Mary L. Card, minor heirs of Joseph N. Card, deceased. A. Adams and George E. Calhoun, securities.

Page 292 - John T. Medearis admr. of estate of Joseph N. Card, deceased. Henry Dean and Edmund Cooper, securities. John W. White, Lemuel Broadaway and Abram Reagor to lay off support to Lucy Card, widow of Joseph N. Card, deceased, and family.

Page 292 - Henry Dean guardian of Mary and Tapenus Lipscomb, minors &c.

Page 292 - Lemuel Broadaway, Nimrod Burrow and M. W. Watson, School Commissioners of Flat Creek Township, each be allowed $10.00 each.

Page 292 - Nancy Blanton and others. Exparte - Petition. Continued to next Court.

Page 292 - Lewis Tucker guardian of Catharine Anderson and Sarah Elizabeth Anderson, minors &c.

Page 293 - John Koonce be reappointed guardian of minor heirs of Jesse Koonce, deceased. Robert Reed and John Reed securities.

Page 293 - John Cortner was reappointed guardian of Martha C. Cortner, his minor child.

Page 294 - David S. Evans guardian of David S. Elkins, a lunatic. J. F. Cummings security.

Page 294 - Waddy S. Taylor admr. of estate of Thomas Wilson, deceased. William T Thompson and John W. Simpson, securities.

Page 294 - Richard H. Powell and Robert J. Powell, executors of the estate of Thomas P. Powell, deceased.

Page 294 - Susan Pennington, a lunatic, 10th District, be allowed $25.00.

Page 294 - Charles Garmon, an aged poor man of the 22nd District be allowed $25.00.

Page 295 - George W. Parsons admr. and others. Petition to sell land. Clerk's report. Abram Claxton purchaser. 41 acres and 37 poles.

Page 296 - William C. King and others. Petition to sell land. Report. William J. Whitthorne purchaser. Lands that belonged to the estate of Daniel C. King, deceased.

Page 297 - George E. Calhoun and others. Petition to sell land. Land belonged to Card & Calhoun, partners in a Saw Mill, situated in Bedford County

1854 July Term

Page 297 - (continued) that Joseph N. Card is dead, and that George E. Calhoun is the surviving partner of said firm. Joseph N. Card left surviving him, his wife Lucy M. and his two children, Mary and Elizabeth Card, minors, having for their guardian John T. N. Card.

Page 299 - John T. Medearis admr. of Joseph N. Card, deceased. Petition to sell slaves. Joseph N. Card is dead, intestate. He left 2 slaves, which will have to be sold.

Page 300 - Herod G. Holt acknowledged he was indebted to D. D. Hix and J. C. Hix, executors of the estate of William Hix, deceased. Holt purchased from Hix in August 21, 1853, land.

1854 August Term

Page 301 - Samuel G. Hays, Randolph Newsom and Richard Phillips to lay off support to Emily Dixon, widow of Robert Dixon, deceased, for herself and family.

Page 301 - James C. Gambill, Samuel Anderson and Samuel Roane to lay off support for widow and family of Eli C. Griffith, deceased.

Page 301 - Wilborne Hiles guardian of Matilda A. Hiles and Thompson Hiles, minor children of Joseph Hiles and heirs at law of Alfred Hiles, deceased.

Page 302 - Charles Smith admr. of estate of Emily Ann Smith, deceased. Gabriel Maupin, security.

Page 302 - Aaron Gambill admr. of estate of Robert Logan, deceased. James C. Gambill and Alexander Dysart, securities.

Page 302 - M. L. Dismukes admr. of estate of Robert Dixon, deceased. J. Dixon and Edmund Cooper, securities.

Page 302 - John Q. Davidson admr. of T. G. W. Wright, deceased. John R. Eakin, security.

Page 302 - John H. Gambill admr. of Eli C. Griffith, deceased. Samuel Doak and J. Dixon, securities.

Page 302 - Joel Coggins admr. of John Swing, deceased. Jesse Rogers, security.

Page 303 - Alexander Downing admr. of William Eoff, deceased. Martin Hoover and Washington Gibson, securities.

Page 303 - Coleman F. Hord guardian of Mary J., William W., Nancy, Robert B., and Susan Hord, minor heirs of E. B. Hord, deceased. John Q. Davidson, security.

Page 303 - James G. Neeley guardian of Joseph B. Dwyer, a son of John S. Dwyer, deceased.

Page 303 - J. C. Hix, Kindred Pearson and Alfred Campbell elected School Commiss-

1854 August Term

Page 303 - (continued) ioners for 2 years in the Flat Creek Township.

Page 303 - Waddy S. Taylor admr. of estate of Thomas Wilson, deceased.

Page 303 - J. M. McCrory admr. of estate of Jarrett Linch, deceased.

Page 303 - Alfred Ransom admr. of Curtiss Snell, deceased. W. R. Ransom,
William Snell, and Thomas H. Coldwell securities.

Page 303 - Archibald Pruitt appointed guardian of Benjamin R.(?) McGuire and
John A. McGuire, instead of John McGuire former guardian who has
resigned. James Mullins, A. E. Mullins, William Mullins and H. C.
Kincaid securities.

Page 304 - J. L. Turner, Commissioner to receive for Mrs. Robinson in the 9th
District, $20.00, in place of Josephus Gregory, former Commissioner.

Page 304 - Robert T. Cannon, J. W. Norville and William Young to lay off support
to Elizabeth Swing and family, widow of John Swing, deceased.

Page 304 - William Pepper, Archibald Murphy and John R. Eakin to lay off support
to Clemenzie Wright, widow of T. G. Wright, and family.

Page 304 - H. H. Price vs J. C. Holt. Delayed to next Court.

Page 305 - William Little, William Holt and J. P. Taylor elected School Commissioners for Rover Township, Range 3, Section 7, for 2 years.

Page 306 - A. M. Cooper and wife and others. Petition for dower. William Little
departed this life intestate some years ago, leaving his widow Delilah
Lytle and other petitioners, his only heirs at law and also owner of
a tract of land. Delilah Lytle has not received her dower out of the
estate. Augustine Wilson, William Floyd, James Lawrence, Albert Knott
and Robert Allison, any two of whom with A. Wilson, surveyor, may act
to lay off her dower. The dower includes the mansion house. 6 heirs.

Page 306 - Jordan Rucker admr. of William Rucker, deceased. Court is to allow
admr. to make contract or compromise which he can do with one William
Landis against whom his intestate had removed judgement in his life
time before Wilie Perry, Esq. on 13 July 1839.

Page 306 - Commissioners appointed to superintend the letting out and building
the bridge across Duck River at Scull Camp Ford (which has been filed
in Court) that the bridge has now been completed by James Wortham. A
committee of B. M. Tillman, Joseph Hastings and William McGill, to
examine the bridge and make report in Nov Term of Court.

Page 307 - Samuel A. Strickler guardian of Christena Strickler, a minor heir of
Benjamin Strickler, deceased.

Page 307 - Mary V. Fogleman guardian of Catharine E. Fogleman, Lewis V. Fogleman, Sallie W. Fogleman, Benjamin F. Fogleman, minor heirs of G. W.
Fogleman, deceased.

1854 August Term

Page 307 - Henry Yancy guardian of his lunatic brother, resigned his guardianship.

Page 308 - Nancy Blanton and others. Petition for dower and sale of land.
Commissioners to lay off to Nancy Blanton formerly Nancy Parker, widow
of Charles H. Parker, her deceased husband, her dower including the
mansion house and improvements. 40 acres which is 1/3 of real
estate.

Page 309 - Nancy Blanton and others. Petition. Clerk's report. Land cannot
be divided which was divided to the remainder heirs, and will have to
be sold. Plat on page 309.

Page 309 - E. D. Winsett, one of the executors of Jason Winsett, deceased, made
report.

Page 310 - Benjamin A. Nelson admr. of estate of Thomas Phillips, deceased. Moses
Nelson and James Anderson, securities.

Page 310 - Aaron Gambill and others. Petition to sell land. Robert Logan died
in Bedford County, seized and possessed of a tract of land. Court
ordered it to be sold.

1854 September Term

Page 313 - H. L. Davidson admr. of Hugh L. Brittain, deceased.

Page 313 - John Q. Davidson guardian of Margarett and Martha Ferril, minors.

Page 313 - W. P. Goodwin guardian of William John, Eliza Jane, James Henry, and
George W. Goodwin, his minor children.

Page 314 - Green L. Neeley admr. of estate of William Cook, deceased. John M.
Warner and Jacob Molder, securities.

Page 314 - Hiram H. Nease guardian to Alice Holt, minor heir of Jordan C. Holt,
deceased.

Page 314 - John Q. Davidson guardian to Eliza Jane, Susan, Judah A., Margarett H.,
Priscilla, James J., Daniel C., and William H. Trigg, minor heirs of
William H. Trigg, deceased.

Page 314 - Robert Bradshaw, H. F. Holt and James Snell elected School Commissioners in Range 4, Section 4, for 2 years.

Page 314 - George A. Reagor guardian of Christopher C. and Sarah E. Hix, minor
heirs of J. R. Hix, deceased, resigned as guardian. John P. Dean
appointed guardian. James B. Hix and Henry Dean, securities.

Page 314 - Joel Coggins admr. of John Swing, deceased.

1854 September Term

Page 314 - John W. Norville, R. T. Cannon and William Young to lay off support to widow of John Swing, deceased.

Page 315 - Samuel R. Whitson admr. of Kenneth Madison, deceased. Ro. B. Davidso security.

Page 315 - John Q. Davidson admr. of Pumphrey Meadows, deceased.

Page 315 - John M. Gibson guardian of Samuel M. Harper and Mary M. Harper, minor heirs of William Harper, deceased, resigned.

Page 315 - John F. Thompson, Samuel H. Card and Thomas Shearin to lay off support to Nancy Cook and family, widow and family of William Cook, deceased.

Page 315 - Henry Dean, Thomas Dean and James B. Reagor to lay off support to Margarett Boone, widow of William Boone, deceased.

Page 315 - G. M. Ray admr. of William H. Miles' Will &c.

Page 318 - George E. Calhoun and others. Petition to sell land and mill. Alfred Campbell purchaser.

Page 318 - H. L. Davidson desires to be released from admr. bond on estate of H. L. Brittain, deceased.

Page 319 - Nancy Word, wife of Thomas S. Word, being an heir and distributee of the estate of William Hix and Sally Hix, deceased. She was examined separately from her husband, she stated that she was willing for her husband to receive money coming to her from said estate.

Page 320 - Joseph Hastings guardian of Elizabeth Cates, minor heir of William H. Cates, deceased.

Page 320 - Johannah Nash and others. Petition to sell land. Land has been paid for by David P. Orr and William C. Orr. 21 acres and 39 poles instead of 22 acres. Land that belonged to Abner Nash, deceased.

Page 321 - Benjamin Boon, one of the witnesses of the Last Will and Testament of Arthur Campbell, deceased.

1854 October Term

Page 322 - John Thomas, James L. Wood and L. C. Shanklin elected School Commissioners for the Fairfield Township.

Page 323 - Thomas S. Mayes, Stephen Freeman and Newton Allen to lay off support to widow of P. J. Thompson, deceased.

Page 323 - Benjamin Decherd admr. of John Bradford, deceased, resigned.

Page 324 - C. W. Black guardian of George J. Black, be removed as guardian.

1854 October Term

Page 323 - (continued) William Campbell was appointed guardian.

Page 325 - Levi Underwood and wife, aged persons, be allowed $30.00.

Page 325 - Mrs. Alfair Trollinger, aged person, be allowed $25.00.

Page 325 - Emeline Stockard, support her insane child, $15.00.

Page 325 - Reubin Williams, pauper, be allowed $25.00.

Page 327 - John H. Scott guardian of Joseph M. Holt, Belinda Holt and Harriett Virginia Holt, minor orphans of Joseph Holt, deceased. Alex. Kimbro and D. R. Vance securities.

Page 327 - Wrencher Spence guardian of Marmoe Edward, John Wesley, Nancy Temple and Margarett Spence, minor children of John M. Spence, deceased. William Mallard and Brittain Spence securities.

Page 327 - Robert Pate guardian of minor heirs of William Lytle, deceased.

Page 327 - Winston W. Gill guardian of John J. Gill, Mary R. Gill, Sarah Jane Gill and Winston W. Gill, his minor children.

Page 327 - William P. H. McCowan guardian of Nathan A. Manly, Susan Ann Manly and Henry H. Manly.

Page 327 - James Cheshire guardian of Nancy Elizabeth Cross, minor heir of James M. Cross, deceased. James B. Reagor security.

Page 327 - G. M. Ray admr. of estate of William H. Miles, deceased.

Page 328 - Martin Thompson admr. of estate of Phillip J. Thompson, deceased. Stephen Freeman and T. S. May securities.

Page 328 - Thomas J. Robinson admr. of estate of Hannah Harrison, deceased.

Page 328 - Winston W. Gill admr. of estate of Sarah Ann Gill, deceased.

Page 328 - Alexander Kimbro admr. of estate of Joseph Holt, deceased, J. H. Scott, D. R. Vance, John L. Ayres, Hosia Green and J. M. Isom, securities.

Page 328 - G. T. Neeley admr. of estate of Henry Pickle, deceased. Jonathan Liggett and William H. Stephens, securities.

Page 328 - William S. Jett admr. of estate of William H. Trigg, deceased.

Page 329 - Rebecca A. Philpot, wife of Charles T. Philpot appeared and was examined apart from her husband, in regards to the monies arising from her father and mother's estate, William Hix and Sarah Hix, deceased.

1854 October Term

Page 330 - Aaron Gambill and wife Nancy H. and others. Petition to sell land.
             Lands belonging to estate of Robert Logan, deceased. Aaron Gambill
             purchaser. 73 acres. Nancy H. Gambill is wife of Aaron Gambill.
             Rosina Davis wife of Samuel Davis, Martha M. Chapel, Margarett Logan
             and guardian of Caledonia and Cincinattia Phillips.

Page 332 - Thomas J. Robinson admr. of Hannah Harrison, deceased, and others.
             Petition to sell slaves and land. Hannah Harrison is dead and that
             she died intestate and that Thomas J. Robinson is the admr. of her
             estate. She died the owner of 3 slaves, which will be necessary for
             them to be sold and proceeds to be divided amongst 6 distributees.
             Hannah Harrison was the widow of John Harrison, deceased.

Page 333 - Commissioners to lay off dower to Margarett Boone, widow of William
             Boone, deceased. She received her dower. The homeplace on which the
             mansion is situated containing about 228 acres and also Lot marked as
             Lot No. 4, known as the John Brown place, containing 93 acres, making
             in all 320 acres.

Page 333 - Margarett Boone and others. Petition for dower. Granted on 3 Oct]85

Page 334 - John, Robert A., Ephraim, Lethe B., and Madison L. Burrow, minors by
             their next friend J. G. Neill. Petition to remove guardianship. The
             minors are minors of Madison L. Burrow, deceased. They together with
             their mother have moved to Carroll County where they now reside and
             do not contemplate removing back to Bedford County and that James B.
             Algee has been appointed their guardian by the County Court of Carroll
             County and that John C. Hix be notified to pay over the amounts due
             his wards &c.

Page 334 - Elias Holt and others, heirs and admrs. of estate of Joseph Holt,
             deceased. Petition to sell land and slaves. The only children and
             heirs at law of Joseph Holt, deceased, are Louisa wife of James Isom,
             Emily wife of Jason Green, Sarah wife of John L. Ayers, Roena wife of
             Hosea Green, Elias Holt, Frances Holt, Mary Ann Holt, Minerva Holt,
             Joseph M. Holt, Belinda Holt, and Harriett Virginia Holt. Land cannot
             be divided and will have to be sold. And that John L. Ayers holds
             the bond of Joseph Holt for one undivided third of the 105 acres.

Page 335 - Johannah Nash and others. Petition to sell land. James C. Tune as a
             creditor of Francis M. Nash attached his interest in said land. Court
             to pay Tune for judgement against land.

Page 335 - John H. Oneal guardian of John R. and Sarah Jane Muse, minors.

Page 337 - Charles M. Norville guardian of John E., Eugene and Rebecca C. F.
             Norville, minors.

Page 337 - Elizabeth Word wife of Joseph Word formerly Elizabeth Stewart, came in
             to Court and was examined apart from her husband touching on her con-
             sent for her husband to receive any monies arising from her mother's
             estate, to wit, Sarah Hix, deceased.

Page 338 - Levi Turner, David R. Vance and George Cortner to lay off support to Mary Holt and family, she is the widow of Joseph Holt, deceased.

Page 338 - William Anderton and wife (blank) Anderton appeal to the matters of probate of William H. Miles' noncupative Will. Continue to next Court.

Page 339 - Elizabeth Spence and others. Petition for dower. Dower to be set off to Elizabeth Spence, formerly the widow of Richard Musgroves, her deceased husband, a tract of land, 38 acres and 136 poles.

Page 340 - Thomas J. Robinson and wife and others. Petition to sell land. Hannah Harrison, widow of John Harrison, deceased, and heirs, he died intestate. Hannah Harrison is now dead and that the petitioners are the only heirs at law of John Harrison, deceased. Land to be sold.

Page 341 - L. A. Wynn and wife and others. Petition to sell land. Sale on 27 September 1854 of 196 acres. No bidders. Then 237 acres was offered and no bidders. Then offered 196 acres, Moses Fortner at a reduced rate. Clerk to pay over to guardian of Martha Ann Wynn wife of L. A. Wynn one share and to J. B. Wynn as guardian of Mary C. Taylor and Josephine Taylor the remaining 2/3 of fund.

Page 342 - B. E. Cooper and others. Petition for dower and partition of land. William Little, deceased. To assign to Delila Little widow of William Little, her dower out of the estate, the remainder of estate to be divided into 6 equal parts or lots. Elizabeth Cooper wife of Absalom Cooper drawed Lot No. 1. Martha wife of B. E. Cooper got Lot No. 3. Alcy wife of J. B. Cooper got Lot No. 6. Rebecca C. wife of Franklin Ray got Lot No. 5. Gemima got Lot No. 4. Amanda got Lot No. 2.

Page 345 - J. H. C. Scales admr. of Noah Scales, deceased. Petition to sell slaves. Noah Scales died intestate some years ago in Bedford County, leaving as his heirs at law, Petitioners J. H. C. Scales who was appointed admr. and Victorah Scales, Moriah who has since intermarried with N. R. Gabbard, Sally Scales, Effie Scales, William Scales, Rebecca Scales, Noah Cooper Scales, and Joel Scales and also being the owner at his death a considerable number of slaves. Some of the slaves are getting old, both men and women. They should be sold.

Page 346 - Granville L. Sharp, a minor aged 5 years, was bound to James R. Reese until he arrives at age of 21 years to learn farming. 3 Oct 1854.

Page 348 - Elias Holt and others, heirs at law of Joseph Holt, deceased. Petition to sell land and slaves. The only children and heirs at law of Joseph Holt, deceased, are Louisa wife of James Isom, Emily wife of Jason Green, Sarah wife of John L. Ayers, Roena wife of Hosea Green, Elias Holt, Francis Holt, Mary Ann Holt, Minerva Holt, Joseph M. Holt, Belinda Holt, and Harriett Virginia Holt. John L. Holt holds the bond of said Joseph Holt for an undivided third of the 105 acre tract. It is necessary to sell land. The first Lot being the 53 acres purchased from the heirs of Jeremiah Kimbro and second Lot being the balance of the home tract, and the third Lot the 105 acres in which John

1854 October Term

Page 348 - (continued) L. Ayers has an interest of 1/3rd. Also, Joseph Holt
at the time of his death owned slaves. He left 11 children and his
widow Mary Holt and that Alexander Kimbro was admr. of estate of
Joseph Holt, deceased. Slaves to be sold.

1854 November Term

Page 351 - Alexander Lee admr. of William Stephens, deceased. The widow, J. P.
Stephens and T. N. Gibson and others, heirs, waving their rights to
admr. and requesting A. Lee to be appointed. Abram McMahan and
John Jakes securities. John Jakes, G. D. Stephenson, Jacob Coffman,
and James Frizzell (any 3 of them) to lay off support to Mrs. Stephens
widow of William Stephens, deceased.

Page 351 - Randolph Newsom admr. of estate of Riley H. Forbes, deceased. Green
B. Newsom his security. James F. Newsom, Hiram H. Holt and H. C.
Hurst to lay off support to Mrs. Martin, widow of R. H. Forbes.

Page 352 - John H. White admr. of estate of Jeremiah Forbes, deceased. Leonard
Bullock and Alex. Sanders securities.

Page 352 - L. Lamb guardian of Giles J. Lamb, a minor.

Page 352 - John Jakes guardian to William Logan Stephens, a minor heir of William
Stephens, deceased.

Page 352 - John H. Oneal resigned as guardian of H. C. Earnhart. John F. Thompson was appointed guardian in his place, to Henry C. Earnhart, minor
heir of Henry Earnhart, deceased.

Page 352 - William Little guardian of Sarah E., Francis M., Charles W., and
Martha A. Gault, minors of J. C. Gault, deceased.

Page 352 - William T. Tune resigned as guardian of minor heirs of E. Whitman,
deceased.

Page 352 - James W. Wallace guardian of minor of William Harper, deceased.

Page 354 - John Reed, age 10 years, was bound to James Hart, to learn farming.

Page 355 - William Stewart came into Court to have funds in the hands of John C.
Hix as Executor of William Hix and Sally Hix, deceased, belonging to
John H. Stewart, Elizabeth Stewart, Sarah Stewart, Sibby Stewart,
Joshua Stewart, and Martha Ann Stewart, minor children of Ailsy Stewart
deceased. William Stewart has been appointed by probate of Lawrence
County, Missouri, to be guardian of said minors.

Page 356 - David G. Deason, wife and others. Petition to sell land. Land to be
sold. 98 acres. The Lot and House in Unionville and the place known
as "Oak Ridge". Petitioners are the children of Thomas C. Rankin,
deceased.

1854 November Term

Page 357 - Price C. Steele admr. of John Woods, deceased. John Wood departed
this life in Bedford County on the __ day of ___]854 after having made
his Will. He died the owner of slaves which are to be sold. Alfred
Mallard is executor and that he died before John Wood and Court appointed Price C. Steele admr.

Page 358 - Jerome Albright and others. Petition to sell land. W. W. Gill was
the purchaser from J. J. Burrow and has paid 1st payment. 1/10 part
to each of the following: Jerome Albright, Eleanor Albright, Jacob C.
Albright, Penny Ann Albright, Catharine Albright, Jane Burrow wife of
Jacob C. Burrow, Nancy Warren wife of Benjamin Warren, and the share
of Ransom White and wife Candace to Jerome Albright his assignee,
Elizabeth Woosley wife of George N(R). Woosley one share, and Rachael
G. Freeman.

Page 359 - J. W. Frizzell admr. of Green B. Majors, deceased, be released from
payment of a note charged to him in inventory of said estate against
N. L. Majors.

Page 360 - Elias Holt, Francis Holt, Mary Ann Holt and others, heirs of Joseph
Holt, deceased. Petition to sell land and slaves. 160 acres.

Page 362 - Randolph Newsom admr. of Riley H. Forbes, deceased. Exparte - Debts.
Forbes was the owner of 2 slaves. Slaves to be sold.

Page 362 - Samuel Parker and others, heirs at law of Charles H. Parker, deceased.
Petition to sell land. Land to be sold.

Page 363 - Jesse W. Brown admr. of Henry More, deceased, and Eliza Catharine Moore
widow and others of said Henry Moore, deceased. John H. Oneal has
collected all monies for sale of land &c.

Page 363 - Samuel Parker and others, heirs at law of Charles H. Parker, deceased.
Petition to sell dower tract. The only children and heirs at law of
Charles H. Parker, deceased, and Samuel Parker, Nancy Baxter wife of
James T. Baxter, James Parker, Elmer Parker, Daniel Parker, William
Parker and Priscilla Parker, that said 40 acres are so situated that
partition thereof cannot be made. Land to be sold.

Page 364 - Nancy Blanton and others. Petition to sell land and slave. Sell
slave at residence of Charles H. Parker, deceased.

Page 365 - Joseph Hastings and wife and others vs Moses Edde and others. Hiram
Edde was the purchaser of the land mentioned in the pleadings, has
paid to Hiram J. Edde, one of the heirs of Candis Edde, a mare.

Page 366 - John T. Medearis and others. Petition to sell slaves. John T.
Medearis as admr. and the widow and heirs of J. N. Card, deceased.
Lucy M. Card bit and purchased nefro woman and her child. Lucy M.
Card, widow of J. N. Card, deceased. She purchased other negroes.

1854 November Term

Page 367 - Rebecca R. Philpot wife of Charles T. Philpot appeared in Court and
         examined apart from her husband, giving consent for his to receive
         any monies from estate of her father amd mother's estate, William
         Hix and Sarah Hix, deceased.

1854 December Term

Page 368 - William T. Barrett, Daniel G. Stephenson and Martin Sims to lay off
         support to Eddith Forbes, widow of Jeremiah Forbes, deceased.

Page 368 - Commissioners to lay off support to Rachael Pickle, widow of Henry
         Pickle, deceased.

Page 368 - Commissioners to lay off support to H. C. Earnhart, son of his
         deceased father Henry Earnhart, deceased.

Page 368 - Commissioners to lay off support to Mary (Nancy?) Cook, widow of
         William Cook, deceased.

Page 369 - Thomas J. Robinson admr. of estate of Hannah Harrison, deceased.

Page 369 - Randolph Newsom, Benjamin F. Greer and James S. Newton to lay off
         support to Mrs. Robinson, widow of Joseph Robinson, deceased.

Page 369 - Robert M. Cheaves proposed to prove the noncupative Will of Mrs.
         Nancy Pearson who died 9 July 1854, leaving two minor children, Thomas
         Newton and Elizabeth A. Pearson. Proven.

Page 369 - John Chapman admr. of Joseph Robinson, deceased.

Page 370 - John Ramsey admr. of Jane Adams, deceased.

Page 370 - Augustus Cannon executor of the estate of Minos Cannon, late of
         Alabama.

Page 370 - Jno. S. Davis guardian of Jno., Millard and Cassander Streeter, minor
         heirs of Jno. Streeter, deceased. William B. M. Brame and W. J. Jett
         securities.

Page 370 - Samuel Doak resigned as guardian of the heirs of Benjamin Delk,
         deceased.

Page 370 - Edith Forbes guardian of Malissa Jane and Thomas Marion Forbes, minor
         children of Jeremiah Forbes, deceased.

Page 371 - Harbert Wiggins guardian of Sarah Jane, Riley H. and infant child not
         yet named minor children of William O. Forbes, deceased.

Page 371 - Harbert Wiggins guardian of James M. Wiggins his minor heir. Jno. W.
         Wiggins, security.

Page 371 - Thomas Musgrave guardian of Margaret Ellen, Lydia P., Eddith E., and

112

1854 December Term

Page 371 - (continued) Mary L. Musgrave, his minor children. Joshua Musgrave
and Joel Stallings securities.

Page 371 - J. C. Coleman guardian of Henry J., Joshua R., and W. S. Coleman,
his minor children. Moses Reavis and Wynn Bearden securities.

Page 371 - G. G. Osborne guardian to Mary B. Reaves formerly Mary B. Shaw,
James B. Shaw and Robert G. Shaw, minor children of C. G. W. B. Shaw,
deceased. Thomas C. Whiteside and J. E. Scruggs securities.

Page 371 - Edmund Word guardian of Mary J. Hastings, a minor heir of Willis
Hastings, deceased. R. C. Jennings and Samuel Doak securities.

Page 372 - William J. Barrett guardian of James Riley Forbes, minor heir of Riley
H. Forbes, deceased. John E. Barrett security.

Page 372 - Susan Hale. Petition for dower. Report at next Court.

Page 372 - Richard Nance guardian of Mary A. Wadley. He was appointed by the
Rutherford County Court, and that Alexander Moon be appointed for
this county. Mary A. Wadley, minor heir of G. W. Wadley, deceased.

Page 372 - Samuel Parker and others, heirs of Charles H. Parker, deceased.
Petition to sell dower tract of land. Report to next Court.

Page 372 - Price C. Steele admr. &c with the Will annexed of John Wood, deceased.
Slave was bid off to Elizabeth Wood, others sold to Thomas Gregory and
Jo. H. Thompson.

Page 374 - Charles L. Cannon and Polly Ann his wife, William Young and Eliza
Catharine his wife and others. Petition to divide land, about 220
acres, in Bedford County on the east side of the Garrison Fork of
Duck River. Land to be divided among Rebecca and Letitia Cannon,
children of Robert T. Cannon and his deceased wife Letsy Morton
Cannon and Polly Ann Cannon wife of Charles L. Cannon and Eliza
Catharine Young wife of William Young.

Page 376 - Harrison Oliver and James B. Oliver by their next friend Pasady
Oliver. Petition to remove guardianship. Passady Oliver was
appointed guardian of Harrison and James B. Oliver by Court at ___
Term 1853. They reported that Passady Oliver has removed to Henry
County, Tennessee and that Henry County has appointed Passady Oliver
as guardian of same. Guardianship removed from Bedford County to
Henry County, Tennessee.

Page 376 - Augustus Cannon produced the Last Will and Testament of Minos Cannon,
Sr., late of Madison County, Tennessee, for probate. Benjamin T.
Moore, William H. Moore and H. T. Brown witnesses. Augustus Cannon,
executor.

Page 377 - William McGrew vs J. H. M. McGrew and G. W. McGrew and R. Newsom.
William McGrew appointed guardian to his minor children.

113

1854 December Term

Page 378 - Edmund Cooper executor of Last Will of Sarah Terry, deceased.

Page 378 - William Galbreath admr. of John Bradford, deceased.

Page 378 - Henry Cooper guardian to William S., Sarah L., and Harriett F.
Powell, minor heirs of Thomas P. Powell, deceased.

Page 378 - Elias Holt and others. Petition to sell land and slaves. Lands
belonging to estate of Joseph Holt, deceased. Alexander Kimbro admr.
Sale on 27 Oct 1854. About 11 slaves sold.

Page 379 - John White admr. of Jeremiah Forbes, deceased. Edith Forbes and other
heirs &c. Petition to sell slaves. John H. White and wife Mary L.,
Edith Forbes the widow, Thomas M. Forbes and Malissa Jane Forbes,
James Riley Forbes, Margarett E., Lydia P., Edith E. and Mary L.
Musgrave, Sarah J. and Riley H. Forbes and an infant girl not yet
named, minor children of William O. Forbes, deceased, and James M.
Wiggins are the only heirs and distributees at law of Jeremiah Forbes
deceased. 8 slaves sold.

Page 381 - James Harris guardian of Ann Harris, a lunatic.

Page 381 - In matters of Eliza Catharine Moore in the case of the widow and heir
and admr. of Henry Moore, deceased. Report. Eliza Catharine Moore
widow and Jesse W. Brown, admrs. of Henry Moore, deceased, and others
heirs of said Moore, deceased. Petition to sell land. Eliza Catharine
Moore to have the value of her life estate, 1/3, of the purchase money
after paying debts.

Page 382 - Jane J. Norville executrix and Jas. L. A. Norville. Petition by his
mother and next friend and guardian, petition to sell slaves. Jas.
L. A. Norville, son of H. J. H. Norville, deceased, to sell slaves.

Page 384 - W. C. King and others, minor heirs of D. C. King, deceased. To sell
land. William A. Buchaloo guardian of the minor heirs was appointed
by the Coffee County Court.

Page 384 - Martha Reed formerly Martha Harrison, came into Court and said it was
her request the the monies arising from the sale of the lands of her
father John Harrison, deceased, also monies arising from sale of the
dower interest of her mother Hannah Harrison, deceased, now in the
hands of the Clerk of this Court. Martha Reed wife of E. Reed to receive her monies.

1855 January Term

Page 387 - State of Tennessee vs William Johnson, John Armstrong, Thomas Holland
G. W. Hobbs and Jack Christopher. For beating a slave without sufficient cause.

Page 387 - State of Tennessee vs John Armstrong. Indictment for A. & B.

1855 January Term

Page 387 - State of Tennessee vs _____ Jones. Indictment for A. & B. affray.

Page 387 - State of Tennessee vs Barney Lester. Gaming.

Page 388 - State of Tennessee vs Wynn Coble. Indictment for beating slave and
         riot.

Page 388 - State of Tennessee vs Jeremiah Bramlett. Gaming.

Page 388 - State of Tennessee vs Arthur Brooks. Indictment for A. & B.

Page 388 - State of Tennessee vs George Solomon.For selling Spt. Liquors.

Page 388 - State of Tennessee vs B. F. Smith. Indictment.

Page 389 - State of Tennessee vs Joseph Bailey. For selling liquors.

Page 389 - State of Tennessee vs Joseph Bailey. Selling liquors.

Page 389 - C. T. Clay, for shrowding furnished L. Hix, $2.00.

Page 389 - C. T. Clay for shrowding furnished for Mrs. Daniel, $4.20.

Page 389 - Thomas H. Allison for 3 pauper coffins, John Baldwin, M. Brown, and
         J. Calton, $19.00.

Page 389 - H. J. Reed for pauper coffin for J. B. Harding, $3.00.

Page 389 - M. F. Thompson, Jailor, to keeping William Yancy, a lunatic for 76
         days, $29.10.

Page 389 - William Henly, blind man, a pauper, $10.00.

Page 390 - John H. White admr. of Jeremiah Forbes, deceased. Inventory and sale.

Page 390 - R. H. Barns guardian of Lucy J. M., Daniel W., and Edward T. Barns,
         minor heirs of Daniel and Susan Barns, resigned as guardian and John
         L. Cooper was appointed guardian.

Page 391 - J. M. Ledbetter guardian of the minor heirs of John K. Lawwell,
         deceased. Henry Lawwell and Thomas Shearin securities.

Page 391 - Edwin F. Kirk guardian of John P. Kirk. Thomas B. Allison security.

Page 392 - J. B. R. Cooper admr. of Jobe W. Cooper, deceased. J. W. Clary and
         Robert Pate securities.

Page 392 - Isaac Troxler and William S. Troxler admrs. of Jacob Troxler, deceased.
         Nicholas Troxler, security.

Page 392 - C. T. Clay admr. of Jonathan S. Hix, deceased. Joel Darnell security.

1855 January Term

Page 392 - John Q. Davidson resigned as admr. of Pumphrey Meadows, deceased. G. W. Anderson appointed guardian.

Page 393 - State of Tennessee vs James M. Oneal. A. & B. against Defendant.

Page 393 - State of Tennessee vs Summerfield Cheek. A. & B. against Defendant.

Page 394 - State of Tennessee vs W. W. Whitesell. A. & B. on A. Trollinger. Fined.

Page 394 - State of Tennessee vs Andrew Trollinger. A. & B. on W. W. White-sell, fined.

Page 394 - State of Tennessee vs George Solomon. A. & B. on Daniel Osteen. Convicted, bound to Court.

Page 394 - State of Tennessee vs John Osteen. A. & B. fined.

Page 394 - State of Tennessee vs Samuel Osteen. A. & B. cleared.

Page 394 - State of Tennessee vs H. M. Dawdy. G. W. Goodwin Tax with cost.

Page 394 - State of Tennessee vs Daniel Osteen. A. & B. on G. W. Solomon, fined.

Page 394 - State of Tennessee vs G. W. Goodwin. For carrying knife.

Page 394 - State of Tennessee vs James Fansett(?). A. & B. on R. Curtiss, fined.

Page 395 - State of Tennessee vs Y. I. Thomas. A. & B. on James Ray, fined.

Page 395 - State of Tennessee vs James Ray. A. & B. on Y. I. Thomas.

Page 395 - Benjamin F. Greer admr. of George W. Fogleman, deceased and others. Petition for division of slaves. George W. Fogleman is dead, he died intestate, leaving Mary V. Fogleman his widow and Catharine E., Lewis V., Sally W., and B. F. Fogleman, only children and that Benjamin F. Greer is his admr. of the estate and slaves. 20 slaves.

Page 396 - David G. Denson and wife and others. Petition to sell land. Sale in the Town of Unionville on 9th day of Dec 1854. William Brown purchaser. J. G. Harrison purchased house and lot in Unionville. Alfred S. Little purchased __ acres.

Page 397 - Nancy Blanton and others. Exparte - To sell land and slaves. Sale 16 Sept 1854 at the late residence of Charles H. Parker. Epps Parker purchaser.

Page 398 - Samuel Parker and others, heirs at law of Charles H. Parker, deceased Petition to sell land. Sale of 3 Nov 1854, land sold to Samuel Parker.

116

Page 398 - Isaac and William S. Troxler admrs. of Jacob Troxler, deceased.
Petition to sell slaves. Jacob Troxler is dead and he left only one
slave, a man named Perry. Sale at Rowesville.

Page 400 - Hugh H. Manly and others. Petition to sell lnad. Reuben Manly departed this life intestate as to his real estate and he owned the
following tracts, one of 72 acres, one of 25 acres and 95 poles on
which he resided at the time of his death, other of 126 acres.
Widow Martha Manly has not received her dower. Jno. McCrory and
William W. Miller to lay off support to Martha, 1/3 of estate, the
remainder goes to the heirs of Reuben Manly.

Page 402 - Randolph Newsom admr. of Riley H. Forbes, deceased. Petition to sell
slave. To sell negro George.

Page 402 - Claiborn McCuistion executor of John McCuistion, deceased.

Page 402 - Daniel B. Shriver and Charlotte Keeling was appointed admrs. of the
estate of James L. Keeling, deceased. J. M. H. McGrew and John H.
Oneal securities.

Page 402 - Stephen Freeman School Commissioner of Richmond Township.

Page 402 - Mrs. E.(Ellen) Thompson wife of John S. Thompson formerly E. Albright,
appeared in Court to be examined apart from her husband, she consenting
for him to receive her monies arising from the sale of the land belonging to the estate of Jacob Albright, deceased. Gerome Albright and
others petitioners.

Page 403 - Thomas J. Robinson and others. Petition to sell land. Clerk to
report to next Court.

Page 404 - Thomas Lipscomb, Commissioner vs Samuel Doak, Robert M. Whitman and
Edmund Cooper. Judgement. Thomas Lipscomb admr. of Michael Meadows,
deceased, with Will annexed. Lipscomb owes defendants.

Page 404 - John H. Oneal, C&M vs John M. Warner and Thomas Thompson. Judgement.
Obligation due out of the purchase of lands of Henry Earnhart, deceased.
(4 Dec 1852)

Page 405 - G. G. Osborne, John S. Davis, R. L. Singleton, John E. Scruggs, and
James Finch to lay off support to widow and family of James L. Keeling,
deceased.

Page 405 - Thomas Lipscomb admr. of Michael Meadows and Commissioner vs Clement
Cannon, Clement Cannon, Sr., and Charles L. Cannon. Judgement.

Page 406 - Charlotte Keeling, Daniel Shriver, Mary Keeling, William T. Keeling,
James Keeling and Eliza Keeling. Petition to sell land. 5 Town lots
in Town of Fairfield, Bedford County, and 1 small tract of land, 15
acres situated in Coffee County, Tennessee.

1855 January Term

Page 407 - Louisa A. Parsons wife of N. B. Parsons formerly Louisa A. Nash, appeared in Court to be examined apart from her husband. She consented for her husband to receive any monies arising from the estate of Abner Nash, deceased.

Page 407 - Charlotte Keeling, Daniel B. Shriver, Mary Keeling, William T. Keeling, James Keeling, and Eliza Keeling. Petition to sell land. They are the heirs of James L. Keeling, deceased.

1855 February Term

Page 410 - Thomas B. Allison guardian of minor heirs of A. Adams, deceased. A. L. Adams security.

Page 410 - William D. Arnold guardian of Minerva A. Arnold. M. F. Earnhart and G. T. Neeley securities.

Page 410 - W. W. Adams guardian of Mary Ester, Malissa, John W., and Jane Adams, minor heirs of Archibald Adams, deceased. John Oneal and John Ramsey securities.

Page 410 - James H. C. Scales admr. of estate of Noah Cooper Scales, deceased. J. H. C. Scales and Edmund Cooper securities.

Page 411 - John Ramsey admr. of estate of Jane Adams, deceased. Report on sale and inventory.

Page 411 - Commissioners to lay off support to Mary Ann Trigg, widow of William H. Trigg, deceased.

Page 412 - B. F. Craig, a blind man, be released from State and County Taxes.

Page 412 - William Yancy, a lunatic now in the County Jail) be sent to the Poor House in Bedford County.

Page 413 - On Petition of Robert Allison, J. W. Allison and John E. Frost it was ordered that the line of Civil District # 11 be changed. Commencing where said District line strikes the lands of Robert Allison running thence north to N. F. Neal's corner, thence east with the lane to the east boundary line of District # 10, thence south to the north east corner of District # 11. Twenty one Justices being present and voted in the affirmative, to wit, John Q. Davidson, J. J. Shriver, William K. Ransom, William Murphree, Willis Ellis, William Galbreath, George W. Ruth, P. C. Steele, F. B. Price, Jno. W. Simpson, Jackson Nichols, Jos. Stallings, William Wood, Jas. H. Harrison, L. W. Barrett, Richard Phillips, H. F. Holt, L. Turner Hooser, William McGill, and Daniel Parker.
On petition of John W. Maxwell and D. A. Ozment it was ordered that the east boundary line of District # 11, be so changed to include petitioner's land in said District # 11, as follows, commencing in the old Nashville Road at James Finney's south boundary line, thence east about 30 poles to J. W. Maxwell's north east corner, thence south

118

1855 February Term

Page 413 - (continued) including the lands of John W. Maxwell and D. A. Ozment to Absalom Reaves' corner where it intersects said District line # 21.

Page 413 - Ordered by the Court that Andrew Howard, an old and decrepid poor man, be released from Poll Tax.

Page 413 - On Petition of John Jackson, William G. Hight, William C. Cook, Thomas Davis, Jno. W. Manier, William King and Jno. Boyce, it was ordered by the Court that the line of Civil District # 11 be changed as follows, to wit, commencing at Weakley's Creek and running with the public road by Hight's to as to include the lands of the petitioners, north to the County line, so as to change the petitioners from District # 9 to # 10. 21 Justices voting in the affirmative.

Page 413 - J. K. Whitson admr. of Kenneth Madison, returned report on estate.

Page 414 - Martin Thompson admr. of P. J. Thompson be allowed more time to make a return on inventory.

Page 414 - William M. Hutson and wife and others. Petition to sell land. Pay their share of land was sold in 1853.

Page 415 - J. C. Bates and wife Sarah Jane Bates vs Elizabeth Thompson and others. Lawrence C. Thompson is dead and that he died intestate in Bedford County, seized and possessed of a tract of land and that he left surviving Elizabeth Thompson his widow and Sarah Jane who has intermarried with J. C. Bates, and John R. Thompson, Benjamin C. Thompson, William P. Thompson, Mary E. Thompson, Judith Ann Thompson, and Levina F. Thompson, his only children and heirs at law. Elizabeth the widow has not received her dower. Christopher S. Dudley, John L. Cooper and Stephen B. Batte to lay off to widow her dower and divide land into seven shares. J. C. Bates and Sarah Jane Bates to get the land upon where they live.

Page 416 - Thomas J. Robinson admr. of Hannah Harrison, deceased. Petition to sell slaves. Purchasers of the slaves were J. W. Greer and T. J. Robinson.

Page 416 - James F. Hudgins guardian of Jackson Hale, Sarah E. Hale, William T. Hale and John Randolph Hale, minor children of John Hale, deceased vs Francis Jackson Executor of Mead Hale, deceased. James F. Hudgins guardian in the State of Missouri, Ray County, of Jackson Hale, Sarah E. Hale, William T. Hale, and John Randolph Hale, minor children of John Hale, deceased.

Page 417 - J. H. C. Scales admr. of Noah Scales, deceased. Petition to sell slaves. 24 slaves.

Page 420 - John W. Norville appointed admr. of estate of Mitchell Mullins, deceased. John P. Steele, his security.

1855 February Term

Page 421 - John H. Oneal, Clerk and Commissioner vs Elisha Reed and Randolph
Newsom. Judgement.

Page 422 - Charlotte Keeling, widow and William T. Keeling, Mary Keeling, John
Keeling and Eliza Keeling. Heirs of James L. Keeling, deceased.
Petition to sell land. Robert L. Singleton purchased the lot on
which the blacksmith shop is situated. L. P. Fields purchased the
15 acres of land in Coffee County, Tennessee.

Page 424 - Isaac and W. S. Troxler admr. of Jacob Troxler, deceased. Petition to
sell slave. George Cortner purchaser.

Page 424 - John H. Oneal, Commissioner vs Elisha Reed and Randolph Newsom.
Martha C. Reed formerly Martha C. Harrison was examined by the Court
apart from her husband Elisha Reed and she consented for her husband
to receive any monies coming out of the sale of land of her father
John Harrison including the dower. She is the owner of 2/6th part
of the same.

1855 March Term

Page 425 - Commissioners to lay off support for the widow and family of James L.
Keeling, deceased.

Page 425 - William H. Anderton admr. of estate of James Anderton, deceased. Isaac
Troxler and Thomas I. Stanfield securities.

Page 425 - John F. Thompson admr. of estate of Jacob Fisher, deceased. Edmund
Cooper security.

Page 425 - Hezekiah Ray, John Powell and H. C. Ferguson to lay off support to
the widow and family of James Anderton, deceased.

Page 426 - Jane J. Norville Extrix. of H. J. H. Norville, deceased, and James L.
Norville, a minor, who petitions by his mother Jane J. Norville as his
next friend and guardian. Petition to sell slaves. Slaves belonging
to the estate of J. H. Norville, deceased.

Page 426 - R. J. Powell, William A. Johnson and William C. Work and A. M. McElroy
any three of them, to lay off support to widow and family of John S.
Nailor, deceased.

Page 427 - J. J. Crunk admr. of estate of George L. Crunk, deceased. J. W. Crunk
and Watson Floyd his securities.

Page 427 - John W. Nailor admr. of John S. Nailor, deceased, estate. R. H.
Powell and W. H. Nailor, securities.

Page 427 - James Vannatta guardian of James R. Nash, a minor heir of John Nash,
deceased. P. E. Clardy and W. K. Ransom securities.

Page 427 - N. P. Moderal guardian of the minor heirs of Alsey Harris, deceased,

Page 427 - (continued) resigned and Jane Harris was appointed guardian. F. B. Price and J. L. Cooper securities.

Page 427 - Jacob B. Delk guardian of minor heirs of George Capley, deceased. N. C. Thompson security.

Page 427 - Martin Sims admr. of estate of William H. Newborne, deceased. William A. Griffis security.

Page 428 - William A. Griffis guardian of minor heirs of William Newborne, deceased. Martin security.

Page 428 - J. W. Norville admr. of Mitchell Mullins, deceased. Returned inventory.

Page 428 - John W. Crunk guardian of the minor heirs of J. J. B. Crunk.

Page 428 - Richard Swanson admr. of estate of John M. Smith, deceased. David Campbell, John B. McEwen and George W. Buchanan securities.

Page 428 - We, Mary Ann Hardin and G. H. Frazer, hereby bind ourselves to the County of Bedford, that a bastard child of the said Mary Ann Hardin, shall never become chargeable to said Court as a pauper, if it should be we will pay all such expense and charges as sworn as they are incured to the Trustee of said County, this the 9th day of October 1854. Atest   John J. Shriver

Signed Mary A. (X) Hardin (Seal)
        G. H. Frazer   (Seal)

Page 429 - State of Tennessee vs A. J. Bigham. Fine. March 9, 1854

Page 429 - State of Tennessee vs John Oneal. Indebted to State of Tennessee.

Page 430 - Mrs. Matilda Holt appeared in Court and was appointes admrix. of the estate of her deceased husband Michael Holt, also A. H. Evans was appointed admr. of said Holt. Commissioners to lay off support to widow and family of Michael Holt, deceased.

Page 431 - Daniel B. Shriver admr. and Charlotte Keeling admrix. of James L. Keeling, deceased. Petition to sell slave. James L. Keeling is dead and that he died intestate sometime in December 1854, and that Daniel B. Shriver and Charlotte Keeling has been appointed admrs. of said J. L. Keeling, deceased. To sell one slave.

Page 432 - John Troxler and others, heirs of Jacob Troxler, deceased. Petition to sell land. Land to be sold at Rowesville and Normandy.

Page 433 - Richard Warner guardian of Thomas Warner, a minor heir of William D. Warner, deceased. Petition to sell land Warrant. On 13 Jan 1855, issued to petitioners ward, Thomas Warner, from the Department of the Interior, by the United States of America Bounty Land Warrant No.

1855 March Term

Page 432 - (continued) 102734 for 40 acres for the services of his father
William D. Warner, deceased, Private in Capt. Hudlow's Company Tennessee Militia Creek War, and that said Thomas Warner is a minor and
only heir at law of said William D. Warner, deceased. They desire
the Warrant to be sold.

Page 433 - Jas. A. McLure (McClure) and others. Petition to sell land.

1855 April Term

Page 434 - Commissioners to lay off support to widow and family of William
Stephens, deceased.

Page 434 - Commissioners to lay off support to widow and family of P. J. Thompson
deceased.

Page 434 - Commissioners to lay off support to Sarah Naylor, widow of John Naylor
deceased.

Page 434 - Commissioner to lay off support to widow and family of Michael Holt,
deceased.

Page 435- Commissioners to lay off support to widow and family of Matthias Cortney
deceased.

Page 435 - Commissioner to lay off support to widow and family of T. G. W.
Wright, deceased.

Page 435 - Jno. W. Naylor admr. of John Naylor, deceased, returned with inventory &c.

Page 435 - John Q. Davidson admr. of T. G. W. Wright, deceased, estate and
report on sale.

Page 435 - Upon Petition of J. C. Bates, S. V. Butts, William C. Brame, Robert
Blankenship, A. Adcock, A. Dickens, Thomas Dickens, Miles B. Damron,
it is ordered by the Court that the line of Civil District # 5 be
changed as follows, to wit, Beginning at the Shelbyville and Murfrees
boro Road, thence east on the south boundary of J. C. Bates to the
lands of William C. Brame, thence south east north and west with the
lands of said Brame and S. V. Butts to the north boundary of said Butts
thence with the line between Preston Frazier and said Bates to said
road, thence north with said Frazier's lines to the south east corner
of Robert Blankenship's land, thence north to the Rutherford County
line. 20 Justices being present and voting in the affirmative, &c.

Page 435 - Commissioners to lay off support to widow and family of. Jas. Anderton, deceased.

Page 436 - James Ogilvie admr. of estate of C. L. Batte, deceased. J. Nichols
and C. P. Houston securities.

1855 April Term

Page 436 - Archibald Murphree admr. of estate of Sarah L. Campbell, deceased.
Robert Buchanan and John Q. Davidson securities.

Page 436 - George Huffman admr. of estate of Laton E. Boone, deceased. G. W.
Heard and John Q. Davidson securities.

Page 436 - John H. Oneal guardian of Mary A. A. McCuistion, heir of John C.
McCuistion, deceased.

Page 436 - George Cortner, Jesse Holt and William Knight to lay off support to
widow and family of Laton Boone, deceased.

Page 437 - John Baxter for 2 coffins for Thomas Lagston and Hezekiah Brown,
paupers, $10.00.

Page 437 - Abram Claxton for coffin for Mary Jane Turner, a pauper, $5.00.

Page 437 - M. S. Rogers for coffin for Martha Farris, a pauper, $4.00.

Page 437 - Jacob Reese for coffin for Allen Cantrill, a pauper, $5.00.

Page 439 - Moses Marshall Coroner of Bedford County.

Page 442 - John P. Steele guardian of P. A. Wheeler, resigned. A. Reeves was
appointed guardian.

Page 443 - John H. White admr. of Jeremiah Forbes, deceased, Edith Forbes and
others. Petition to sell slaves. Sold at the residence of late
Jeremiah Forbes, deceased, 8 slaves.

Page 444 - John R. Troxler, Elizabeth Wright and others, heirs of Jacob Troxler,
deceased. Petition to sell land. A. L. Landis purchaser.

Page 447 - J. J. Crunk and others. Petition to sell slaves. Martha Crunk wife
of J. J. B. Crunk, is dead, that she died leaving surviving her,
George J. Crunk, W. C. Crunk, Sally Ann Brantley formerly Sally Ann
Crunk, Harriett R. Crunk, Eliza H. Crunk, Letitia Crunk, Anna Crunk,
Martha Crunk, Margarett J. Crunk, and Jefferson P. Crunk, her only
children and as such under a Deed of Gift executed by Gabriel E.
Lowe their grandfather entitled to the slaves. And it also appearing that George J. Crunk one of Martha Crunk's children has departed
this life intestate since the death of his mother and that J.J. Crunk
is his admr. And that Sally Ann has intermarried with William C.
Brantley, and that W. C. Crunk is of age, and that they also desirous
of obtaining their shares.

Page 447 - In the matter of Mary J. Hopkins upon Petition of lunacy. Petition
of W. W. Hopkins, it is ordered by the Court that a writ of lunacy
issue to the Sheriff of Bedford County requiring him to summon
Joseph Anderson, A. B. Moon, Samuel Sutton, John B. Jones, Jesse M.
Ledbetter, Merriman(?) Burns, Thomas Ray, Benjamin Crowell, William
Crowell, Augustine Wilson, John C. Wilson, and William Wortham free

1855 April Term

Page 447 - (continued) holders residing in Bedford County, who are to examine the condition of Mary J. Hopkins and report to next Term of Court.

Page 446 - Matilda Holt and others. Petition for Dower. Michael Holt is dead, that he died intestate, that he left surviving him Matilda Holt his widow and other petitioners his only heirs at law and that was the owner of a tract of land. Matilda Holt desires her dower. C. S. Dudley County Surveyor, Demarcus D. Hix, and Samuel G. Hays be appointed to lay off the dower.

Page 447 - In the matter of Sarah McFarlin upon petition of lunacy. A jury was appointed to inquire into the condition of Sarah McFarlin as to whether she is an idiot or is capable to care and manage for herself.

Page 447 - Thomas Lipscomb admr. with the Will annexed vs William C. Holt, J.J. Phillips and W. F. Cooper. Judgement.

Page 448 - Daniel B. Shriver and Charlotte admrs. of James L. Keeling, deceased Petition to sell slave. To sell slave to pay debt.

Page 448 - Hugh H. Manley and others. Petition to sell land. Sale of 3 Feb 1855 of several tracts of land.

Page 451 - Charlotte Keeling, admrix. and D. B. Shriver admr. and other heirs at law of James L. Keeling, deceased. Petition to sell land. Land in Town of Fairfield, Bedford County.

1855 May Term

Page 454 - James Carlisle guardian of Benton Gabbert, a minor heir of William Gabbert, deceased.

Page 454 - Barnett Stephens guardian of his minor children.

Page 454 - B. F. Whitworth guardian of the minor grandchildren of W. P. Elkins, deceased, and children of B. F. Bowers in the place of R. H. Majors who resigned.

Page 454 - Emily Dixon guardian of William R. and R. B. Dixon, minor heirs of Robert Dixon, deceased.

Page 454 - William Shearin guardian of Edward M. Shearin, a minor heir of Thomas Shearin, deceased.

Page 455 - Thomas Shearin guardian of H. L. and Newton C. Shearin, minor heirs of Thomas Shearin, deceased.

Page 455 - John F. Thompson guardian of Willie F. Shearin, a minor heir of Thomas Shearin, deceased.

Page 455 - Mrs. Emily Baxter wife of Thomas Baxter appeared in Court and was

Page 455 - (continued) examined apart from her husband and gave her consent to receive any monies arising from the sale of the lands of her father Henry Earnhart, deceased.

Page 457 - G. G. Osborne appeared in open Court and made application to have the funds in the hands of Joseph W. Couch belonging to Susan J. Couch, removed to the State of Texas, County of Ellis. Joseph W. Couch was appointed guardian to the personal and estate of Susan J. Couch in this County of Bedford and has since removed with his ward to the State of Texas. Granted.

Page 457 - Mary J. Hopkins. Petition for lunacy. The Jury stated that she is now in the asylum in Nashville, Tennessee, and that she is not capable of caring or manageing for herself. Her property is in 30 acres of land, a dower, and household and kitchen furniture, stock &c. Allen Morris her guardian.

Page 458 - Robert McFarlin. Petition for lunacy. Jury found Sarah McFarlin to be of sound mind and that she is capable of controlling her own affairs and she owns one room of furniture, a negro boy and about $128.00 in cash.

Page 459 - Emily Dixon widow of Robert Dixon, deceased, resigned her right as exrix. of the Will of Robert Dixon, deceased.

Page 459 - R. H. Majors guardian of minor grandchildren of W. P. Elkins and children of B. F. Bowers, resigned and was received.

Page 460 - James Russ guardian of Mary Johnson.

Page 460 - Joseph H. Thompson and Robert N. Jones. Petition to be released as securities of George W. Hobbs. Released. Also, George W. Hobbs failed to give other security.

Page 461 - John Burrow and others. Petition to sell land. John Burrow and other heirs at law of M. L. Burrow, deceased. The title to be vested in William M. Goggin the purchaser.

Page 461 - Green T. Neeley admr of William Cook, deceased vs Nancy Cook and others, widow and heirs of said William Cook, deceased. Nancy Cook, Thomas J. Cook, Mary E. Cook, and George W. Cook the adult defendants failed to answer complainants Bill. The Defendants are Andrew J. Cook, Sarah A. Cook, Emily M. Cook, Hugh L. W. Cook, Zachary T. Cook and Nancy Frances Cook are minors with no guardian. James L. Oneal was appointed guardian. William Cook late of Bedford County departed this life intestate, leaving Nancy Cook his widow and Thomas J., Mary E., George W., Andrew J., Sarah A., Emily M., Hugh L. W., Zachary T., and Nancy Frances Cook, his children and heirs at law. It is necessary to sell his real estate to pay his debts.

Page 462 - Upon application of Christopher Couch by his next friend, that Christopher Couch a minor now residing in the State of Missouri, County of

1855 May Term

Page 462 - (continued) Ray, and that Joseph E. Couch has been appointed his
guardian by probate Court of Ray County, Missouri. Thomas H. Coldwell to pay over to Joseph Couch, his interest &c.

Page 463 - Green T. Neeley admr. of William Cook, deceased. vs Nancy Cook and
others, widow and heirs of William Cook, deceased. Petition to sell
land to pay debts.

Page 464 - John M. Warner and others. Petition to sell land. Lands belonging
to the said John Warner, deceased. 207 acres.

Page 466 - J. J. Crunk and other heirs at law of Martha Crunk, deceased. Petition to sell slaves. John W. Crunk purchaser.

1855 June Term

Page 468 - Smith Arnold guardian of Mariah Simmons formerly Mariah Mullins, a
minor. John A. Moore security.

Page 468 - Manuel Ray guardian of James, Mary, Marion, Melvina, Catharine, and
Martha C. Ray, minor heirs of Charles Ray, deceased.

Page 468 - William M. Goggins guardian of Thomas H., Sarah J., Martha E., Tennessee V., and Isaac C. Davidson, minor children of Bluford Davidson,
deceased.

Page 468 - Isaac Vickery guardian of Francis M. Vickery, his minor child. John
Jordan security.

Page 469 - Thomas M. Davidson admr. of estate of Richard M. Davidson, deceased.

Page 469 - Isaac Vickery admr. of estate of Owen Vickery, deceased.

Page 470 - John S. Thompson guardian of Sarah Jane Brown, a minor heir of Rufin
Brown, deceased. Samuel Roan and Jarel Smith, securities.

Page 470 - Smith Arnold guardian of William Cortner, a minor heir of Levi Cortner
deceased.

Page 470 - James G. Barksdale guardian of William Cortner, a minor heir of Levi
Cortner, deceased. Smith Arnold who resigned as same.

Page 470 - Commissioners to lay off support to widow and family of Thomas
Hensley, deceased.

Page 471 - William M. Meadows by his next friend William Jones vs Daniel Stephen
William M. Meadows is a minor now a resident of Wayne County and that
John C. Throgmorton has been appointed guardian.

Page 471 - Daniel B. Shriver admr. and Charlotte Keeling admrx. of James L. Keel
ing, deceased. Petition to sell slaves.

1855 June Term

Page 472 - State of Tennessee, Bedford County - On motion of William F. Bradford, Esq. and it appearing to the satisfaction of the Court that
Melvin N. Fowler is and has been a resident citizen of Bedford County
in the State of Tennessee for more than twelve months previous to
this application and is over twenty one years of age and a gentleman
of good moral character and is desirous of obtaining license to
practice law. It is therefore ordered by the Court that these facts
be so certified in confirmity with the Acts of the Legislature of
Tennessee in such cases made and provide for the purpose of his
obtaining License to practice law in this State.

Page 473 - Richard Warner executor and Commissioner vs J. M. Warner and J. W.
Rutledge. Judgement. Richard Warner executor of John Warner,
deceased.

Page 474 - John W. Maxwell, Phillip Sprouse and Willis Carson to lay off support
to the widow and family of John W. Wheeler, deceased.

Page 474 - Joseph Haynes, Drury Martin and R. A. Gault to lay off support to
widow and family of Owen Vickery, deceased.

Page 474 - Power of Attorney signed by James H. Curtiss, Jr. and wife Theresa
Curtiss. Theresa Curtiss was examined by Court apart from her husband
and she gave consent for his to receive any monies of hers.

Page 475 - Emily Dixon and William R. Dixon and Robert Barksdale Dixon vs James
B. Dixon and M. L. Dismukes. Petition for dower. Robert Dixon late
of Bedford County departed this life having first made his Will which
was proven. James B. Dixon executor and Emily Dixon admrix. and M.L.
Dismukes admr. Emily Dixon widow of Robert Dixon, deceased, and the
other petitioners his only children. He died possessed of a tract of
land in Bedford County of about 140 acres on which he lived at the time
of his death. Emily Dixon is entitled to her dower.

Page 476 - Jacob Harrison admr. of the estate of Robert Harrison, deceased. John
Harrison security.

Page 476 - Mary Vance Fogleman admr. of estate of Sarah W. Fogleman, deceased.

Page 476 - Mary Vance Fogleman admr. of estate of Benjamin F. Fogleman, deceased.
A. J. Greer security.

Page 477 - James Hastings and others vs Hiram Eddy and others. Candis Eddy one
of the minor defendants has died since the sale of the land and Hiram
Eddy admr. of her estate.

Page 477 - Green T. Neeley admr. of William Cook, deceased vs Nancy Cook, widow
and Thomas J. Cook, G. W. Cook, Mary E. Cook, Andrew J. Cook, Sarah A.
Cook, Hugh L. W. Cook, Zachary T. Cook and Nancy Francis Cook, heirs
of William Cook, deceased. Petition to sell land. G. W. Cook purchaser, land in Civil District # 18 of Bedford County on both sides of
Sinking Creek.

BEDFORD COUNTY COURT MINUTE BOOK - 1857

1857 November Term

Page 6 - State of Tennessee vs Jno. H. Holt. Bastardy.

Page 7 - Calvin E. Jenkins guardian of Margaret J. Jenkins, his minor child. A. L. Landis security.

Page 7 - David R. Vance guardian of Eliza J. and Robert B. Vance, minor children of Robert Vance, deceased.

Page 8 - Andrew Reed guardian of Warren Reed, William G. Reed and Almeda Reed minor children of C. W. Reed, deceased.

Page 8 - Absalom Reavis guardian of Nathan Thompson, Phillip Thompson, Ann Thompson, Joseph Thompson, Mary Thompson, and Ellen Thompson. Jackson Nichols security.

Page 8. W. C. Arnold, late a citizen of this County, Bedford, has departed this life intestate. George W. Cunningham admr. of the estate.

Page 8 - R. F. Norman, late a citizen of Bedford County, had departed this life intestate. Jackson Nichols security.

Page 9 - F. F. Fonville admr. of estate of Sarah Parks, deceased.

Page 9 - William King has departed this life intestate.

Page 9 - John F. Phifer, late a citizen of Bedford County, had departed this li: intestate. Edmund Cooper admr.

Page 9 - Power of Attorney, dated 2 Nov 1857, executed by G. H. Castleman and h. wife Alcy Castleman and Abram Reagor and Elizabeth Reagor his wife, to Moses Lacy.

Page 11 - Margaret M. Hastings, late of Bedford County, departed this life inte: ate. Robert Hastings admr.

Page 11 - Hartwell J. Ray, late a citizen of Bedford County, has departed this life intestate. John Reed admr. George Reed security.

Page 11 - Robert S. Worke, late of Bedford County, has departed this life intes ate. W. T. Hughes admr. B. F. Whitworth security.

Page 11 - Henry Hart, late of Bedford County, has departed this life intestate. James B. Morris(?) and D. J. Hart admrs. Watson Floyd and William Campbell securities.

Page 12 - W. P. Temple admr. of Dempsey P. Temple, deceased. Preston Frazier security.

Page 13 - Robert Cannon, D. G. Deason and Capt. Jno. Bennett to lay off support

128

1857 November Term

Page 13 - (continued) to widow and family of Wilson C. Arnold, deceased.

Page 13 - B. F. Whitworth, James Ogilvie and George W. Bell to lay off support
to widow and family of Robert S. Worke, deceased.

Page 13 - William Caruthers and others. Petition to divide slaves. 7 slaves
to be divided between Eliza, George and William Caruthers.

Page 14 - George W. Frankford of Bedford County appeared in open Court and
acknowledged the execution of a Deed of Conveyance to James Gosling of
Alleghany County, Pennsylvania, dated 10th October 1857.

Page 15 - W. T. Hughes admr. and others. Petition to sell slaves. Robert S.
Worke departed this life intestate in Bedford County on the __ day of
Oct 1857 and that he left Matilda his widow and Robert H., William A.,
and Sally F., as his children and only distributees. W. T. Hughes admr.
of estate. He was owner of two slaves. They cannot be divided and will
have to be sold.

Page 15 - James S. Maupin guardian of Jane, Betty, Thompson B. Maupin, a portion
of the minor children of Blan Maupin, deceased. Petition to sell horses
&c.

Page 16 - Daniel Parker admr. et al. Petition for dower. We asign to Delilah
Walsh land. (Plat on page 16) J. W. C. Walsh her deceased husband.

Page 18 - State of Tennessee vs Jno. H. Holt. Bastardy. Court found in favor
of Defendant.

Page 18 - Sarah Johnson et al. Petition for dower. Sarah Johnson, widow of Edwin
Johnson, deceased.

Page 18 - Jno. C. Aiken. Petition to remove guardianship. John C. Aiken has removed from Bedford County to Warren County, Tennessee and desires the
guardianship be removed from Bedford County to Warren County, he is
guardian of Sarah A. Lane, William H. and Robert T. Lane who are residents of Warren County.

Page 20 - A. Freeman and Jno. T. Brown and others. Petition to sell land.

Page 22 - W. M. Ray and others. Petition to divide land. Heirs &c. of Robert
Ray, deceased. The widow has had her dower allotted to her.

Page 22 - Daniel Parker et al. Petition to sell land.

Page 23 - M. A. A. McCuistion vs Jno. H. Oneal. Report.

Page 23 - James Carlisle and others. Petition to sell land. To report.

Page 23 - William Murphree and others. Petition to establish Will. Case dismissed.

1857 November Term

Page 24 - William H. Wisener requiring William S. Brown to appear and enter into a new bond with other security in place of Jesse Phillips.

1857 December Term

Page 25 - T. P. Welles guardian of Charity, Tabitha, John W., Ranson B., and William C. welles, his minor children. William T. Tune, security.

Page 25 - Edwin Butler guardian of W. H., Jno. R., and Acthen Butler. G. W. Harrison, Security.

Page 25 - Sarah Smith guardian of her minor child, Mary J. Smith. W. R. Smith security.

Page 25 - Robert N. Jones renewed his guardianship of minor children of Samuel Pratt, deceased. Thomas Holland security.

Page 26 - Thomas H. Coldwell resigned as guardian of the minor children of A. G. Snell. Jno. C. Snell appointed guardian of Jno. T. Snell, Sarah H. Snell and Eliza C. Snell. W. P. Bridges and W. B. Snell securities.

Page 26 - G. W. Tilford, late of Bedford County, had departed this life intestate W. C. Blanton admr. Jno. W. Tilford and C. S. Dudley securities.

Page 26 - Mary F. Snell, late a citizen of Bedford County, had departed this life intestate. W. P. Bridges admr. Wilie B. Snell and J. C. Snell securities.

Page 27 - John Revis, late a citizen of Bedford County, had departed this life intestate. James R. Revis admr. William Armstrong and A. Helton, securities.

1857 December Term

Page 28 - Quarles T. Sutton, late a citizen of Bedford County, had departed this life intestate. Jno. T. Stephens admr. Jno. W. Cowan and William Brown securities.

Page 28 - Thomas B. Karr resigned as Justice of the Peace in District # 4.

Page 28 - Commissioners to lay off support to widow and family of W. C. Arnold, deceased.

Page 29 - W. M. Hutson guardian of his minor sister Jane Hutson. H. N. Hutson security.

Page 29 - Thomas D. Garrett guardian of Lipscomb Garrett, a minor child of Stephen Garrett, deceased.

Page 29 - P. H. Reaves guardian of Elenor Phelps and Mary Phelps. J. J. Burrow and A. S. Reaves securities.

Page 30 - James B. Wheeler by his guardian Jno. W. Maxwell. Petition to sell horse. They desire to sell the horse because the horse will become useless before James B. Wheeler becomes of age.

Page 31 - Blackman A. Koonce, a late citizen of Bedford County, departed this life intestate. John J. Koonce admr.

Page 31 - Elizabeth J. Koonce, late a citizen of Bedford County, departed this life intestate. Jno. J. Koonce is her admr.

Page 32 - James Carlisle resigned as guardian of Benton Gabbert. S. W. Barrett was appointed guardian.

Page 32 - Robert Parks executor of Will of Joshua Parks, resigned. F. F. Fonville was appointed his admr.

Page 32 - J. N. Phelps departed this life intestate. Thomas H. Coldwell admr.

Page 33 - Miles Phillips, Thomas S. Mays and John Armstrong to lay off support to widow and family of John Revis.

Page 34 - Sarah Johnson et al. Petition for dower. Dower allotted out of the lands of Edward Johnson, her deceased husband. Land in the 19 District on which said Johnson lived at the time of his death. Other land in District # 5 of Marshall County. Dower tract includes the mansion house and improvements. Plat on page 36.

Page 37 - Jno. H. Oneal, C & M and Commissioner vs John McQuiddy and Loton Shofner. Judgement. John H. Oneal to sell land belonging to the heirs of Martha Yell, deceased. Judgement against John McQuiddy and Loton Shofner which is now due. John McQuiddy became purchaser of land of Martha Yell, deceased, on 28 Nov 1855 and Loton Shofner his security.

Page 38 - Daniel Parker et al. Petition to sell land. Estate of J. W. C. Walsh, deceased.

Page 39 - Commissioners to lay off support to widow and family of J. P. Gillinan(?).

Page 39 - Settlement with Morgan Smith Executor of J. B. Webb.

Page 39 - Settlement with Joseph Hornady and Sarah Proby executors of J. W. Proby.

Page 39 - State of Tennessee for the use of the heirs of J. Meadows, deceased vs George W. Cunningham admr. Settlement.

Page 40 - John C. Hix admr. and et al. Petition to sell land. Land of heirs of Finney Norman, deceased, who are all of age. Desires land to be sold.

Page 40 - Jesse Rogers, Robert Reed and William Hime are to take charge of the bridge across Duck River at the "Sckull Camp Ford" and report.

1857 December Term

Page 41 - Commissioners to lay off support to the widow and family of James Gant, deceased.

Page 41 - Settlement by the Judge with D. G. Blessing admr. of H. W. Blessing, deceased.

Page 42 - William M. Ray et al and others. Petition to sell land. To report.

Page 42 - Joseph W. Trigg and others. Petition to sell slaves. Joseph W. Trigg purchased 7 slaves.

1858 January Term

Page 54 - Sarah Clark wife of Robert Clark, appeared in Court and was examined apart from her husband. She gave consent for her husband to receive any monies arising from the sell of land.

Page 54 - Matilda E. Brown, a citizen of Bedford County, departed this life intestate. George W. Brown admr.

Page 55 - Allen T. Tune resigned as guardian of Sarah V. and Susan P. Whitman, minor children of Edmond Whitman, deceased. George W. Gregory was appointed guardian. Thomas Gregory, Sr. and Thomas Gregory, Jr., securities.

Page 55 - Jeremiah Culverhouse renewed guardianship of Elizabeth and Jane Culverhouse.

Page 55 - Jeremiah Culverhouse admr. of Dicey Jones, deceased. H. W. Jones security.

Page 56 - Joseph Trice exr. of Benjamin Gambill with Joseph H. C. Scales, Jno. Cortner and William Wood, securities.

Page 56 - Monroe Pratt and others by their next friend. Petition to remove guardianship. Petitioners Monroe Pratt, Columbus Pratt, Mary Jane Pratt and Willis Pratt who reside in Travis County, State of Texas. They are the legatees of their grandfather George Pratt, deceased, which is in the hands of John Wallace and Drury M. Pratt, the executors of the Will and of George W. Thompson the local guardian. Desire guardianship be changed to Texas &c.

Page 57 - Mary A. Cunningham guardian of Joseph H., Sarah E., Martha Adeline and Susan A. Cunningham, her minor children. Thomas W. Buchanan and John Cortner securities.

Page 57 - Mary Jane Hasty executed a Power of Attorney, now in Court, that she did so freely .... (?)

Page 57 - Henry Dean declined to serve as Trustee of James R. Reese.

1858 January Term

Page 58 - Hiram Harris and others. Petition to sell land. Land belonged to the heirs of George W. Tilford, deceased.

Page 59 - John S. Woods guardian of Martha P. Muse.

Page 59 - John McQuiddy asked to be released as one of the securities of Alfred Gwynn. Granted.

Page 59 - Hiram Harris et al. Petition to sell land. Land cannot be divided and desires the land to be sold.

Page 60 - Mathew Shearin and others. Petition to sell slaves. James Gant is dead, that he died intestate, that he left surviving him as his only heirs at law the parties named in the petition. They desire to sell a slave.

Page 61 - Rachel Craycroft and others. Petition to sell slaves. Rachel Craycroft, Jacob Stilwell, Margaret R. Craycroft, Gustavus Stilwell, Thomas Stilwell, Henry C. Stilwell and Eliza Banks, interest in slaves, and that the above named being the owners of 7/8 of the slaves. The death of William Sorrell leaving as his heirs &c. his widow Elinor Sorrells and children, Catherine wife of T. R. W. Crane, Joseph, James, Jane wife of James Richardson, William, Margaret, Nancy, Needham, Marion, Isom, Henry, and Newton Sorrells.

Page 62 - State of Tennessee for the use &c. vs Wilie B. Snell admr. &c. Wilie B. Snell admr. of Albert G. Snell, deceased.

Page 63 - Court desires the guardianship be removed as guardian of the minor children of Henry Collins, deceased, and granted or appoint Joel Whirly as guardian. They are all residents of Marshall County, Tennessee.

1858 February Term

Page 65 - J. G. Norman, special guardian of his brother William Norman, his minor brother. Jno. H. Thompson, Clerk to receive any monies arising from the estate of Fanney Norman, deceased. G. A. **Renegar,** security.

Page 65 - M. E. W. Dunaway, Register of Bedford County, asked the Court to appoint his brother Finis E. Dunaway, his Deputy.

Page 66 - Power of Attorney executed by Thomas and Nancy Taylor to Logan D. Stephens.

Page 66 - John W. Maxwell guardian &c. Petition to sell stock.

Page 67 - John Bussey and others. Petition to sell land warrant. Elliott Bussey was at the time of his death the owner of a Land Warrant No. 60440 for 100 acres and the petitioners John Michael, George, Elizabeth and Mary Bussey and Mary C. and Martha J. Hill are the only heirs at law of said Elliott Bussey, deceased, and they are the owners of the Land Warrant mentioned. It is necessary to sell the Land Warrant.

1858 February Term

Page 68 - H. H. Nease (Hiram H.)(his Emily J., 1850 Census) went into Court to
make bond to receive money from sale of land belonging to the estate
of Jordan C. Holt, deceased.

Page 68 - J. F. Jenkins guardian of Matilda Brown, a minor child of George W. Brown
deceased. James Carlisle security.

Page 68 - B. W. Nowlin guardian of the minor children of Thomas Musgrave. James
Stallings security.

Page 68 - Price C. Steele guardian of Mills M. Puckett. John L. Cooper security.

Page 69 - Joshua Crowell guardian of Francis, Mary Jane and John Crowell, minor
children of Jacob Crowell. John Crowell and Samuel Crowell securities.

Page 69 - William Reaves guardian of John Swing's minor children. Isham Reaves
security.

Page 69 - John L. Cooper guardian of Lucy S., William W., Joseph L., Martha A. L.
Thomas J., and Nancy Puckett, minor children of William S. Puckett.

Page 69 - John S. Thompson guardian of Asberry, Mary, Elizabeth, Thomas Thompson,
his minor children. Samuel Roane security.

Page 70 - Elenor Hawkins, late a citizen of Bedford County, departed this life
intestate. Daniel Parker admr. J. M. Ray and R. H. Terry securities.

Page 70 - William B. Swing, late of Bedford County, departed this life intestate.
Stephen Rogers admr. Jesse Rogers and J. H. McGrew securities.

Page 70 - Edwin L. Bryan, late a citizen of Bedford County, departed this life
intestate. Robert B. Davidson admr.

Page 72 - James A. Puckett guardian of Benjamin A. and Samuel E. Puckett. J. L.
Cooper and John W. Key securities.

Page 72 - Thomas Jeffries guardian of his minor children. J. R. Stem security.

Page 72 - Susan Walker, late a citizen of Bedford County, departed this life
intestate. Calloway Walker admr. John T. Martin security.

Page 74 - Abram Evans, Justice of the Peace of District # 25.

Page 74 - Tuesday Feb 2, 1858. This day ordered by the Court that no person
shall hitch his horse nearer than fifteen feet on either side of the
north, east, south and west gates that enter the Court House Yard and
that the Mayor and Aldermen of Shelbyville enforce this order and en-
flect such penalty by them make them just for as violators of this
order and that no person shall any a sale of any kind nearer than 20
feet of said gayes.

Page 75 - Jno. T. Stephens admr. &c. Petition to sell slaves. Report.

1858 February Term

Page 75 - James H. Neil guardian of Justina Terry, Martha Terry, Raford Terry,
Mary Terry, Eliza Terry, minor children of James Terry, deceased.

Page 75 - John T. Stephens admr. &c. Petition to sell slaves. The only heirs
of Quarles T. Sutton, deceased. Slaves to be sold, that they cannot be
divided equally. Quarles T. Sutton died intestate in Bedford County
and he was the owner of slaves. Ordered slaves to be sold.

Page 76 - John C. Hix et al. Petition to sell slaves. Mary Norman, one of the
distributees of Finny Norman, deceased, has intermarried with H. R.
Rainey and is a minor and is entitled to a fund in the hands of the
C & M, arising from slae of slaves. H. R. Rainey is to take possession of Mary Rainey's fund.

1858 March Term

Page 78 - Robert S. Clarke admr. of Madeline Finch, deceased. L. P. Fields and
W. G. Miller his securities.

Page 78 - John M. Nash guardian of William Nash. Thomas C. Allison and N. B.
Parsons securities.

Page 78 - Thomas Thompson resigned as guardian of H. C. Earnhart. M. B. Thompson appointed guardian.

Page 78 - W. C. Blanton, Augustus Wilson, R. H. Thompson to lay off support to
widow Emily Norman.

Page 79 - James Scruggs, James Frizzell, Samuel McMahan and John McCrory to lay
off support for widow of Thomas Hutchen, deceased.

Page 79 - Ordered by the Court, then being also 20 magistrates present and voting
that the line between the 7th District and the 21st Civil District of
said Bedford County be so changed as to throw the plantation upon which
Joseph Thompson now resides into the 7th Civil District of Bedford
County and that from and after the passage of this order, that the said
plantation and residence of the said Joseph Thompson shall be consider-
ed as a part of the 7th Civil District, and it is also ordered that the
line between the 8th and 5th Civil District of said County be so changed as to throw Price C. Steele's residence into the 5th Civil District
of Bedford County. (Thompson's land on Flat Creek)

Page 79 - Alex. Kimbro et al. Petition to sell land. To report by C & M.

1858 March Term

Page 80 - Thomas Hatchet, late a citizen of Bedford County, had departed this
life testate and that the widow has waved her right to admr. upon estate.
Alexander Lee was appointed admr. A. McMahahan and Nathan Chaffin
securities.

135

1858 March Term

Page 80 - James S. Newton guardian of Martha and Amanda Gabbert, minor children of William Gabbert, deceased.

Page 81 - Daniel Parker et al. Petition to sell slaves.

Page 81 - Clemenza Sugg resigned as guardian of the minor children of T. G. W.
Wright. Nehemiah Sugg was appointed guardian.

Page 81 - James Scruggs, James Frizzell, Sam McMahan and Nathan Chaffin to lay
off support for widow of Thomas Hatchett, deceased.

Page 82 - Daniel L. Reaves, James B. Shaw et al. Petition to sell land.
Thomas G. Mosly to examine this cause and report.

Page 83 - Mrs. Mary Troxler, daughter of John Koonce, Jr. appeared in Court to
be examined apart from her husband W. S. Troxler and gave consent for
him to receive any monies from estate of John Koonce, Jr., which had
belonged to the estate of John Koonce, Sr.

Page 84 - Margaret Koonce, late a citizen of Bedford County, had lately departed
this life intestate. Thomas P. Wilhoite admr.

Page 84 - Rachel Craycroft and others. Petition to sell slaves. Sale of slaves
to be at Richmond. Isaac S. Davidson and Jackson Wallis purchasers.

Page 87 - Daniel Parker and others. Petition to sell slaves. Slaves of Elinor
Hawkins, deceased, to be sold.

Page 88 - Benjamin Mosly entered into bond. Funds belonging to Maria Isora Holt,
a minor of Jordan C. Holt, with R. S. Dwiggins and H. H. Holt securities.

Page 89 - John S. Davis, John E. Scruggs and Robert S. Clarke to lay off support
for the widow of Robert L. Singleton, deceased.

Page 89 - L. P. Fields executed a Power of Attorney to John H. Morgan, dated
3 March 1858.

1858 April Term

Page 123 - Court allowed Reuben Williams $10.00, he being a cripple.

Page 123 - Mr. and Mrs. Garman, aged, allowed $15.00 each.

Page 125 - Jno. T. Neil admr. and others. Petition to sell slaves. Ann Jordan
wife of J. F. Jordan and daughter of Smith Arnold, deceased, appeared
in Court on 5 April 1858 and was examined apart from her husband. She
gave consent for him to receive any monies or interest.

Page 128 - Thomas D. Tarpley guardian of Henry E., F. C., and Samuel G. McGowan,
minor children of Samuel McGowan, deceased.

1858 April Term

Page 128 - P. H. Reaves guardian of Mary E. Phelps and Josephine Phelps. A. S. Reaves and Moses Reaves securities.

Page 128 - Mrs. Thomas Pettus appeared in Court and was examined apart from her husband and gave consent for him to receive any monies from the sale of land belonging to the Manly heirs.

Page 129 - Power of Attorney by William King and his wife Elizabeth King. Elizabeth having given her husband right to collect any monies &c.

Page 129 - Power of Attorney by Acton Young, Nancy Young, William Young, J. W. Dickerson, Nancy Dickerson to James Young.

Page 129 - Mary H. Hendon guardian of Keziah and John M. Hendon, her minor children. J. R. Hendon security.

Page 129 - John H. Oneal vs Smith Bowlin, R. W. Pearson, and W. F. Freeman. Motion for judgement. Report to next Court.

Page 129 - Preston Frazier guardian of John S. Frazier, Jr.

Page 130 - Nancy Mitchell, late a citizen of Bedford County, had departed this life intestate. J. H. Job admr. W. C. Scott and John I. Davidson securities.

Page 131 - Daniel Parker and others. Petition to sell slaves. Epps Parker security.

Page 131 - Thomas J. Warren guardian of Miss Julia Gurnee(?).

Page 131 - Malissa A. Killingsworth, an infant of 16 months, had been deserted by its parents. The infant is placed with William Givins until she is 18 years of age.

Page 131 - El Bowden guardian of G. E., William T. and Priscilla Parker, minor children of Charles H. Parker, deceased. Bowden is now a resident of Coffee County, Tennessee. Court removed Bowden and Epps Parker was appointed guardian. Daniel Parker and Thomas L. Roberts securities.

Page 132 - Alexander Dysart guardian of Caledonia and Cincinnatie Phillips.

Page 132 - Hiram Harris and others. Petition to sell land. Land belonged to estate of George W. Tilford at the time of his death. W. C. Blanton admr. Land to be sold.

Page 134 - Elliott Bussey and others. Petition to sell Land Warrant. To report.

Page 134 - Mathew Cotner vs Robert F. Arnold. Contested election. Continued.

Page 136 - William T. Hughes admr. &c. Petition ro sell slaves. Slaves in the estate of Robert S. Worke, deceased.

1858 April Term

Page 143 - John T. Stephens and others. Petition to sell slaves. To report.

Page 144 - George A. McClure and others. Petition to sell land. Lewis Lynch purchased land.

Page 145 - Mathew Cortner vs Robert F. Arnold. Contested election. Continued.

Page 148 - Mathew Shearin. Petition to sell slave. A. G. Woods purchaser.

1858 May Term

Page 150 - John H. Floyd guardian of John Floyd, William Floyd, James Floyd, with William Floyd security.

Page 150 - Martin Hancock guardian of minor children of Orville Muse, deceased. D. H. Skeen and Reuben Curry securities.

Page 150 - Peter Cotner guardian of his minor children, with Thomas S. Mays and J. H. Harrison securities.

Page 151 - W. S. Troxler and others. Petition to sell slave. A portion of the fund going to Mrs. Eran Shofner, arising from the sale of the slave sold to Martin Euliss be paid to her Attorney Thomas C. Whiteside.

Page 152 - W. J. Davis guardian of Rebecca Taylor, a free person of color and also a minor.

Page 152 - Feliz Turrentine guardian of his minor daughter Frances E. Turrentine.

Page 152 - Thomas Pearson had departed this life intestate. Court appointed Dr. John Bell admr. with J. H. Harrison security.

Page 154 - John H. Oneal, C & M vs Smith Bowlin, William F. Pearson and R. W. Pearson. Motion for judgement.

Page 156 - Edmund Cooper resigned as executor of Erwin J. Frierson, deceased.

Page 157 - John Q. Davidson, Jonas Myers and Robert Buchanan to lay off support to widow and family of Archibald Murphy, deceased.

Page 157 - W. W. Gant and others. Petition to sell land. 7 shares to be divided equally. W. W. Gant is entitled to 2 shares and one share purchased by him of Annie Russell and husband and that Martha Shaddie is entitled to 2 shares. One in her own right and the other she purchased of Annie Bryant and also that Mary Broughton to get one share, and that Elizabeth Gant gets one share and that the heirs of John Gifford, deceased, are entitled to one share.

Page 159 - That the daughter of the "widow Ship" is a lunatic. Jury to examine her and report.

Page 159 - Levi Thornberry guardian of his minor children.

1858 May Term

Page 160 - Claiborn McCuistion, late a citizen of Bedford County, had departed this life intestate also his widow declined to serve as admr. of
his estate. Garrett Phillips appointed admr.

Page 160 - William Hardin is now a resident of Marshall County, Tennessee and he
be released from paying taxes in this County.

1858 June Term

Page 161 - James Carlisle and others. James Carlisle admr. sold land.

Page 161 - Jane R. Murphy appeared in Court and signified her dissatisfaction
with the provision made for her by the Will of her late husband,
Archibald Murphy.

Page 161 - W. J. Hill resigned as guardian of minor children of John D. Hill.
Philip Hodges was appointed guardian.

Page 161 - Court ordered Jno. T. Medearis to pay over to Samuel Card, guardian
of the minor children of Joseph N. Card, deceased.

Page 162 - W. B. Wilson, late of Bedford County, departed this life intestate.
J. D. Wilson admr. J. F. Davidson security.

Page 163 - R. B. Davidson resigned as guardian of Robert P. and John W. Frierson,
minor children of E. J. Frierson, deceased. Thomas Lipscomb appointed guardian.

Page 163 - Jackson Nichols resigned as Trustee of W. H. Kellon. W. C. Blanton
was appointed Trustee.

Page 163 - Wiley F. Daniel guardian of Scott, Elizabeth, James, John N., and Woody
Edmondson.

Page 163 - S. G. Miller guardian of Robert Uselton, for the first coming to him
from the estate of James Taylor.

Page 164 - B. F. Cobb guardian of Miss Malissa Jane Thomas. A. M. Webb and
Reuben Curry securities.

Page 164 - John A. Ganaway admr. of Margaret Garrett, deceased. R. W. McClure
security.

Page 165 - Robert B. Blackwell constable of the 19th Civil District.

Page 166 - Michael Capley be released from paying taxes on 35 acres.

Page 166 - Jane A. Murphy vs Robert B. Murphy and others. Archibald Murphy died
intestate in January 1858 and he was the owner of about 525 acres of
land on waters of the Garrison Fork of Duck River in Bedford County,
in Civil District # 2, which was the home at the time of his death.

139

1858 June Term

Page 167 - Thomas J. Robinson and others. Exparte - Report of J. H. Thompson
that he had collected money from sale of a slave, pay to John W. Green
as admr. of his wife who was a distributee.

Page 168 - Robert B. Davidson resigned as guardian of William and Albert Frierso
minor children of E. J. Frierson, deceased. W. S. Jett appointed
guardian.

Page 168 - Dr. Thomas Lipscomb guardian of John W. and Robert P. Frierson, resign
ed. Ann P. Frierson appointed guardian.

Page 168 - Edmund Cooper resigned as executor of E. J. Frierson, deceased. Robert
B. Davidson admr.

Page 169 - Commissioners to lay off support to widow and family of J. P. Gillman
deceased.

1858 July Term

Page 170 - Gen. Robert Cannon be paid $60.50 for damages by reason of a road
being changed which runs upon his plantation.

Page 171 - Court ordered $250.00 be approporated to build a bridge across Duck
River at Fairfield.

Page 173 - Moses Marshall coronor of Bedford County.

Page 175 - State of Tennessee vs F. M. Anderson and State of Tennessee vs Thomas
Crutchfield. To divide District 10 and 11 in Bedford County to make
a new District.

Page 177 - Thomas J. Robinson and others. Petition to sell slaves. Slave sold
by Mrs. Elisha Reed and Mrs. Robert J. Greer. They appeared in Court
and was examined apart from their husbands and gave consent for their
husbands to receive money they received from sale of slave woman.

Page 178 - Hannah Harrison and others. Petition to sell land. Mrs. Elijah Reed
in Court and consented for her husband to receive money arising from
sale of land.

Page 178 - Power of Attorney by J. R. Hendon, William McDowell, M. E. McDowell,
Sarah Jane Hendon and Mary H. Hendon to R. G. Stewart of Kentucky.

Page 180 - J. P. McCuistion guardian of Rufus, Thomas and Margaret F. Robinson,
in place of C. McCuistion, deceased. G. Phillips and A. Sanders
securities.

Page 180 - Lucy Mosly, late a citizen of Bedford County, departed this life
intestate. Benjamin Mosly admr. A. Mosly security.

Page 180 - Mrs. Susan Burt resigned as guardian of Sara, Lucy and Richard Burt.
John L. Burt appointed guardian. Mrs. Susan Burt security.

1858 July Term

Page 181 - John W. Naylor and others vs G. B. Hale and others. Preston Frazier
purchaser of one of the tracts of land from John W. Naylor, Sarah
Nailor, Martha Stover, Alfred Naylor, Woodfin Nailor, George W. Nash
and wife Amanda, G. B. Hale and wife Harriett, James A. Nailor, C. P.
Nailor, Calvin Nailor and Joshua Nailor, land in Bedford County on
the east side of the Turnpike Road leading from Shelbyville to Murfreesboro. (Woodfin Graveyard is located on this land).

Page 182 - Hiram Harris and others. Petition to sell land. Report to next Court.

Page 182 - Susan Garrett, late a citizen of Bedford County, departed this life
intestate. Hardy Prince admr. A. E. Mullins and William Johnson
securities.

Page 182 - Samuel Hopper, late a citizen of Bedford County, departed this life
intestate. B. W. Nowlin admr. T. H. Bell security.

Page 183 - Benjamin Fugitt guardian of Harriet Clark, a minor who now resides in
Cannon County, Tennessee.

Page 183 - Jane R. Murphy. Petition for dower. Commissioners to lay off dower
out of the land of the late Archibald Murphy, deceased. Land in
District # 2, containing 525 acres. (Graveyard located on this dower
also plat on page 184).

Page 185 - Joseph W. Trigg and others. Petition to sell slaves. Slave to be
sold to pay debt. Power of Attorney executed by William Hitch and his
wife Esther, that they had appointed D. C. Trigg as their Attorney.
Esther is daughter of her deceased father Hayden Trigg. Part of the
share of W. H. Trigg goes to his children. Also, to Susan Trigg and
reserve the share of Eliza Jane Hale.

Page 187 - Jos. H. Thompson Commissioner vs James B. Dixon and James Dixon.
Motion for judgement.

Page 187 - Jos. H. Thompson, C & Commissioner vs Robert Cannon, James M. Elliott,
and T. W. Jordan. Sale of land belonging to the heirs of Wilson
Coats, deceased, (Celia widow of Wilson Coats, her name was marked out
and Wilson written in). Robert Cannon purchased a portion of the said
land. James M. Elliott and T. W. Jordan securities.

Page 188 - Jos. H. Thompson Commissioner vs Robert N. Jones, Thomas Holland and
Moses Marshall. Motion for judgement. Sale of land belonging to the
heirs of Wilson Coats, deceased.

Page 189 - Jos. H. Thompson Commissioner vs Thomas G. Holland, Robert N. Jones
and Thomas Holland. Sale of land belonging to the heirs of Wilson
Coats, deceased.

Page 190 - Jos. H. Thompson Commissioner vs James F. Cummings, Jacob F. Thompson
and S. D. Coble. Sale of land belonging to the heirs of Wilson Coats,
deceased.

1858 July Term

Page 191 - Jos. H. Thompson Commissioner vs Blackman Koonce, Robert Maupin and Gabriel Maupin. Sale of land belonging to the heirs of John Koonce, Jr.

Page 192 - Jos. H. Thompson Commissioner vs H. C. Blessing, D. G. Blessing and Robert Cannon. Judgement. Continued to next Court.

Page 195 - This day ordered by the Court that the District Line between District # 9 and # 10 be so changed that where said line shall reach the land of W. C. Cook &c.

Page 196 - Jos. H. Thompson vs L. P. Fields admr. Judgement. L. P. Fields admr. of Robert L. Singleton.

Page 196 - Jos. H. Thompson vs John J. Koonce admr. Judgement. John J. Koonce admr. of Elizabeth Koonce.

Page 196 - Jos. H. Thompson vs Daniel Parker. Judgement. Daniel Parker executor of John _. Hawkins, deceased. Also Elendor Hawkins.

Page 197 - Jos. H. Thompson vs J. F. Jenkins. Judgement. J. F. Jenkins guardian of _____ Brown.

Page 197 - Jos. H. Thompson vs B. W. Nowlin guardian. Judgement. Nowlin guardian of the Musgrove children.

Page 197 - Jos. H. Thompson vs George W. Brown admr. Brown admr. of Mahala E. Brown.

Page 198 - Jos. H. Thompson vs Thomas D. Garrett. Garrett guardian of Lipscomb Garrett.

Page 198 - Jos. H. Thompson vs Erwin Butler. Butler guardian of John R. Butler and A. Butler.

Page 198 - Jos. H. Thompson vs G. G. Osborne executor and Hosea Green executor. Osborne and Green, Executors of Willis Green.

Page 198 - Jos. H. Thompson vs James F. Calhoun admr. Calhoun admr. of Thomas Henderson.

Page 199 - Jos. H. Thompson vs N. J. Calhoun. Calhoun guardian of Mary Henderson.

Page 199 - Jos. H. Thompson vs Joseph Anderson. Anderson admr. of Mary Thompson.

Page 199 - Jos. H. Thompson vs Robert Dennis. Dennis guardian of minor children of _____ Blessing.

Page 200 - Jos. H. Thompson vs C. A. Warren admr. Judgement. Warren admr. of Martha Dobbins.

1858 July Term

Page 200 - Jos. H. Thompson vs William Hoover. Judgement. William Hoover guardian of Joseph Loyd.

Page 201 - Jos. H. Thompson vs W. S. Arnold. W. S. Arnold executor of C. G. Arnold.

Page 201 - Jos. H. Thompson vs W. S. Arnold. W. S. Arnold, Constable.

Page 201 - Jos. H. Thompson vs James G. Nealy. James G. Nealy guardian of Joseph Dwyer.

Page 202 - Jos. H. Thompson vs H. T. Montgomery. H. T. Montgomery admr. of W. E. Montgomery.

Page 202 - Jos. H. Thompson vs N. Thompson, 3rd and James Dixon. N. Thompson, 3rd. admr. of Nancy Dixon.

Page 203 - Jos. H. Thompson vs B. A. Nelson. B. A. Nelson guardian of W. J. Blessing.

Page 203 - Jos. H. Thompson vs J. M. Hicks. J. M. Hicks guardian of Martha Kizer, William Kizer and John Kizer.

Page 203 - Jos. H. Thompson vs Wrencher Spence. Wrencher Spence guardian of John W. Spence and others.

Page 204 - Jos. H. Thompson vs A. Reaves. A. Reaves guardian of Ann Wheeler.

Page 204 - Jos. H. Thompson vs Jackson Nichols admr. Jackson Nichols admr of R. F. Norman.

Page 204 - Jos. H. Thompson vs B. F. Duggan executor. Duggan executor of Thomas Cheatham, deceased.

Page 205 - Jos. H. Thompson vs W. T. Hughes admr. W. T. Hughes admr. of Robert S. Worke, deceased.

Page 205 - Jos. H. Thompson vs James B. Morris admr. and D. J. Burt admr. of Henry Hurt, deceased.

Page 205 - Jos. H. Thompson vs John L. Cooper. John L. Cooper guardian of the minor heirs of Pucket and his transcript made out by him for Rutherford County &c.

Page 206 - Jos. H. Thompson vs James A. Pucket. Pucket guardian of Pucket children.

Page 206 - Jos. H. Thompson vs John C. Hicks admr. of Margaret Stewart, deceased.

Page 207 - Jos. H. Thompson vs A(rcena) Pruit executor &c. of Willis Pruit, deceased.

1858 July Term

Page 207 - Jos. H. Thompson vs P. H. Reaves, guardian of the Phillips'
children.

Page 207 - Jos. H. Thompson vs A. Erwin. A. Erwin executor of Archibald Murphy,
deceased.

Page 208 - Jos. H. Thompson vs Nancy Stephens executrix of H. M. Stephens,
deceased.

Page 208 - Jos. H. Thompson vs John Bell admr. of Thomas Pearson, deceased.

Page 208 - Jos. H. Thompson vs F. B. Lipford executor of Julia Lipford.

Page 209 - Jos. H. Thompson vs John A. Ganaway admr. of Margaret Garrett, deceased.

Page 209 - Jos. H. Thompson vs J. D. Wilson admr. of W. B. Wilson, deceased.

Page 209 - William Galbreath resigned as guardian of Elizabeth Virginia Beaty.

1858 August Term

Page 210 - Cambell Tribble, late a citizen of Bedford County, departed this life
intestate. Isaac Shook admr. A. Reagor and Daniel Nealy securities.

Page 210 - Thomas H. Allison guardian of James, Malissa and Easter Adams. Alexander Dysart and L. D. Stockton securities.

Page 211 - Joanna Nash, late a citizen of Bedford County, departed this life
intestate. W. T. Tune admr. John T. Tune security.

Page 211 - W. E. Davis resigned as guardian of his minor child, Susan J. Davis.
Thomas W. Davis appointed guardian.

Page 211 - Jos. H. Thompson vs R. N. Jones guardian. Judgement. R. N. Jones is
guardian of his children.

Page 212 - J. W. Stem guardian of Susan C., Warren V., Thomas H., Martin, Arthur
E., Nathaniel, and Mary J. Wilson. D. A. Ozment and B. F. Kimmons
securities.

Page 212 - Jonas Sykes, late a citizen of Bedford County, departed this life
intestate. Thomas A. and R. M. Sykes admrs. P. H. Thompson and
David C. Jones securities.

Page 212 - John Noblett guardian of Nancy and John Noblett. D. N. Wise security.

1858 August Term

Page 213 - E. J. Hamilton guardian of A. J. Hamilton. M. B. Hamilton and W. H.
Wisener securities.

144

1858 August Term

Page 213 - Deed from Wiley Riggins and wife Margaret Riggins to Thomas M.
Gordon. Margaret Riggins was examined apart from her husband and
gave consent for him to receive her monies.

Page 213 - Stephen Hurt guardian of Elizabeth V. Beaty. F. B. Price and John Hurt
securities.

Page 214 - Abigal Culp, late of Bedford County, departed this life intestate.
John Lentz admr. Hiram Harris security.

Page 214 - F. M. Guthrie, late of Bedford County, departed this life intestate.
J. F. Farrar admr. J. B. Reagor security.

Page 214 - Henry Dean, Isaac Williams and John W. White to lay off support for
the widow of J. K. Spence.

Page 215 - J. P. Davis guardian of C. C. Hicks and Sarah E. Hicks. H. Dean and
J. B. Reagor securities.

Page 215 - John S. Davis guardian of John, Mildred, and Cassander Streater.
W. S. Jett and W. B. M. Brame securities.

Page 215 - William Carlisle guardian resigned. He was guardian of Joseph and
Jno. W. Phillips. James Phillips was appointed guardian. Benjamin
Phillips security.

Page 217 - Robert S. Dwiggins guardian of "W. W. Lacy". Edmund Cooper and J. C.
Hicks securities. and also Jarrell Smith security.

Page 217 - Joel Stallings guardian of Mary and Richard Musgrove. John H. Oneal
and James C. Gammill (Gambill) securities.

Page 218 - Joel Stallings guardian of Nancy E., Margaret E., J. N., Phaney, and
W. J. Stallings, his minor children. John H. Oneal and James C. Gambill securities.

Page 218 - Jos. H. Thompson guardian of Franklin Robinson. John W. White security.

Page 218 - Robert S. Dwiggins vs Benjamin Mosly. Benjamin Mosly guardian of
Miss I.(Isodore) Holt. Robert S. Dwiggins security.

Page 219 - John H. Oneal vs Hiram Holt and W. H. Wisener. Case continued.

Page 219 - Joseph H. Thompson Commissioner vs James Dixon and J. B. Dixon.
Judgement. Sale of land of estate of William Thompson, deceased.
James Dixon and J. B. Dixon securities. James Dixon purchaser.

Page 220 - Aaron Gambill, Jr. and others. Petition to sell land. Aaron Gambill,
Jr. has paid for land he purchased of Robert Logan, deceased.

Page 221 - Daniel Parker and others. Petition to sell slaves. Jacob Harrison
purchaser.

1858 August Term

Page 222 - Commissioners to lay off support to widow of J. P. Gillman.

Page 222 - Commissioners to lay off support to widow and family of C. McCuistion.

Page 222 - The executor of Joseph Thompson, deceased. Report.

Page 223 - N. Thompson, 3rd. resigned as admr. of Nancy Dixon, deceased. John E Davis was appointed admr. J. B. Dixon security.

Page 223 - Joseph H. Thompson Commissioner vs James Dixon and James B. Dixon. Judgement.

Page 224 - John W. White resigned as guardian of minor children of F. B. Norvill deceased, David, James, Louisa, Mary, John D., William, and Samuel Norvill. Joseph H. Thompson appointed guardian.

Page 224 - Samuel Pratt vs Robert N. Jones guardian &c. Defendant to appear in next Court.

Page 224 - G. _. Calhoun and others. Petition to sell land. Alfred Campbell purchaser. Land that belonged to Samuel N. Card and others.

Page 225 - A 12 man jury to examine the idiocy or lunacy of Walter Dixon and Mariah Dixon and report.

Page 225 - Jos. H. Thompson Commissioner vs D. G. Blessing, J. P. Blessing and James Coats. Case continued.

Page 225 - Jos. H. Thompson Commissioner vs H. C. Blessing and D. G. Blessing. Case continued.

Page 226 - William Campbell guardian of Nancy Connell.

Page 226 - Margaret J. Arnold, late a citizen of Bedford County, had departed this life intestate. G. W. Cunningham admr. J. M. Johnson security.

Page 227 - Settlement with John W. Rutledge as Trustee of John M. Warner.

Page 227 - John H. Oneal Commissioner vs Hiram Edde and W. H. Wisener. Judgement In case of James Edde, James Hastings and wife Ellen, Silas Pratt and wife Patience, and Hiram J. Edde vs Jane Edde, Elizabeth Edde and Cand is Edde, Francis Edde, and Mary Edde. Court ordered the land belonging to the Defendants be sold. Hiram Edde purchaser.

Page 228 - A payment allowed ($200.00) to Sutton and wife Jane is due at June Term 1855.

Page 228 - Robert Cannon and Jno. P. Steele to lay off for the children of Margaret J. Arnold, deceased.

146

1858 August Term

Page 228 - John T. Neil guardian of William, James, Sam, Daniel, Elizabeth, and John Arnold.

Page 229 - A. Freeman and others. Petition to sell negroes. Elenor Freeman had failed to prosecute as approve guardian of negro girl, Dicy.

1858 September Term

Page 230 - John Larue, Thomas H. Bell and H. M. Oneal to lay off support for the widow of Samuel Hopper, deceased.

Page 230 - A jury of 12 to examine the lunacy of Nicholas Anthony.

Page 230 - Epps Parker resigned as guardian of the minor children of Charles Parker, deceased.

Page 230 - Jno. T. Neil resigned as guardian of (blank) Cortner.

Page 231 - Thomas W. Coffey guardian of James B. and Jno. L. (twins) and Elizabeth Bradley, children of Joel Bradley. (6 male). C. S. Coffey and James W. Coffey securities.

Page 231 - Catherine E. J. Mount, late of Bedford County, departed this life intestate. Hannah H. Mount her admrix. W. C. Harpley and James R. Endsley securities.

Page 231 - David J. Wheeler guardian of Jno. L. Jacobs. Horatio Coop security.

Page 232 - W. T. Myers guardian of Thomas R. and A. E. Myers. L. S. Myers and John Q. Davidson securities.

Page 232 - A. L. S. Hufman guardian of Sarah A. Hufman. John Q. Davidson security.

Page 232 - Rebecca Springer, late a citizen of Bedford County, departed this life intestate. David R. Hooker admr. J. G. Neely security.

Page 232 - Samuel McMahan, late a citizen of Bedford County, had departed this life intestate. Alexander Lee admr. G. G. Osborne and Abram McMahan securities.

Page 233 - Samuel T. Carr, late a citizen of Bedford County, had departed this life intestate. Samuel H. Carr admr. John T. Neil security.

Page 233 - John England, late a citizen of Bedford County, had departed this life intestate. Rezin England admr.

Page 233 - Winn R. Williams, late a citizen of Bedford County, departed this life intestate. Joseph Morton admr. W. D. William security.

Page 234 - Commissioners to lay off support for Martha M. Smalling, widow of James M. Smalling, deceased.

1858 September Term

Page 234 - Jackson Nichols, Esq. resigned as Justice of the Peace of 11th District

Page 235 - L'Nathan Davis, Estate. F. M. Prewett and Rebecca Davis executors. Estate settled.

Page 236 - W. W. Gill, James Carlisle and Jesse Evans to lay off support for widow and family of Wynn R. Williams, deceased.

Page 236 - James Ogilvie, Elisha Harmon qualified as School Commissioners for Crowell Township of Bedford County.

Page 238 - Jackson Nichols resigned as guardian of Thomas J. and Amanda C. Deason. Dr. D. G. Deason appointed guardian.

Page 239 - G. G. Osborne, Thomas S. Davis and R. S. Thomas to lay off support for widow and family of Samuel McMahan, deceased.

Page 240 - Jane R. Murphy guardian of Robert, Mary A., Ellen C., Charles B., and Patrick Murphy, minor children of A. Murphy, deceased.

Page 242 - Daniel Parker and others. Petition to sell land.

Page 242 - Jos. H. Thompson vs H. C. Blessing and others. Judgement.

Page 243 - Mary E. Pratt and others vs Robert N. Jones guardian &c. Motion to remove guardian.

1858 October Term

Page 244 - E. D. Winsett elected Justice of the Peace of the 11th District.

Page 248 - This day ordered by the Court that the District Line between 23rd and 25th Civil District of Bedford County be so changed as to throw the present residence of James Rippy, Sr. into the 25th Civil District of Bedford County. 25 magistrates voting for change.

Page 251 - James Stallings guardian of a minor child of Nancy Pearson.

Page 252 - J. W. C. Keller admr of Ann Keller, deceased.

Page 252 - Walter S. Stephens admr. of Redding Stephens, deceased. John T. Stephens security.

Page 253 - Jno. Q. Davidson admr. of Joseph Keller, deceased. J.W. C. Keller and Jno. M. Keller securities.

Page 253 - A jury appointed to examine the lunacy of Nicholas Anthony. Reported that he was a lunatic and unable to take care of his business. Court appointed S(L). J. Anthony guardian.

1858 October Term

Page 255 - Thomas Gaddiss admr. of William Williams, deceased. James T. Arnold and Peter E. Clardy securities.

Page 255 - Jos. H. Thompson vs D. G. Blessing. Judgement

Page 255 - Mary Pratt and others vs R. N. Jones. Case dismissed.

Page 256 - Mily Dixon guardian of minor children of Robert Dixon, deceased, re-signed and Court appointed John C. Hix as guardian.

Page 256 - Jesse Ledbetter, Joseph Anderson and John W. Mayfield appointed as Bridge Commissioners for the location of the bridge across Duck River between Crowell's Mill and the County Line.

Page 256 - Jackson Nichols admr. of R. F. Norman, deceased, resigned and Solomon G. Reaves appointed admr.

Page 257 - Robert Pate resigned as guardian of Amanda Lytle. A. M. Cooper was appointed guardian. A. Reaves and W. C. Blanton securities.

Page 257 - Elias Holt guardian of Harriett V. Holt. J. L. Ayers and Joseph M. Holt securities.

Page 257 - Mrs. Thomas J. Robinson appeared in Court apart from her husband and was examined. She gave consent for her husband to receive any monies coming to her from the estate of Hannah Harrison, that is now in the hands of Jos. H. Thompson.

Page 259 - Mrs. E. T. Barnes appeared in Court apart from her husband and gave her consent for her husband to receive her portion of the fund now in the hands of John H. Oneal.

Page 259 - Ethan Loyell and others. Petition to divide land. Jno. K. Loyell, a citizen (late) of Bedford County, departed this life intestate leav-ing a widow and five children. He owned 200 acres of land. Widow Mary Loyell has received her dower. Ethan, Henry, Elizabeth, William, and Burnice Loyell, heirs of Jno. K. Loyell, deceased. C. S. Dudley appoint-ed Commissioner and Robert Allison, Jno. Rucker, Thomas Tarpley and William Brown to divide and set apart the dower tract and assign the heirs their share of land.

Page 261 - Jury to determine the idiocy or lunacy of Walter Dixon and Maria Dixon. They were found to be incompetent to handle their own affairs. J. N. Dunaway guardian of said "idiots". James Dixon security.

Page 261 - James Coates and others. Exparte - Andrew Reed asked to have his wife's portion of the fund arising from the sale of the land. Court stated the fund had not been paid to Andrew Reed but was paid to the children of said Reed.

1858 November Term

Page 263 - J. G. Neely and G. W. Parsons qualified as School Commissioners for
for the Sulphur Spring Township and R. S. Thomas qualified as same
for the Coldwell Township.

Page 263 - Mary Pratt and others vs Robert N. Jones. Thomas H. Coldwell security

Page 264 - Jason T. Brittain, late a citizen of Bedford County, departed this li
intestate in Bedford County. G. W. Thompson admr. N. Thompson, Jr.
security.

Page 265 - Andrew Erwin and others. Petition to sell negro. Sale at residence
of A. Murphy on 9 Oct 1858. Sold negro man to Mrs. Jane Murphy.

Page 266 - Jno. T. Neil guardian of minor children of Wilson C. Arnold.

Page 266 - John C. Hix and others. Petition to sell slaves. Jno. C. Hix admr.
of Fanny Norman, deceased, to sell negroes.

Page 266 - John Caruthers renewed his guardianship of William Caruthers.

Page 267 - Martin Sims, Thomas Montgomery and Samuel H. Card to lay off support
for widow and family of Redding Stephens, deceased.

Page 267 - Wiley J. Ussery guardian of Samuel and John Arnold, minor children of
W(ilson). C. Arnold, deceased.

Page 267 - James H. Harrison guardian of James Arnold, minor child of Wilson C.
Arnold, deceased.

Page 267 - Pierce Wilhoite guardian of his child, Wilborn Wilhoite.

Page 268 - J. M. Frizzell resigned as guardian of W. G. Majors. John W. Frizzel
was appointed guardian.

Page 268 - Joseph H. Thompson resigned as admr. of Elizabeth Meyers, deceased.

Page 268 - Martha Robinson, late a citizen of Bedford County, departed this life
intestate. John W. Greer admr.

Page 269 - Francis Robinson, late a citizen of Bedford County, departed this lif
intestate. John W. Greer admr.

Page 269 - Fanie Lyon guardian of W. B. Lyon and Sarah M. Lyon, her minor children. Benjamin Brown and Lemuel Broadaway her securities.

Page 269 - Fanie Lyon guardian of her children, W. B. and Sarah M. Lyon, to a
friend in State of Alabama.

Page 270 - A jury of John Wilson, George Hemphill, William Floyd, William Brown,
James P. Taylor, George Taylor, William Knott, A. F. Knott, Alfred
Little, Jno. W. Simpson, and A. Ransom to examine Burrell Word. Repor

1858 November Term

Page 270 - W. W. Gant and others. Petition to sell land. Cherokee County,
Texas, Americus Gifford guardian of S. E. Gifford, Edward S. Gifford,
John William and Amanda C. Gifford, his minor children.

Page 271 Joseph H. Thompson vs D. G. Blessing and others. To report to next Court.

Page 271 - Joseph H. Thompson vs H. C. Blessing and others. Report to next Court.

Page 271 - Mary Pratt and others vs R. N. Jones. Held over to next Court.

Page 271 - William Brown, William Little and W. B. M. Brame to lay off support
to widow and family of Jason T. Brittain, deceased.

Page 273 - Mary E. Pratt and others by next friend vs Robert N. Jones. R. N.
Jones guardian.

Page 274 - Middleton Holland guardian of Mary Jane, Martha Ann, Moses A.,
Mitchell B., and William M. Holland, minor children of Franklin
Holland, deceased.

Page 275 - James B. Coats and others. Petition to sell land. W. J. Blessing
one of the heirs to receive any monies arising from sale of land.
Land sold to Dr. J. H. McGrew.

1858 December Term

Page 276 - G. W. Cunningham guardian of William Cotner. W. K. Ransom and A. L.
Landis securities.

Page 277 - John Reid guardian of Cynthia Reid, with Andrew Reid and Robert Reid
securities.

Page 277 - G. W. Cunningham guardian of Elizabeth Arnold and (blank) Arnold,
minor children of W. C. Arnold, deceased.

Page 279 - Robert S. Clark guardian of Fanny P. Finch, Elizabeth A. Finch, and
Magdeline A. Finch. L. P. Fields, E. F. Scruggs, Asa Thomas and
J. L. Woods securities.

Page 279 - W. S. Eakin guardian of James H. Eakin. Edwin H. Ewing, John W.
Cowan and Alexander Eakin securities. Also guardian of George N.
Eakin.

Page 280 - A. J. Drumright guardian of William B. Drumright. B. G. Drumright and
Presley Jones securities.

Page 280 - Manuel Ray guardian of Melvina, Catherine, Martha, Marion, and Mary
Jane Ray. John Hastings security.

Page 280 - W. P. H. McGowan guardian of Henry H. Manley, to receive any monies
from sale of land belonging to Manley estate.

1858 December Term

Page 280 - A jury of men appointed to ascertain the idiocy of Sarah Shipp and to report to next Court.

Page 281 - William T. Thompson, late a citizen of Bedford County, departed this life intestate. John W. Simpson and A. T. Thomason admrs. He left a widow and family.

Page 282 - John B. McGhee, late of Bedford County, departed this life intestate. John T. Edgen admr.

Page 286 - Jos. H. Thompson vs H. C. Blessing and others. Continued.

Page 286 - Jos. H. Thompson vs D. G. Blessing and others. Continued.

Page 286 - Willis Bearden and others. Petition to sell land. Willis Bearden purchased land. Payment is now due and that he owns a tract of land in his own right and has purchased another from James K. Claunch. Court orders Bearden to pay his two ninths of money, 1/9th goes to Wynn Bearden, 1/9th to James A. Bearden. Elizabeth Philpot wife of Burton Philpot is entitled to 1/9th of amount of money.

Page 287 - James Mullins and others. Exparte - Joseph H. Thompson pay over to A. E. Mullins his share of note upon James Mullins, when collected.

Page 287 - George Pratt resigned as Trustee of Ann Frances Black. William Campbell was appointed in his place. Pierce Wilhpite security.

Page 288 - Hugh Manley and others. Exparte to sell land. Rebecca Frizzell and Elizabeth McCowan (femme coverts) appeared in Court apart from their husbands and gave consent for them to receive any monies arising from the sale of land. Court ordered that David W. Frizzell and J. F. McCowan to receive the shares.

Page 288 - G. G. Osborne guardian of Bettie McMahan. Alexander Lee and A. McMahan securities.

Page 289 - Elizabeth Shipp, late a citizen of Bedford County, departed this life intestate. W. J. Raney her admr. John T. Martin security.

Page 289 - Daniel Parker and others. Exparte to sell land. Daniel Parker purchased

Page 290 - William Little guardian, gave the receipts of Martha A. Gant, R. C. Hail, Mary Gant, James H. Elmore, William Elmore and Joseph Bennett for money own them from Little as admr. of Hugh M. Gant.

Page 290 - Joseph H. Thompson vs William R. Smith, I. L. Davidson and J. G. Smith Note due on land purchased belonging to the estate of John Phillips, deceased.

Page 292 - Jos. H. Thompson, Clerk, settled with Robert S. Clark admr. of William K. Finch, deceased.

1858 December Term

Page 292 - Jos. H. Thompson settled with executors of Alexander B. Moon, deceased.

Page 292 - Jos. H. Thompson settled with W. J. Whitthorne admr of Minos Cannon, deceased.

Page 294 - Elizabeth P. Kingree guardian of her minor children.

Page 294 - Nancy L. Phillips executrix of J. _. Phillips, deceased.

Page 294 - John W. Burton and wife Mary A. vs William and Albert Frierson and others. Defendants, William, Albert, Robert and John Frierson, minors through their guardian W. S. Jett and Ann P. Frierson. Ervin J. Frierson had died seized of land. The land known as "White Cottage Farms" also slaves. Mary A. Burton is a daughter of said Ervin J. Frierson and entitled to 1/5 share of said land. The above named are the only children of E. J. Frierson, deceased.

Page 296 - Mary Loyell, Henry Loyell and others. Exparte to divide land &c. Nancy Lawrence has conveyed by Deed to the petitioners, Henry, Ethan, Elizabeth, William, and Burnice Lowyell, all her interest in the tract of land. Land purchased of William Allison's executors.

Page 297 - Joseph H. Thompson settled the estate of John B. Wynn with John Cheatham admr.

Page 297 - Richard Anderson and others vs Joseph Anderson. O. Bill.

1859 January Term

Page 301 - Rebecca Lowell(?), a pauper, be allowed $25.00.

Page 301 - William Given be given $60.00 for taking care of an infant child.

Page 303 - M. W. Wilson and others vs John Bennett. Motion to be released as security.

Page 304 - Martin Sims, Samuel Card and D. G. Stephenson to lay off support for widow and family of W. H. Aaron, deceased.

Page 304 - Presley Prince guardian of Sophia, Martha and William Crisco, minor children of Jordan Crisco, deceased.

Page 304 - Samuel T. Gilliland guardian of Kitty E. J. and Samuel Gilliland, his minor children.

Page 305 - Burrell Waid, late of Bedford County, departed this life intestate. Burrell Word admr.

Page 305 - Thomas A. Sykes guardian of James B., Jonas S., Robert A., Martha T., and Ann E. Jones.

1859 January Term

Page 305 - John R. Thompson to obtain a Law License.

Page 306 - Robert N. Jones resigned as guardian of minor children of Samuel Pratt, deceased.

Page 306 - J. Y. Norman guardian of W. G. Norman. Jno. C. Hicks and George A. Reagor securities.

Page 307 - Margaret Bradshaw guardian of her minor children. Thomas Dryden and Thomas A. White securities.

Page 307 - M. W. Watson and others vs John Bennett. Mathew W. Watson, William Perry, John Wilson, Rufus Smith and Jarrell Smith securities for John Bennett a constable of 22nd District of Bedford County.

Page 308 - Spencer Brown, late of Bedford County, departed this life intestate. John W. Brown admr. Henry Brown and John Wallace securities.

Page 308 - Jos. H. Thompson vs D. G. Blessing and others. Case continued.

Page 308 - Jos. H. Thompson vs H. C. Blessing and others. Case continued.

Page 308 - H. A. Williams and wife and Mary V. Whitman vs Sarah and Susan P. Whitman. Case continued.

Page 308 - Rachel Craycroft and others. Petition to sell slaves. Isaac S. Davidson, Power of Attorney, executed by Rachel Craycroft, Jacob Stillwell, Jacob Rich, Margaret H. Rich, Gustavus B. Stillwell, A. J. Banks W. H. Stillwell, Thomas D. Stillwell and S. C. Stillwell to Isaac S. Davidson to attend to and manage their interests in sell of slaves. Jackson Wallis purchased slaves.

Page 309 - Burrell Word vs Pleasant Word and others. Pleasant Word, ---ions Word, William Word, Neoma Word, Mary E., James and Samuel and John Stockard. James, Pleasant, Thomas B., and Ava Thompson, Joseph Burleson and wife Patience and Pleasant Word are non-residents of Tennessee.

Page 310 - Joseph H. Thompson vs Burrell Word et al. Burrell Word, a lunatic, lately had departed this life intestate and that Burrell Word, Jr. has been appointed admr. of estate.

Page 310 - Edmond S. Wortham and wife and others vs Jno. S. Clark and wife and others. John S. Clark and wife Elizabeth and Daniel Anderson and wife Susanah has failed to answer said cause.

Page 311 - George Terry, late a citizen of Bedford County, departed this life intestate. J. C. Bell admr. of estate.

Page 311 - William Murphy and Emeline Jacobs vs John L. Jacobs and David J. Wheeler. Petition to sell slaves. Slaves to be sold.

1859 January Term

Page 312 - Settlement with Thomas Shearin admr. of John K. Loyell.

1859 February Term

Page 313 - H. A. Williams and others vs Sarah and Susan P. Whitman. John K.
Baskette guardian of Sarah and Susan P. Whitman, minors.

Page 313 - Willis Bearden and others. Petition to sell land. To report.

Page 316 - B. C. Thompson had departed this life intestate. F. P. McElwrath admr.
John R. Thompson and Elizabeth Thompson securities.

Page 316 - H. A. Williams and wife et al vs Susan V. and Sarah P. Whitman. To
sell slaves and divide funds from estate of Edmond Whitman, deceased.

Page 317 - George Cotner guardian of minor children of Isaac M. West. Riley
Riggins and Blackman Koonce securities.

Page 317 - Elizabeth Thompson guardian of Lawrence T. Bates.

Page 318 - B. B. Bomar guardian of Thomas J., James W., Sarah E., and S. Jane
Harrison. R. J. King and James H. Bomar securities.

Page 318 - Martin Friddle guardian of James A. Friddle.

Page 318 - William Hime admr. of D. K. J. Hime, deceased. N. Burrow and John A.
Hime securities.

Page 320 - R. F. P. Jones admr. of Judith I. Jones. S. W. Jones and John A. Jones,
securities.

Page 320 - R. F. P. Jones admr. of F(Francis). E. Collins.

Page 320 - R. F. P. Jones admr. of Samuel R. Jones.

Page 320 - R. F. P. Jones admr. of R. M. Jones, deceased.

Page 320 - R. F. P. Jones admr. of Alsey Jones, deceased.

Page 322 - Commissioners to lay off support for widow of W. H. Aaron, deceased.

Page 323 - Hillsman Bledsoe guardian of Preston L. and Hillsman Bledsoe.

Page 323 - Commissioners to lay off support for widow and family of David
Whiteside.

Page 323 - James B. Coates and others vs Jno. M. Stewart and others. Rent for
said land is due.

Page 324 - Jesse Coleman guardian of William, James, and John Coleman, his minor
children.

1859 February Term

Page 324 - Augustine Wilson guardian of Sarah E. and Mary T. Ogilvie.

Page 324 - William H. Wisener admr. of Sarah J. Burditt.

Page 324 - Simion W. Jones and others. Petition to divide slaves. Simion W.,
Samuel R. Jones, Francis E. Collins, Robert M., Judith E., Jno. A.
and Dicy M. Jones to divide slaves.

Page 325 - John W. Burton and wife vs W. S. Jett and others. Report to next Court

Page 325 - Edmond S. Wortham and wife vs John S. Clark and wife and others. John
Moon departed this life intestate in Bedford County about the __ day
of ___ 1846 and at his death he was owner of a tract of land, 160 acre
and that Elizabeth Wortham and the defendants, Pleasant B. Moon and
Susanah Anderson, his only children and heirs and he left his widow
Elizabeth who has since intermarried with the Defendant John S. Clark.

Page 326 - Ethan Loyell, Henry Loyell and others. Petition to divide land.
Commissioners not to divide lands of Jno. K. Loyell, known as the
"Allison Tract". They assigned to Elizabeth Loyell a tract of land.
Plat of land on page 329. (Name spelled Lowell on plat)

Page 331 - William Murphree and others vs John L. Jacobs. Case continued.

Page 331 - Settlement with Executors of John Shofner, deceased.

Page 332 - Settlement with admrs. of James Hart's estate.

Page 332 - Settlement with executors Edmund Cooper, estate of Charles S. Byrn.

Page 332 - Moses Marshall, Coronor, reported of inquest over bodies of Keeble
Terry and James Coop.

Page 334 - Benjamin Mosely guardian of Izora (Isadorah), daughter of Margaret
(Wilhoite) Holt and Jordan Holt. Izora is now married to A. J. Long.

1859 March Term

Page 335 - John V. Biddle guardian of Samuel E., Thomas Vance and Joseph D.
Biddle, minors.

Page 336 - James T. Snoddy guardian of M. V. Hazelett. B. Stephens and Wynn
Bearden and Jno. C. Ray securities.

Page 336 - Edwin F. Kirk guardian of Jno. P. Kirk.

Page 336 - Theofelus Revall admr. of Mary Word, deceased. Burrell Word security.

Page 336 - M. W. Watson admr. of Hiram Burnett, deceased. John Byron security.

Page 337 - H. A. Williams and wife vs G. W. Gregory guardian and others. To
divide slaves belonging to estate of Edward Whitman, deceased, leaving

Page 337 - (continued) the following children, Sophronia wife of H. A. Williams, Mary V., Sarah V., and Susan P. Whitman.

Page 338 - Commissioners to lay off support for widow and family of David J. Norvill.

Page 338 - N. Thompson, 2nd admr. Petition to sell land. Joseph H. Thompson to pay over to N. Thompson money arising from sale of land.

Page 339 - Samuel W. Jones and others. Petition to divide slaves. To divide among Simeon W. Jones, John A. Jones, Francis Collins, Dicy Jones, S. R. Jones, Robert M. Jones and Judith E. Jones. The admr. R. Jones, resigned and S. W. Jones admr.

Page 341 - Jno. H. Floyd guardian of Jno. M., William and Jonas Floyd.

Page 341 - Thomas C. Whiteside admr. of David Whiteside, deceased.

Page 341 - E. M. B. Norville admr. of D. J. Norville, deceased.

Page 342 - Willis Bearden and others. Exparte - William Hicks and William Walsh distributees.

Page 343 - James B. Coats vs James M. Stewart. Fund belonging to wife of John Reed also wife to Isaac Reed, arising from payment in this cause, the wives gave consent for their husbands to receive the payment.

Page 343 - Daniel Parker, Kindred Pearson and John Brinkley to lay off support for widow and formerly Hiram Bennett, deceased.

Page 343 - J. C. Searcy appointed Trustee for R. S. McConnell.

Page 343 - Dr. Isaac N. Jones shall purchase a grub tool as having been necessary for the work of the road on which he oversees.

Page 348 - M. E. W. Dunaway guardian of his daughter Margaret.

Page 349 - G. W. Cunningham was appointed guardian of William Cotner.

Page 349 - James B. Coates and others vs James M. Stewart. Andrew Reed appeared in Court and made bond &c. W. M. Reed security.

Page 349 - James L. Keeling's estate. Settlement with Daniel B. Shriver admr. of estate.

Page 349 - Terry D. Thompson, Elijah Arnold and Redding George to lay off support for Mrs. Martha Norville and her children.

Page 350 - John W. Mayfield admr. vs M. Ray and others. Petition to divide slaves. Slaves belonged to Robert Ray, deceased. They met at the residence of Robert Ray, deceased to divide slaves &c. William M. Ray gets Lot # 1, Lindy and child and receive cash of Thomas M. G. Ray, Mary Ray, the

1859 March Term

Page 350 - (continued) widow gets Lot # 2, Gennie and Richard and pay cash to Lot
5, J. W. Shearin and wife Polly gets Lot # 3, George and receive
cash of Thomas M. G. Ray, Thomas M. G. Ray gets Lot # 4, Charlott an
child and Tony and pay. Martha C. Ray and A. J. Ray gets Lot # 5 and
4 slaves &c. Nancy J. Ray, Martin C. Ray, Rosanah H. Ray and John W.
Ray gets slaves and cash.

Page 353 - Edmond S. Wortham and others vs P. B. Moon and others. Petition to
sell land of John Moon, deceased. John Moon owned a tract of land
in Bedford County, District # 11 on the North Fork of Duck River, the
plat is on page 355.

Page 356 - William Murphree and others vs John L. Jacobs. To sell negro boy.

Page 356 - Thomas Cox admr. of George M. Morgan. John Smith, W. S. Arnold and
Jonathan Erwin securities.

Page 357 - John W. Burton and wife vs Robert B. Davidson and others. To report
at next Court.

Page 357 - Burrell Word admr. of B. Word, deceased vs Pleasant Word and others.
S----- Word, William Word, William Word, Joseph Burleson and wife
Patience, Naomi Word and Nancy E. and James Stockard, John and James
Thompson vs Pleasant Word, W. C. Word, Theophilus Reid and wife Mary,
Sarah Patterson, _____ Patterson and wife Elizabeth are Defendants.
The Defendants failed to appear in Court to answer cause.
Report to next Court. Those appearing are Samuel and John Stockard,
Pleasant and Thomas B. and Ava Thompson and John Word are minors with
no regular guardian. Mary Reid, deceased, her admr. was Theophilus
Reid. Burrell Word departed this life in December 1859 intestate,
owning slaves.

Page 361 - William Yancy, who is a lunatic, was brought to Court and a jury of
men to examine him and determine if he is able to tend to his own
business. They determined he was unable to tend to his own business.

1859 April Term

Page 362 - Mrs. Skidmore, a pauper, be allowed $15.00.

Page 362 - W. T. Thompson, a pauper, be allowed $40.00.

Page 364 - Mrs. G. W. Ruth was dismissed from the Will of her deceased husband,
G. W. Ruth.

Page 365 - James Smith and (blank) Chandler to take Wilson, a lunatic, to the
asylum.

Page 366 - Henry Cates, a blind man, be released from paying taxes.

Page 367 - J. Y. Norman vs J. B. Bedwell. Contested election.

1859 April Term

Page 372 - C. P. Houston guardian of William Houston, Jr.

Page 373 - David R. Hooker admr. of Samuel Robinson. John W. White security.

Page 374 - William Murphree and others vs John L. Jacobs and others. To sell
negro boy.

Page 375 - D. B. Shriver. Petition to ___ settlement as admr. of James L. Keeling.
David B. Shriver admr.

Page 375 - Commissioners to lay off support for widow of D. J. Norville.

Page 378 - Andrew Reed guardian of minor children of Claiborn Reed, deceased.

Page 379 - John W. Burton and wife Mary vs William Frierson and Albert Frierson,
by their guardian W. S. Jett and Robert P. and John W. Frierson who
defend by their guardian Ann Frierson. Sell of slaves.

Page 380 - J. C. Bates and wife Sarah Jane Bates vs Elizabeth Thompson and others.
To assign dower &c. Elizabeth Thompson gets the dower tract. She is
widow of L. C. Thompson, deceased, and gets the mansion house and 105
acres and 43 poles. Lavenia F. Thompson got tract of 30 acres and 65
poles. Judith Thompson got 28 acres and 90 poles. Mary E. Thompson
got 28 acres and marked as Lot # 3. W. P. Thompson got 30 acres and
44 poles and marked as Lot # 4. Benjamin C. Thompson got 27 acres and
67 poles and marked as Lot # 5. John R. Thompson got 30 acres and marked as Lot # 6. Sarah Jane Bates wife of J. C. Bates got 30 acres and
marked as Lot # 7. Plat on page 383.

Page 384 - John R. Freeman guardian of his minor brothers and sister, to wit,
Lewis, Baily and Martha Freeman. John T. Brown security.

Page 385 - Andrew Mathews appointed by Trust Deed a Trustee for John E. Bennett
had departed this life. James Mullins appointed Trustee.

Page 386 - W. W. Gill guardian of Henrietta and Jane B. Holt, resigned. A. J.
Long appointed guardian.

1859 May Term

Page 387 - Simeon W. Jones and John A. Jones vs Dicey M. Jones. Petition to sell
slaves. Dicey M. Jones is a minor under age 21 and without a guardian
and James H. Neil appointed guardian.

Page 387 - John C. Hicks admr. of Margaret Stewart. William Campbell security.

Page 389 - Micajah Payne elected a Constable of 2nd District.

Page 390 - James S. Newton guardian of Martha Ann, Amanda Gabbert. L. W. Barrett
and James Carlisle securities.

159

1859 May Term

Page 391 - Prior J. Crunk by E. J. Hunter vs John W. Crunk. Petition to remove guardian.

Page 391 - Burrell Word and others vs Pleasant Word and others. Report.

Page 392 - John H. Oneal vs William W. Manley, R. S. Thomas and Smith Bowlin. To sell land belonging to the estate of Reuben Manley, deceased. William W. Manley purchaser.

Page 394 - James Dennison admr. of Robert Dennison, deceased. W. J. Davis and J. R. Clardy securities.

Page 394 - W. G. Cowan, Jas. L. Scudder and R. P. ___?___ to lay off support for the widow and family of Andrew Mathews, deceased.

Page 394 - John C. Hicks, admr. of his deceased wife Elenor Hicks.

Page 396 - John C. Hicks admr &c. vs William Stewart and others. Benton H., Barrett, Jemima, Greely, William, and John Stewart are also the grand children of Joshua Stewart whose names are unknown and the grandchild of Samuel Stewart non resident of Tennessee.

Page 396 - Jane Adams and others. Petition to sell land. Edward Osteen purchase of land and the purchase money is now in the hands of Joseph H. Thomp son. A record of Perry County that H. Barham is the guardian of Jose W. Adams, Mary E. Adams, George M. Adams, and Henry J. Adams, minor children of W. G. Adams. H. Barham made bond with Dr. Jennings Moore security.

Page 397 - J. Y. Norman vs J.B. Bedwell. Contested election. Case dismissed.

Page 398 - W. S. Troxler and others vs John P. Koonce and others. Petition to sell land and negroes. E. Shofner wife of A. J. Shofner and Mrs. Reed wife of W. C. Reed came into Court apart from their husbands and gave their consent for their husbands to receive any monies from sale of land and negroes.

Page 399 - Allen Morris guardian of the minor children of E. H. Hopkins.

Page 399 - Richard Phillips elected Treasurer of the Board of Trustees of Dixon Academy.

Page 400 - Settlement with William S. Troxler admr. of John Koonce, Jr., decease

Page 400 - In the matter of James L. Keeling's estate. Daniel B. Shriver admr.

1859 June Term

Page 401 - Burrell Word and others vs Pleasant Word and others. Petition to sell slaves. Sale at village of Rover, Bedford County on 20 April 1859, 10 slaves to be sold.

1859 June Term

Page 403 - M. W. Watson admr. of H. Bennett brought in inventory.

Page 403 - Joel W. Harris guardian of Phebe, Thomas, George W., Harriett, and James Hatchett.

Page 403 - Robert B. Davidson admr. of Rhoda Conway, deceased.

Page 403 - J. F. Vannoy admr. of Robert Miller, deceased. F. P. McElwrath and J. R. Clardy securities.

Page 404 - Henry Cooper admr. of Ann P. Frierson, deceased.

Page 404 - James Dixon. Petition to change road. To report.

Page 404 - James Coates and others vs James M. Stewart et al. Benjamin Coates on 28 May executed Power of Attorney to James Coates of Bedford County to receive any monies arising from the estate of his father Wilson Coates to Bedford County.

Page 405 - George Cotner admr. of Elizabeth Wright.

Page 406 - Thomas J. Robinson and others. On application of James C. Alexander and wife Mary Ann Alexander by their Attorney Thomas J. Robinson, Court ordered that John H. Oneal former Commissioner and Joseph H. Thompson, pay over the share of James C. Alexander and wife Mary Ann Alexander their share in full arising from sale of land and slave belonging to the estate of Hannah Harrison and John Harrison.

Page 406 - W. S. Troxler and wife and others vs W. C. Reed and others. Mrs. W. C. Reed consented for her husband to receive her share as she is a minor under age of 21 years.

Page 406 - John C. Hicks admr. &c. vs William Stewart and others. Petition to sell slaves.

Page 408 - Edmond Cooper guardian of Robert P. Frierson.

Page 408 - John W. Burton guardian of John W. Frierson. W. A. Ransom and W. R. McFadden securities of Rutherford County, Tennessee.

Page 408 - Rebecca Mathews (widow) admr. of her deceased husband Andrew Mathews. Robert Mathews security.

Page 408 - Robert Mathews guardian of William H., Arthur P., Andrew F., John and Mary Mathews. Rebecca Mathews security.

Page 409 - Daniel Parker admr. &c vs C. Cannon, Jr., C. Cannon, Sr. and James Wortham. Judgement. Daniel Parker to sell slaves belonging to the estate of Elenor Hawkins, deceased, on 7 May 1858, he sold slaves and C. Cannon, Jr. became purchaser.

]859 June Term

Page 409 - Nancy Jane Bates and others vs William Bates and others. B. F. White
          purchaser of land belonging to Nancy Jane Bates, heir of Charles Bates
          deceased, of District # 11 of Bedford County.

Page 410 - D. G. Deason. Petition. D. G. Deason guardian of minor heirs of Eliza
          beth Word, deceased, to wit, Rebecca, Nancy E., and W. D. Word who has
          removed to the State of Kentucky and that the two oldest Rebecca and
          Nancy E. Word are married, the former, Rebecca, to Thomas J. Nichols
          and latter, Nancy E. to Enoch S. H-----(?) (Herning?). They are entitl
          ed to receive their share of their mother's estate. T. P. Word exr.

Page 411 - Henry C. Blessing admr. of Polly Blessing, deceased. J. P., D. G.Bless
          ing and James Stallings securities.

Page 411 - Daniel Parker admr &c. vs Jacob Harrison, John Harrison and John Brink
          ley. Judgement. Sale of slave belonging to the estate of Elinor
          Hawkins, deceased.

Page 412 - Ab. J. Long guardian and wife vs Benjamin Mosley, former guardian.
          Ab. J. Long husband of and guardian of Maria I. Long, formerly Maria
          I. Holt and minor child of Jordan C. Holt, deceased. She is to receive
          her share of funds from Benjamin Mosly former guardian. He was also
          former guardian of Maria Isom Holt now the wife of Ab. J. Long.

Page 414 - Commissioners to lay off support to widow and family of Andrew Mathews

Page 414 - Commissioners to lay off support to widow and family of G. W. Ruth,
          deceased.

Page 414 - Daniel B. Shriver vs Jos. H. Thompson. D. B. Shriver admr. of James
          L. Keeling, deceased. Settlement.

Page 415 - Jos. H. Thompson vs V. K. Stevenson and W. G. Hight. Judgement.

1859 July Term

Page 417 - John E. Pearson admr. of Tarlton J. Newsom, deceased. Kindred Pearson
          and M. W. Watson securities.

Page 418 - Mrs. Bates and Mrs. Underwood, heirs at law of Austin Rowland, appeare
          in Court apart from their husbands and gave consent for their husbands
          to receive funds arising from estate of Austin Rowland.

Page 419 - James Coates and others vs James M. Stewart and others. Funds arising
          from slae of Benjamin Coates be paid to James Coates and others.

Page 420 - Commissioners to lay off support to widow and family of R. C. Miller,
          deceased.

Page 420 - Abram Evans, Justice of the Peace of 25th District.

162

1859 July Term

Page 420 - Jos. H. Thompson vs J. F. Cummings. Judgement. Thompson and S. D.
Coble, commissioners, to sell lands belonging to estate of Wilson Coates.
Cummings purchaser of part of the land.

Page 421- Joseph H. Thompson vs Thomas G. Holland, R. N. Jones and Thomas Holland.
Sale of land belonging to estate of Wilson Coates, deceased.

Page 422 - Joseph H. Thompson vs Robert Cannon, J. M. Elliott and T. W. Jordan.
Sale of land belonging to Wilson Coates, deceased.

Page 422 - Jos. H. Thompson vs R. N. Jones, Thomas Holland and Moses Marshall.
Sale of land belonging to estate of Wilson Coates, deceased.

Page 423 - Joseph H. Thompson vs Robert Dennis, Thomas Dalton and James Wortham.
Sale of land belonging to the estate of Wilson Coates, deceased.

Page 424 - Joseph H. Thompson vs Blackman Koonce, Gabriel Maupin and Robert B.
Maupin. Sale of land belonging to the estate of John Koonce, Jr.,
deceased.

Page 425 - Elizabeth Hatchett and others. Petition for dower. Elizabeth Hatchett
widow of the late Thomas Hatchett, deceased. Alexander Lee executor
of estate. Archard Hatchett, Nathan C. Hatchett, Phebe Elizabeth
Hatchett, Thomas Hatchett, George W. Hatchett, Harriett A. Hatchett and
James Hatchett are the children he left surviving him, the last five
are minors and had as guardian Joel W. Harris. Thomas Hatchett died
seized of tracts of land in the Civil District # 4 of Bedford County,
about 140 acres and 180 acres, in all about 320 acres. Elizabeth asks
for widow's dower.

Page 426 - James Coates and others vs James M. Stewart and others. David Blessing and Polly Blessing are dead and that H. C. Blessing, D. G. Blessing, Minerva E. Blessing and Celia C. and wife of Joshua Reed are the
only children and heirs of David and Polly Blessing, deceased. All are
over 21 years of age.

Page 427 - James Coates and others vs James M. Stewart and others. Petition to
sell land. Polly and David Blessing are both recently departed this
life, that Polly Blessing survived her husband for a few weeks. H. C.
Blessing admr. of Polly Blessing's estate. Land sold and H. C. Blessing became the purchaser.of Lot # 12, 6 acres and 107 poles. David G.
Blessing, James P. Blessing and James Coates jointly purchased Lot #
13, 2 acres and 103 2/3 poles.

Page 431 - James L. Keeling. Exparte - Daniel B. Shriver admr. Settlement.

Page 431 - Daniel Parker and others. Petition to sell land. Land of J. W. C.
Walsh.

Page 431 - A. J. Greer guardian of Sarah Short, Mary Burditt, Robert Burditt,
Joseph Burditt and Lafayette Burditt, all are grandchildren of Elenor
Hawkins, deceased. Jacob Harrison security.

1859 August Term

Page 432 - Willis Bearden and others. Exparte - Clerk to pay over to James W.
Bearden proceeds from sale of lands of Nimrod Burrow.

Page 432 - B. F. Whitworth guardian of the minor children of B. F. B(owers) or
(Brown).

Page 433 - Dr. Preston Frazier resigned as guardian of John S. Frazier, Jr.
R. H. Temple appointed guardian.

Page 433 - Thomas B. Marks admr. of Elizabeth M. Bell. G. W. Bell and Thomas
J. Ogilvie securities.

Page 434 - Joel H. Parker, the widow declined to serve admr. of Jesse J. Parker,
deceased. Nehemiah Parker and Timothy Parker securities. Morgan
Smith, Elisha Harmon and H. Jones to lay off support for widow and
family of Jesse Parker, deceased.

Page 434 - Harriett Tarpley guardian of her minor children.

Page 434 - Isaac Vickery guardian of Frances M. and Isaac N. Vickery.

Page 434 - John M. Maddon, an orphan of 9 years, without property to Thomas Sander
until Maddon arrives at the age of 21 years, to learn farming.

Page 435 - William W. Maddon, an orphan of 13 years, assigned to Philip Spencer,
until he is 21 years. He is to learn farming.

Page 435 - Thomas H. Allison admr. of Mary J. Adams, deceased.

Page 435 - Broadaway & Boon, Executors of William Boon, deceased.

Page 436 - John T. Stephens and others. Petition to sell slaves. To report.

Page 436 - State of Tennessee vs Wilson Capley. Bastardy. For the use of Fanny
Freeman. Case dismissed for failure of Plaintiff's proof.

Page 436 - Simeon W. Jones vs D---- M. Jones. To report at next Court.

Page 437 - John C. Hicks admr. vs William Stewart and others. Moses Smiley and
wife Lucinda Smiley are Defendants.

Page 437 - John L. Harmon admr. of Celia P. Harmon, deceased.

Page 437 - John L. Harmon admr. of Simeon J. Harmon, deceased.

Page 437 - John C. Hicks admr. &c. vs William Stewart et al. Petition to sell
slave. Margaret Stewart departed this life in Bedford County and John
C. Hicks admr. At the time of her death she owned a slave. Court
ordered the slave to be sold.

Page 439 - Joel W. Harris and others. Petition to divide land. Others: Julia
Frizzell, Archibald Frizzell, Thomas F. Frizzell and John Frizzell.

1859 August Term

Page 439 - Alexander Eakin executor of Mary J. Eakin.

1859 September Term

Page 442 - William Taylor guardian of Louisa, Mary, George, Pinckney, and Elizabeth Bullock. H. W. Jones and John A. McLain securities.

Page 443 - Joel W. Harris et al. Petition to divide land. To report.

Page 443 - John C. Hicks admr. vs Heirs of Fanny Norman. C & M pay over to W. P. Wilkes the share of his wife Sarah L. Wilkes. She is under the age of 21 years.

Page 444 - Simeon W. Jones and others vs Dicy M. Jones. Petition to sell slaves. Simeon W., John A., and Dicy M. Jones are the owners of two slaves. They will have to be sold.

Page 445 - John C. Hicks admr vs William Stewart and others. To sell slaves.

Page 446 - William Taylor and others. Petition to sell land. To sell the Bullock Land. Elizabeth Lisle wife of Jackson Lisle, Jr., to get the land and at her death to be equally divided amongst her five daughters, Mariah Stem, Rebecca Bullock, Nancy Jones, Clara Taylor and Elizabeth Bullock, the latter of whom has departed this life leaving as her only heirs at law, her children, Permelia Elizabeth, Louisa, Mary, George, and Pinkney Bullock, the last five of whom are minors under the guardianship of William Taylor. Elizabeth Bullock is now dead. Jackson Lisle is deceased.

Page 447 - Power of Attorney executed by Rachel Culverhouse, Lydia R. Culverhouse, and Hiram G. Culverhouse, to Jno. G. Culberton(?) of Rowan, North Carolina.

Page 448 - A. M. McElroy admr. of James Taylor.

Page 448 - Willis Bearden guardian of minor children of John T. Bearden, deceased.

1859 October Term

Page 450 - Mary Shearrin, a pauper, be allowed $20.00.

Page 452 - O. P. Arnold be allowed $16.50 for support of Lucy Taylor, a pauper.

Page 453 - Lucy Taylor, a pauper, be allowed $25.00 for support.

Page 453 - Thomas G(owan) is a cripple and unable to work on road. Excused.

Page 455 - John T. Johnson resigned as guardian of minor children of Edward Johnson.

Page 455 - L. B. Waite admr. of Elizabeth Knott.

1859 October Term

Page 455 - Widow, waved her right, as admr. of A. G. Brown. William Wood and
Alexander Dysart securities.

Page 457 - William Wood, E. H. Hayslett and Thomas Pickle to lay off support to
Cynthia Brown, widow of A. E. Brown, deceased.

Page 457 - Andrew Erwin and others. Petition to sell slaves. Sale at residence
of late Archibald Murphy on 9 July 1859. Slaves sold to Mrs. Jane R.
Murphy.

Page 458 - Jos. H. Thompson vs W. R. Smith, J. S. Davidson and James G. Smith.
Commissioners to sell land of estate of John Phillips, deceased. W. R
Smith purchased the land.

Page 459 - John L. Neill guardian of Thomas V. Parrish. John C. Coldwell security

Page 459 - Emily Hatchett and others. Petition for dower. Commissioners to assist
dower to Emily Hatchett.

Page 461 - W. S. Knott executor of Augustine Rowland, deceased, to pay over to
Josiah Ely the portion of estate belonging to said Ely's children as
he is guardian of said children.

Page 461 - D. B. Shriver and others vs J. L. Keeling and others. Report on sale
of land &c.

Page 463 - John T. Stephens and others. Petition to sell slaves. Clerk to pay
the portion of funds collected from that belongs to John Sutton over
to Charles Sutton, F. Sutton, he having produced proper Power of
Attorney. Also, Clerk to pay over funds collected and belongs to Mrs.
Terry. Also the portion of fund belonging to Sallie Stephens to be paid
to John T. Stephens her husband, which she gave consent to receive fund

Page 463 - V. K. Stephens vs Joseph H. Thompson and others. Case continued.

Page 464 - George Porter is dead. He died without making a Will. J. H. Blakemore admr. J. H. Coldwell security.

Page 464 - Martha Omahondro guardian of her minor children. John T. Wilson her
security.

Page 464 - J. B. Cooper guardian of John C. Cooper. C. T(A). Haskins security.

Page 464 - B. E. Cooper guardian of George N(?). Cooper.

1859 November Term

Page 466 - Simeon W. Jones. Petition to sell slaves. Report at next Court.

Page 466 - Jos. H. Thompson vs ?. K. Stevenson. Report to next Term of Court.

1859 November Term

Page 466 - Alexander Sanders, Garrett Phillips and William Word to lay off
support for widow and family of George Porter, deceased.

Page 466 - John H. Oneal guardian of Mary A. McCuiston.

Page 468 - Eppes Parker admr. of William Parker, deceased. Daniel Parker
security.

Page 468 - Jane Harris and others. Petition for dower &c. Alsa Harris had
departed this life some years since and seized and possessed of land
and that he left a widow and three children, whom are asking for dower
and shares. Dower to get dwelling house and commissioners were appointed to allott each child their share.

Page 469 - Young Wilhoite resigned as guardian of Eliza E. Koonce. W. S. Taylor
appointed guardian.

Page 470 - John Stammers. Petition to remove guardianship. John Stammers desires
the guardian of Mary Jane Stammers and Robinson Bigger to be transferred
from Bedford County to Marshall County, Tennessee.

Page 470 - Commissioners to lay off support for widow and family of A. E. Brown,
deceased.

Page 470 - Robert Allison and others. Petition to adopt a child. Robert Allison,
N. B. Reddick and Harvey P. Reddick petitioners state that Robert
Allison desires to adopt Harvey P. Reddick, the child of N. B. Reddick,
as his own child, and make him his heir &c. Robert Allison desires the
name of Harvey P. Reddick to that of Harvey P. Allison. Robert Allison
has had the said Harvey P. Reddick ever since he was 15 hours old, his
mother having died at that time. He is 18 years old. The father N. B.
Reddick gave his consent for the adoption and name change. Robert
Allison has no children of his own. The Court so ordered.

Page 472 - Emily Hatchett. Petition for dower. Emily Hatchett widow of Thomas
Hatchett, deceased. There were 2 tracts of land in Bedford County,
District # 4 and known as Hays Tract. Plat on page 474.

Page 475 - Alexander Eakin guardian of Robert Moffatt Majors.

Page 476 - Joseph H. Thompson presented a settlement with Mathew Shearin admr.
of James Gant, deceased.

Page 476 - Simeon W. Jones and others. Petition to sell slaves. Sale of slaves.

Page 478 - B. K. Cobb admr. of R. Mosly, deceased. J. M. Elliott and J. D. Cobb
securities.

Page 478 - Martin C. Ray and others. Petition to divide land. Lands of estate
of Robert Ray, deceased. Martin C. Ray got 15 acres. Martha C.
Shearin got 12 acres. Mary R. Shearin got 24 acres. Andrew J. Ray got
10 acres. Thomas M. Ray got 10 acres. America Ray got 23 acres. John
W. Ray got 12 acres. W. M. Ray got 48 acres. And Nancy J. Ray got 53

1859 November Term

Page 478 - (continued) acres. Plat on page 482. NOTE: A graveyard is on the lands of Martin C. Ray's Lot, marked as No. 1.

Page 487 - John H. Oneal vs James A. Marr and John L. Cooper. Petition to sell land. Land belonging to the estate of John Taylor, deceased. John A. Marr purchaser.

Page 489 - Thomas R. Wilhoite admr. of W. H. Koonce, Jr., deceased. John D. Wilhoite security.

Page 490 - Martha Omohundro guardian of her minor children.

Page 491 - Zepheniah Weaver admr. of Franklin Stephens. Barney Patterson and F. T. Burrow securities.

Page 491 - John S. Thompson guardian of his minor children, resigned and H. H. Muse appointed guardian., to wit, Mary, Asberry, Thomas, and Elizabeth Thompson. K. M. Pybas security.

Page 491 - Orville Hensley guardian of Mary E., John T., and Clara Jane Mason. Benjamin M---- and Harrison Hensley securities.

Page 492 - James F. Arnold guardian of Lewis Vance Fogleman and Catherine Fogleman. A. J. Greer and G. W. Greer securities.

Page 492 - William Kimmons guardian of Martha E. Kimmons his wife. A. J. Greer and G. W. Greer securities.

Page 492 - J. B. Reagor guardian of L(?). Reagor with L. Broadaway and J. W. Reagor securities.

Page 492 - J. B. Boothe guardian of W. S(T). Mullins. F. R. Price security.

Page 493 - John E. Hall guardian (John Q. Davidson formerly guardian) of Joseph, Margaret, Priscilla, James, Daniel, and William Trigg, minor children of William H. Trigg, deceased. L. W. Hall and D. R. Vance securities.

1859 December Term

Page 494 - Mary A. Campbell vs J. A. B. Campbell. J. A. B. Campbell is a minor with Joseph H. Thompson guardian.

Page 494 - Elizabeth Reaves guardian of her minor children, Daniel A., Martha E., William C., Rutha C., Nancy T., and Solomon L. Reaves. James R. Revis security.

Page 494 - Jos. W. Trigg, executor of Hayden Trigg. Settlement on estate by D. C. Trigg.

Page 495 - Elizabeth Tune. Petition to change name. Elizabeth Tune petition to change name to Elizabeth Gillmore because of the fact that John Tune her former husband and from whom she was divorced, has married again

168

Page 495 - (continued) and there are now two Mrs. Tune, and these facts fully
appearing to the satisfaction of the Court and the proof. Court ordered that the name be changed from Elizabeth Tune to Elizabeth Gillmore
and from this day she shall be known as Mrs. Elizabeth Gillmore.

Page 495 - Dr. Smith Bowlin who was named as executor in the Will of E. W. Giles,
deceased, entered into bond with W. J. Davis and C. S. Dudley securities.

Page 496 - Isaac Boaz admr. of Sarah Boaz, deceased. A. M. McElroy security.

Page 496 - Elizabeth Bennett. Petition for dower. Hiram Bennett has departed
this life intestate and that he was at the time of his death the owner
of a tract of land. His land in District # 24 of Bedford County. M.W.
Watson admr. of said Bennett's estate. Hiram Bennett having died without issues, Elizabeth Bennett is the widow and that she desires her
dower.

Page 498 - Daniel W. Barnes et al. Petition to divide slaves. Daniel W. Barnes
who is now nearly 21 years of age and Lucy J. Barnes are part owners
of 6 slaves. Harriett and her three children and Lucinda and Ida, they
and their guardian John L. Cooper desires a division of slaves.

Page 499 - John W. Burton and wife and others. Petitioners, William, Robert and
John Frierson and Mary A. Burton are part owners of 15 slaves. William
Frierson is now nearly 21 years of age and desires his share of slaves.

Page 500 - William Wood and others, Jane Harris and others. Petition for dower.
Alsea Harris died. His land was in the 9th District of Bedford County
and where Alsea Harris resided at the time of his death. Jane Harris
desires her dower. She gets the homeplace. William Wood and his wife
Elizabeth Wood gets 50 acres marked as No. 2. Harriett Marbury wife
of James K. Polk Marbury gets 30 acres. Plat on page 500.

Page 503 - V. K. Stevenson vs Joseph H. Thompson and others. Petition. Case
dismissed.

Page 503 - Joseph H. Thompson vs Willis Bearden, Jesse Rogers and Wynn Bearden.
Judgement. Land sold belonging to the heirs of (blank) Bearden, deceased. Willis Bearden purchaser.

Page 505 - A. L. Landess vs E. C. Holt, et al. Petition. Defendants, Elias C.
Holt and wife Henrietta Holt, William A. Loyd and Tempy Loyd has failed
to answer this cause. The Complainants and Defendants are joint owners
of a tract of land. Tempy B. Loyd are entitled to dower and remainder
to go to A. L. Landess and defendants.

Page 505 - Mary Campbell and others vs J. A. B. Campbell. Petition to sell land.
Continued to next Court.

Page 506 - James S. Garrett guardian of Thomas C., Nancy L., Robert C., and William
C. Garrett, minor children of Darrington Garrett. William Collins
security.

1859 December Term

Page 507 - William Taylor and others. Petition to sell land. 2 tracts of land.
William Taylor purchaser of one tract, Willis Jackson purchaser of ot
tract.

Page 509 - William S. Troxler and wife and others vs John P. Koonce. Death of
William H. Koonce and of Margaret Koonce. Thomas D. Wilhoite admr of
estate.

Page 509 - Simeon W. Jones et al vs Exparte - Concerning negro David.

Page 510 - H. H. Manly and others. Petition to sell land. Smith Bowlin purchase

Page 510 - William S. Troxler and wife and others vs John P. Koonce and others.
A. L. Landis and Blackman Koonce purchaser and has paid in full.

Page 511 - Walker Hurst. Petition for free person. Walker Hurst, a free man of
color desires to travel and go to parts where he is not known, he desires the Court to certifying to him being a free person. He about 2
years of age, straight hair, inclined to curl and has light complexion
and that he was born a free person of color and that he had lived in
Bedford County several years, every since he was born.

Page 512 - David G. Deason and wife and others, heirs at law of Thomas C. Rankin
deceased. Petition to sell land. A. L. Little purchaser of a tract
of land belonging to heirs of Thomas C. Rankin, deceased and lying in
Bedford County, about 97 acres. Nancy E. Rankin, Amanda Rankin, Ermi
Rankin, David G. Deason and wife Margaret L., W. S. Brame and wife
Mary A. Brame, Samuel G. Thompson and wife Eleanor J., and James C. M
Rankin had interest in the land be devested of them and vested in Alf
L. Little and his heirs. G. W. Harrison purchaser of the Town Lot in
Unionville on which the dwelling house and which lot joins lands of D
A. Ozment and Nancy Morgan and that G. W. Harrison has paid for the
purchase. N. F. Neil purchased small tract on which a house formerly
used as "Poor House" and known as "Oak Ridge" and has paid for same.

Page 514 - Margaret Musgrave and others. Petition to sell land. Joel Stallings
purchased the land in 18th District of Bedford County, containing about
112 (marked above 105) acres and has paid for same. Land belonging to
Margaret Musgrave, Lydia Musgrave, Mary Murgrave and Edde Musgrave,
minors and only children of Thomas Musgrave. Also, Jane Liggett became
purchaser of a tract of land in the same District of Bedford County,
about 50 acres.

Page 515 - James S. Garrett et al. Petition to divide negroes. Darrington
Garrett died intestate (1856), leaving as his children and only heirs
at law, the petitioners, James S., Famey, Thomas C., Nancy L., William
C., and Ruth C. Garrett. They are entitled to his estate. Presley
Jones admr. of estate. Darrington Garrett was owner of 11 slaves.

Page 517 - Joseph H. Thompson vs Benjamin Reaves, Jesse Rogers and William Rogers
Petition to sell land belonging to the heirs of John Koonce, Sr.,
deceased. Benjamin Reaves was purchaser. Jesse and William Rogers
securities.

170

1860 January Term

Page 522 - Commissioners to see whether the line of the 7th District should be so
changed as to include W. M. Stewart. Preston Holland, W. A. Holland
and D. B. S---son. It is ordered that James Mullins, Robert Cannon,
and John A. Moore commissioners.

Page 522 - Lucy Taylor, a pauper, be allowed $35.00.

Page 522 - Noble L. Majors reported that he had in hand $37.00 belonging to the
County and was turned over to the Trustee.

Page 524 - Jason T. Cannon admr. of Robert A. Brown. A. C. Word security.

Page 524 - Mahala Bonner. Petition for inquest of lunacy. Thomas Conwell of
unsound mind to be examined and report to next Court.

Page 524 - W. S. Stephens guardian of Cornelia Smith.

Page 526 - W. H. Sims and others vs Mary H. Sims and Anna A. Sims and others.
Anna A. Sims, Mary H. Sims are minors with Sarah A. Cortner guardian.

Page 526 - W. H. Sims and others vs Sarah A. Sims. To sell land and report.

Page 526 - W. H. Sims and others vs Mary H. Sims and Anna A. Sims. Sale of land.

Page 528 - Mary Blessing vs Joseph H. **Thompson**. Order. Thompson is to pay over
to Mary Blessing the fund arising from sale of land.

Page 528 - James C. Snell guardian of the minor children of A. G. Snell, deceased.
W. B. Snell and W. P. Bridges securities.

Page 529 - Jos. S. Owen to purchase a suit of clothing for William Yancy and
report cost to Court.

Page 531 - Middleton Holland resigned as guardian of the minor children of T.
Holland, deceased. Charles C. Phillips appointed guardian.

Page 532 - Thomas A. Gattis and Riley J. Kimbro admrs. of John Kimbro, deceased.
J. E. Couch and W. S. Evans securities.

Page 532 - Daniel B. Shriver vs John H. Oneal. Sale of land and negroes belonging
to the estate of James L. Keeling, deceased.

Page 533 - Mary Blessing guardian of her minor children. J. G. Barksdale
security.

Page 534 - Thomas C. Allison guardian of Thomas G. Stewart. B. G. Green and
Thomas Shearin securities.

1860 February Term

Page 535 - Hosea Green guardian of the minor children of Francis Keller, deceased.
G. G. Ozborne and John S. Davis securities.

171

Page 535 - Mary A. Cunningham guardian of S. A. Cunningham and Adeline M. Cunningham, two of the minor children of J. W. Cunningham, deceased. Thomas W. Buchanan and John Cortner securities.

Page 535 - Joseph H. Cunningham guardian of Sarah E. Cunningham, one of the minor children of J. W. Cunningham, deceased. J. E. Couch and Thomas W. Buchanan securities.

Page 535 - John E. Hall guardian of the minor children of William H. Trigg, deceased.

Page 536 - Benjamin Boone guardian of Daniel Boone. Jordan Hale security.

Page 536 - Joseph Anderson former guardian resigned. William Shearin appeared in Court and appointed as guardian of Nancy J., Martin C., Rosana A. and John W. Ray. Thomas Shearin and John F. Thompson securities.

Page 536 - William Carlisle guardian of Margaret B. Smith. Wesley Sutton and William S. Stephens securities.

Page 536 - J. N. Dunaway guardian of Margaret J., Robert N. and Samuel H. Chambers, minor children of H. C. Chambers, deceased. M. E. W. Dunaway security.

Page 536 - John W. Burton and wife and others. Petition to divide slaves. Distributees are, Mary A. Burton and William Frierson, of E. J. Frierson their father, deceased. 15 slaves.

Page 539 - Andrew Erwin executor &c. Jane R. Murphy and others, legatees of Archibald Murphy, deceased. Petition to sell slaves. 7 lots of slaves.

Page 540 - Nicholas Welch admr. of W. L. Walch, deceased, who died intestate. N. Walsh had as his security, A. M. McElroy.

Page 541 - Rebecca Leverett died intestate. Price C. Steele admr. of estate. G. W. Parsons security.

Page 541 - Mary Craig died intestate. Daniel Davis admr. and John E. Davis his security.

Page 541 - M. A. Stem died intestate. J. W. Stem admr. with J. R. Stem and J. W. Maxwell securities.

Page 541 - Edwin Batte guardian of his minor children, William and Benjamin Batte G. W. Harrison and H. R. Stem securities.

Page 542 - A. L. Landis vs Tempy Loyd and others. To allot the dower and petition of land. Dower is 74 acres. Tempy D. Loyd gets the dower and included the mansion house and improvements. Henrietta Holt wife of Elias C. Holt gets 24 acres. A. L. Landis gets 24 acres. Plat on page 553.

1860 February Term

Page 545 - John Jakes allowed $40.00 as guardian of W. L. Stephens.

Page 545 - James H. Neil former guardian of minor children of James R. Terry, deceased, resigned and John T. Stephens appointed guardian.

Page 545 - Margaret Bradshaw guardian of minor children of Robert E. Bradshaw, deceased. Thomas Dryden security.

Page 546 - Edmund Cooper guardian of minor children of F. F. Fonville. Henry Cooper as security.

Page 546 - W. W. Stanfield guardian of Charles W. Kirby. Joseph Hastings, Esq. and Thomas J. Stanfield securities.

Page 546 - Settlement with P. H. and W. P. F. Thompson executors of estate of John Thompson, deceased.

Page 546 - B. G. Green and Thomas Shearin filed an inventory of the estate of Grayson H. Stewart, deceased.

Page 547 - Thomas A. Gattis admr. of John Kimbro, R. J. Kimbro and others vs Charity Kimbro and others. Report as to whether land and slaves can be divided without a sale. C. E. Jenkins and William J. Shofner reported that land was 50 to 70 acres and is so small and that it should be sold. Also, the slaves to be sold.

Page 549 - Settlement with N. Thompson,2nd admr. of estate of William Thompson, deceased.

Page 549 - James B. Coates and others vs James M. Stewart and others. Sale of land and purchased by Thomas G. Holland and is paid in full.

Page 550 - Joel W. Harris guardian of Joseph M. and Noble M. Giles, minor children of Milton Giles, deceased. Mary E. Lynn and William M. Howlin securities.

1860 March Term

Page 551 - Joshua M. Hix guardian of minor heirs of Enoch and Nancy Kizer.

Page 551 - G. W. Gregory guardian of Susan P. Whitman, one of the minor heirs of Edward Whitman, deceased. James Gregory and H. A. Williams securities.

Page 551 - Mary Gant guardian of Lewis T. Gant and Edmond C. Gant, two of the minor heirs of Lewis Gant, deceased. Thomas S. Gant and J. M. Ledbetter securities.

Page 551 - J. M. Ledbetter guardian of Sarah E. Gant and Rebecca A. Gant, two minor heirs of Lewis Gant, deceased. William Crowell and Thomas Shearin securities.

Page 552 - James A. Gant, a citizen of Bedford County, had departed this life intestate. At the request of James A. Gant's mother and brother

Page 552 - (continued) Andrew Gant, the Court appointed Gen. Robert Cannon admr. with Patrick Fay, A. D. Fugitt and William Murphree securities.

Page 552 - Lewis Gant, a citizen of Bedford County, had lately departed this life intestate. Mathew Shearin appointed admr. and Thomas S. Gant to be al admr. Edmund Cooper and Thomas Shearin securities.

Page 552 - Lewis Whitsell had lately departed this life intestate. William F. Barnett admr. Thomas Kimmons security.

Page 553 - Thomas Montgomery, D. G. Stephenson and John Oneal to lay off support to the widow of Lewis Gant, deceased.

Page 553 - G. W. Cunningham vs Wiley J. Usery. Case continued.

Page 553 - William M. Reed guardian of Malinda E. Reed. Andrew Reed security.

Page 553 - Hiram Edde guardian of Francis Trott, Nancy Edde, Mary Edde, and Eliza Edde, his minor children.

Page 553 - Isham Sorrells, guardian &c. presented the following paper &c. State of Tennessee, Lincoln County. At County Court at Lincoln County Tennessee in Town of Fayetteville on 1st Monday in September 1858, it being the 6th day of the month, Robert Farquaharson, chairman and presiding Justice Benjamin F. Clark and F. Motlow. "Copy of appointment of guardianship Isham Sorrels appeared and moved the Court to grant him guardianship of Margaret P., Nancy C., Needham J., Ephraim M., Isham S., Henry C., and Newton A. Sorrels, minors. Thomas M. Harkins, T. R. W. Crane and J. W. Barham securities."

Page 555 - Mary Ann Brittain guardian of her minor children, Newcomb T., James W. Joseph F., Mariah E., Mary Ann, Martha Jane, Letitia T., Mary F., and Jason T. Brittain. G. W. Thompson and N. Thompson, Sr. securities.

Page 556 - Phillips Brooks admr. of Giles Burditt, deceased.

Page 556 - P. A. Hall guardian &c presented the following paper. State of Tennessee, Rutherford County. Court in Murfreesboro met on]st Monday in February it being 5th in year 1860. Joseph Lindsey chairman and M. L. Fletcher and John Lytle, associate Justices presiding, John A. Hall came into Court and was appointed guardian of David A., William J., and Mary L. Hall, his own children and minor heirs at law of David Orr, deceased. E. F. Lytle and M. L. Fletcher securities.

Page 558 - Joseph Anderson admr. of his father's estate asked for additional credit on final settlement.

Page 558 - William Galbreath, J. _. Cummings and H. F. Holt to lay off support of widow of Giles Burditt, deceased.

Page 558 - Mrs. (blank)(Nancy)Walsh, one of the heirs at law of the estate of Nancy Bearden, deceased, and wife of (blank) (George) Walsh appeared in Court apart from her husband and consented that her brother-in-law, William

1860 March Term

Page 558 - (continued) Hix, to receive any monies arising from estate.

Page 559 - William H. Elle (Ely?) guardian &c. vs R. N. Jones. Report to next
Court.

Page 559 - Frances Butler guardian of her minor children, William K(?). M. and
John P. R. Butler. John G. Fulghum security.

Page 559 - Thomas N. Gattis admr &c. vs W. W. Kimbro and others. Heirs of John
Kimbro, deceased. Admr. is to sell property to pay debts.

Page 559 - James Hastings and wife and James Edde and others vs Mariah Edde and
others. Candis Edde one of the defendants is dead and that Hiram Edde
is her admr. and as such is entitled to her share of the purchase money
of the lands sold, it being 1/10 of the same.

Page 560 - W. H. Sims and others vs Anna A. Sims and others. To sell land. John
A. Moore bid off the land. Anna A. and Manervia Sims.

Page 562 - Edward T. Barnes and wife and others vs Louisa Rankins and others.
Cause dismissed.

Page 562 - Thomas C. Whiteside admr and others. Petition to sell slaves. David
Whiteside died intestate in Bedford County on 6 January 1859. Thomas
C. Whiteside appointed admr. Louisa Whiteside widow of David Whiteside,
deceased. There are children and grandchildren of David Whiteside,
deceased. He was owner of 6 slaves. Slaves to be sold.

Page 563 - J. F. Jordan and others vs Wilie Arnold and others. Petition to sell
land. Sarah Davis purchaser of the tract of land in Coffee County.
Smith Arnold died having interest in 40 acre tract in Coffee County,
District # 5, on waters of Spring Creek.

DEASON: 4, 9, 15, 29, 54, 98, 110, 128, 148, 162, 170
DECHARD (DECKARD): 71, 106
DEDMON: 23, 66
DEERY: 78
DELK: 55, 66, 77, 85, 88, 90, 112, 121
DENNIS: 142, 163
DENNISON: 160
DENNISTON: 33, 89
DENSON: 50, 55, 67, 86, 116
DIAN: 72
DICKENS: 122
DICKERSON: 37, 137
DILLARD: 16
DISMUKES: 103, 127
DIXON: 20, 27, 32, 46, 57, 67, 93, 103, 124, 125, 127, 141, 143, 145, 146, 149, 161
DOAK: 5, 18, 28, 39, 51, 53, 69, 85, 89, 90, 103, 112, 113, 117
DOBBINS: 142
DOBSON: 35
DOLLAR: 22, 41
DOUGAL: 89, 95
DOWNING: 103
DROMGOOLE: 33, 35, 58
DRUMRIGHT: 151
DRYDEN: 34, 154, 173
DUDLEY: 119, 124, 130, 149, 169
DUGGAN: 79, 143
DUNAWAY: 39, 133, 149, 157, 172
DUNHAM: 53, 68
DUVAL: 42
DWIGGINS: 26, 66, 72, 136, 145
DWYER: 103, 143
DYER: 62
DYSART: 102, 103, 137, 144, 166

EAKIN: 3, 9, 13, 16, 18, 20, 37, 41, 67, 76, 81, 103, 104, 151, 165, 167
EARNHART: 57, 58, 61, 63, 76, 110, 112, 117, 118, 125, 135
EATON: 76
EDDINS (EDINS): 7, 37, 42, 43
EDDE (EDE, EDDY): 45, 48, 49, 51, 53, 70, 75, 88, 111, 127, 146, 174, 175
EDGEN: 152
EDMONDSON: 78, 93, 139

ELKINS: 1, 12, 13, 14, 31, 39, 41, 50, 52, 74, 89, 95, 99, 102, 124, 125
ELLIOTT: 33, 35, 57, 71, 79, 141, 163, 167
ELLIS: 118
ELMORE: 26, 44, 56, 82, 152
ELY (ELLE): 166, 175
ENDSLEY: 147
ENGLAND: 26, 32, 62, 63, 64, 66, 147
EOFF: 103
ERWIN: 49, 76, 83, 93, 144, 150, 158, 166, 172
EULESS (EULISS): 36, 138
EVANS (EVINS, IVINS): 11, 17, 18, 20, 34, 38, 39, 45, 49, 63, 65, 78, 80, 85, 90, 102, 121, 134, 148, 162, 171
EWELL: 28, 50
EWING: 19, 43, 151

FAIN: 73
FANSETT: 116
FARQUAHARSON: 174
FARRAR: 46, 145
FARRIS: 71, 123
FAY: 174
FELPS: 23, 52
FERGUSON: 54, 69, 101, 120
FERRELL (FERRIL): 83, 105
FIELDS: 74, 120, 135, 136, 142, 151
FINCH: 117, 135, 151, 152
FINNEY (FINEY, FINNY): 75, 95, 118
FISHER: 10, 11, 39, 40, 41, 42, 72, 120
FLETCHER: 174
FLINT: 22, 48
FLOYD: 17, 44, 45, 55, 66, 88, 89, 90, 104, 120, 128, 138, 150, 157
FOGLEMAN: 85, 90, 104, 116, 127, 168
FONVILLE: 5, 19, 39, 43, 64, 97, 128, 131, 173
FORBES: 66, 110, 111, 112, 113, 114, 115, 117, 123
FORTNER: 109
FOSTER: 2, 6, 9, 48, 60, 61, 64, 89, 90, 93
FOWLER: 127
FRANKFORT: 129
FRAZIER (FRAZER): 15, 25, 28, 30, 32, 58, 64, 96, 121, 122, 128, 137, 141, 164

FREEMAN: 17, 25, 51, 53, 62, 82, 97, 101, 106, 107, 111, 117, 129, 137, 147, 159, 164
FRIDDLE: 155
FRIERSON: 19, 26, 138, 139, 140, 153, 159, 161, 169, 172
FRIZZELL: 35, 56, 85, 110, 111, 135, 136, 150, 152, 164
FROST: 118
FUGETT (FUGITT): 68, 101, 141, 174
FULGHUM: 175
FULLER: 31, 44

GABBARD: 109
GABBERT: 69, 70, 81, 96, 124, 131, 136, 159
GADDISS: 149
GALBREATH: 18, 22, 29, 42, 53, 84, 90, 99, 114, 118, 144, 174
GALLEGHY: 19
GAMBILL: 1, 2, 3, 9, 15, 22, 28, 38, 39, 40, 42, 48, 57, 60, 64, 79, 103, 105, 108, 132, 145
GAMMILL (GAMEL): 61, 62, 145
GANAWAY: 83, 139, 144
GANT: 4, 7, 32, 51, 54, 132, 133, 138, 151, 152, 167, 173, 174
GARDNER: 20
GARMON (GARMAN): 102, 136
GARRETT: 7, 20, 29, 32, 34, 48, 75, 81, 83, 93, 130, 139, 141, 142, 144, 169, 170
GATTIS: 171, 173, 175
GAULT: 51, 54, 55, 58, 77, 110, 127
GAUNT: 1, 8, 79
GENTRY: 12, 37
GEORGE: 157
GIBSON: 32, 62, 65, 66, 67, 83, 88, 103, 106, 110
GIFFORD: 138, 151
GILBERT: 2
GILES: 169, 173
GILL: 15, 62, 63, 86, 107, 111, 148, 159
GILLILAND: 153
GILLINAN: 131
GILLMAN: 140, 146

GILMORE (GILLMORE): 22, 168, 169
GIVINS (GIVENS): 137, 153
GLENN: 21
GOGGIN (GOGGINS, GOGIN): 33, 97, 125, 126
GOODWIN: 45, 105, 116
GOOSBY: 12
GORDON: 93, 145
GOSLING: 129
GOWEN (GOWAN): 92, 165
GRAHAM: 3, 44, 78
GREEN (GREENE): 59, 82, 84, 85, 94, 101, 107, 108, 109, 142, 171, 173
GREER (GREAR): 24, 38, 48, 51, 52, 53, 54, 55, 56, 59, 64, 74, 82, 85, 88, 100, 112, 116, 119, 127, 140, 150, 163, 168
GREGORY: 37, 74, 100, 104, 113, 132, 156, 173
GRIFFIS: 121
GRIFFITH: 103
GURNEE: 137
GUTHRIE: 145
GUY: 25
GWYNN: 133

HAGGARD (HAGGART): 18, 76, 96
HAILE (HAIL): 17, 43, 44, 152
HALE: 2, 85, 113, 119, 141, 172
HALEY: 4
HALL: 1, 15, 34, 54, 83, 168, 172, 174
HAMILTON: 42, 144
HAMLIN: 42, 44
HAMMILL: 51
HANCOCK: 138
HANEY (HANIE, HAINEY): 53, 60, 63, 82
HARDIN (HARDING): 115, 121, 139
HARKINS: 174
HARMON: 148, 164
HARPER: 29, 30, 32, 34, 55, 62, 63, 64, 65, 66, 67, 83, 88, 106, 110
HARPLEY: 147
HARRIS: 2, 3, 6, 11, 21, 29, 32, 36, 42, 51, 59, 65, 75, 83, 87, 96, 97, 98, 114, 120, 133, 137, 141, 145, 161, 163, 164, 165, 167, 169, 173
HARRISON: 35, 53, 55, 56, 58, 59, 63, 83, 84, 87, 88, 90, 92, 98, 107, 108, 109, 112, 114, 116, 118, 119, 120, 127, 130, 138, 140, 145, 149, 150, 155, 161,

JAKES (JACKES): 10, 22, 35, 87, 100, 110, 173
JAMISON (JAMESON, JIMERSON): 33, 77
JARNAGAN: 71, 75, 79, 82, 84
JEFFRIES: 37, 92, 95, 134
JENKINS: 20, 36, 128, 134, 142, 173
JENNINGS: 28, 59, 62, 113
JETT: 107, 112, 140, 144, 153, 156
JOB: 137
JOHNSON: 2, 18, 30, 35, 49, 50, 67, 70, 71, 100, 101, 114, 120, 125, 129, 131, 141, 146, 165
JONES: 16, 19, 28, 33, 34, 53, 56, 57, 73, 76, 82, 92, 94, 115, 123, 125, 126, 130, 132, 141, 144, 146, 148, 149, 150, 151, 153, 154, 155, 156, 157, 159, 163, 164, 165, 166, 167, 170, 175
JORDON (JORDAN): 88, 89, 93, 126, 136, 141, 163, 175

KEELE (KEEL): 74, 76, 100
KEELING: 117, 118, 120, 121, 124, 126, 157, 159, 160, 162, 163, 166, 171
KELLER: 83, 96, 98, 148, 171
KELLEY: 36
KELLON: 139
KERBY: 59, 63
KERR (KAAR, KAAR): 37, 130
KEY: 134
KILLINGSWORTH: 1, 24, 137
KIMBRO: 2, 3, 7, 12, 28, 37, 38, 43, 44, 45, 47, 107, 109, 110, 114, 135, 171, 173, 175
KIMMONS: 3, 5, 10, 15, 18, 29, 83, 144, 168, 174
KINCAID: 35, 104
KINDLE: 86, 91, 97
KING: 18, 34, 35, 38, 59, 77, 82, 92, 94, 96, 97, 101, 102, 114, 119, 128, 137, 155
KINGREE: 23, 36, 97, 98, 153
KINNEY: 33
KIRBY: 60, 61, 80, 173
KIRK: 115, 156

KIRKLAND: 23
KIZER: 143, 173
KNIGHT: 19, 56, 85, 123
KNOTT: 2, 9, 17, 26, 27, 35, 55, 78, 86, 104, 150, 165, 166
KOONCE: 24, 102, 131, 136, 142, 155, 160, 163, 167, 168, 170

LACY: 10, 13, 26, 30, 36, 64, 79, 128, 145
LAGSTON: 123
LAINE: 45
LAMB: 26, 50, 57, 72, 75, 77, 110
LAMBERT: 74, 76, 80
LANDERS: 9, 11, 63, 73
LANDESS: 169
LANDIS: 28, 50, 59, 61, 104, 123, 128, 151, 170, 172
LANE: 5, 9, 10, 18, 38, 78, 129
LARUE: 9, 11, 25, 36, 56, 90, 147
LAUGHRY: 74, 76, 80
LAWRENCE: 73, 74, 104, 153
LAWWELL (LOWWELL, LOWELL, LOYELL): 77, 86, 95, 115, 149, 153, 155, 156
LEATHERS: 40
LEDBETTER: 2, 9, 26, 35, 77, 81, 100, 115, 123, 149, 173
LEE: 5, 74, 110, 135, 147, 152, 163
LEECH: 53
LEFTWICH: 15
LENTZ (LENTS): 11, 23, 37, 50, 51, 73, 75, 76, 77, 82, 87, 90, 95, 145
LESTER: 115
LEVERETT: 172
LIGGETT: 107, 170
LINDSEY: 92, 174
LIPFORD: 59, 144
LIPSCOMB: 7, 42, 85, 87, 90, 91, 93, 102, 117, 124, 139, 140
LISLE: 165
LITTLE (LITLE): 2, 3, 7, 23, 25, 72, 73, 75, 77, 104, 109, 110, 116, 150, 151, 152, 170
LOCKE: 11, 40, 53, 58, 95
LOGAN: 103, 105, 108, 145
LONG: 95, 156, 159, 162
LOONEY: 4, 5, 12, 40, 79, 88
LOW (LOWE): 71, 79, 123
LOWELL: 153
LOYD: 20, 25, 46, 50, 52, 90, 142, 169, 172
LYNCH (LINCH): 36, 56, 92, 99, 101, 104, 138

LYNN: 55, 173
LYON: 150
LYTLE: 104, 107, 149, 174

MACCOWEN: 68
MADDON: 164
MADISON: 106, 119
MAJORS: 12, 56, 64, 66, 72,
    74, 111, 124, 125, 150,
    167, 171
MALLARD: 16, 36, 39, 40,
    68, 74, 107, 111, 112
MANIER: 119
MANKIN: 7, 17, 22, 25, 26,
    44, 56, 57
MANLEY (MANLY): 88, 89, 107,
    117, 124, 151, 152, 160,
    170
MARBURY: 169
MARKS: 28, 30, 164
MARR: 168
MARSH: 12
MARSHALL: 64, 123, 140, 141,
    156, 163
MARTIN: 4, 5, 6, 19, 25, 33,
    51, 52, 84, 99, 110, 121,
    127, 134, 152
MASON: 27, 30, 100, 168
MASSEY: 72
MATHEWS (MATTHEWS): 13, 14,
    71, 159, 160, 161, 162
MAUPIN (MOPPIN): 14, 33, 44,
    51, 52, 65, 66, 74, 77,
    98, 99, 103, 129, 142,
    163
MAXWELL: 118, 119, 127, 131,
    133, 172
MAYFIELD: 1, 24, 72, 77, 90,
    149, 157
MAYS (MAY, MAYES): 21, 79, 88,
    98, 106, 107, 131, 138
MEADOWS: 3, 5, 24, 82, 85, 87,
    90, 91, 106, 116, 117, 126,
    131
MEDEARIS: 32, 42, 66, 69, 92,
    102, 103, 111, 139
MERRITT: 27, 43, 65
MEYERS: 150
MILES: 17, 18, 20, 35, 46,
    49, 90, 106, 107, 109
MILLER: 8, 11, 20, 23, 36, 39,
    41, 56, 66, 101, 117, 135,
    139, 161, 162
MILLS: 75, 83

MITCHELL: 137
MOBLEY: 50
MODRELL (MODREL, MODERAL): 3, 29,
    32, 51, 98, 120
MOFFATT: 28, 43
MOLDER: 105
MONTGOMERY: 41, 143, 150, 174
MOON: 7, 12, 49, 50, 56, 76, 82,
    88, 113, 123, 153, 156, 158
MOORE (MOOR, MORE): 1, 7, 10, 11,
    17, 21, 37, 48, 49, 52, 53, 55,
    58, 61, 73, 77, 79, 82, 83, 86,
    88, 111, 113, 114, 126, 160, 171,
    175
MORGAN: 17, 27, 34, 47, 49, 66, 93,
    98, 100, 136, 158, 170
MORRIS: 1, 26, 74, 94, 125, 128,
    143, 160
MORRISON: 22, 24, 43, 46
MORROW: 10, 22, 35
MORTON: 20, 58, 62, 147
MOSELEY (MOSLY): 4, 6, 7, 11, 37,
    45, 51, 58, 68, 82, 136, 140,
    145, 156, 162, 167
MOSS: 42, 47, 52
MOTLOW: 174
MOULDER: 20, 21, 58
MOUNT: 147
MULLINS: 5, 10, 20, 23, 33, 39, 65,
    75, 76, 80, 84, 92, 96, 104, 119,
    121, 126, 141, 152, 159, 168,
    171
MURPHREE: 118, 123, 129, 158, 159,
    174
MURPHY: 76, 104, 138, 139, 141, 144,
    148, 150, 154, 156, 166, 172
MUSE: 14, 18, 26, 28, 30, 31, 34,
    41, 44, 45, 46, 47, 48, 71, 85,
    108, 133, 138, 168
MUSGRAVE (MUSGRAVES): 21, 33, 47,
    91, 112, 113, 114, 134, 170
MUSGROVE (MUSGROVES): 43, 46, 109,
    142, 145
MYERS: 13, 16, 46, 47, 76, 99, 138,
    147

McADAMS: 15, 28, 33, 66, 92
McCLURE (McLURE): 43, 65, 85, 92,
    122, 138, 139
McCOMBS: 52
McCONNELL: 157
McCOWN (McCOWAN): 62, 107
McCRORY: 13, 21, 24, 25, 26, 99, 100,
    104, 117, 135

183

McCUISTION: 27, 29, 48, 50, 82, 84, 87, 91, 92, 117, 123, 129, 139, 140, 146, 167

McCUTCHEON (McCUTCHEN): 9, 11, 59, 62

McDOWELL (McDOWEL): 84, 85, 140

McELROY: 80, 81, 120, 165, 169, 172

McELWRATH: 14, 28, 63, 155, 161

McEWEN: 121

McFADDEN: 161

McFARLIN (McFARLAND, McFARLING): 21, 98, 124, 125

McGHEE: 152

McGILL: 86, 88, 98, 104, 118

McGIMSEY: 76

McGOWAN: 136, 152

McGOWEN: 72, 73, 79, 80, 81, 87, 92, 151

McGREW: 18, 89, 113, 117, 134, 151

McGUIRE (McGUYER): 8, 21, 53, 81, 85, 87, 101

McKELBY (McKILBY): 92

McKINLEY: 3, 13, 28, 57

McLAUGHLIN: 23, 36, 97, 98

McLEAN (McLAIN): 9, 86, 165

McMAHAN (McMAHAHAN): 74, 110, 135, 136, 147, 148, 152

McQUIDDY: 38, 131, 133

NANCE: 9, 23, 68, 84, 113

NASH: 3, 4, 8, 9, 31, 43, 46, 48, 69, 71, 74, 75, 76, 78, 80, 87, 106, 108, 118, 120, 135, 141, 144

NAYLOR (NAILOR): 81, 120, 122, 141

NEAL: 118

NEALY: 143, 144

NEASE: 100, 105, 134

NEELEY (NEELY): 11, 14, 28, 32, 33, 58, 76, 77, 86, 93, 102, 103, 105, 107, 118, 125, 126, 127, 147, 150

NEESE: 65

NEIL (NEILL): 4, 7, 11, 17, 18, 24, 25, 30, 32, 34, 40, 42, 45, 55, 62, 65, 66, 67, 83, 88, 108, 135, 136, 147, 150, 159, 166, 170, 173

NELSON: 105, 143

NEWBORNE: 121

NEWSOM: 1, 6, 41, 43, 47, 49, 50, 52, 54, 56, 58, 68, 72, 88, 95, 100, 101, 103, 110, 111, 112, 113, 117, 120, 162

NEWTON: 38, 69, 96, 136, 159

NICHOLS: 5, 12, 54, 55, 118, 122, 128, 139, 143, 148, 149, 161

NIVENS: 31

NIX: 38

NOBLITT (NOBLETT): 4, 5, 15, 24, 46, 61, 69, 144

NORMAN: 4, 8, 34, 128, 131, 133, 135, 143, 149, 150, 154, 158, 160, 165

NORVILLE (NORVILL): 1, 12, 18, 21, 53, 65, 83, 84, 98, 100, 101, 104, 106, 108, 114, 119, 120, 121, 146, 157, 159

NOWLIN: 4, 36, 41, 134, 141, 142

OAKLEY: 2, 43, 44, 85

OGILVIE: 18, 54, 55, 58, 60, 61, 64, 67, 73, 74, 89, 93, 122, 129, 148, 156, 164

OLIVER: 25, 56, 58, 61, 88, 89, 90, 113

OMAHONDRO: 166, 168

ONEAL: 14, 20, 46, 50, 56, 57, 58, 70, 71, 73, 75, 76, 80, 82, 84, 87, 91, 102, 108, 110, 111, 116, 117, 118, 120, 121, 123, 125, 129, 131, 137, 138, 145, 146, 147, 160, 161, 167, 168, 171, 174

ORR: 80, 100, 106, 174

OSBORNE: 22, 29, 44, 66, 76, 95, 99, 113, 117, 125, 142, 147, 148, 152

OSTEEN: 116, 160

OVERCAST: 2

OWENS: 55, 171

OZMENT: 10, 72, 73, 77, 79, 81, 90, 92, 98, 118, 119, 144, 170, 171

PARKER: 14, 28, 29, 43, 85, 95, 101, 105, 111, 113, 116, 118, 129, 131, 134, 136, 137, 142, 145, 147, 148, 152, 157, 161, 162, 163, 164, 167

PARKES (PARKS): 5, 39, 128, 131

PARRISH: 166

PARSONS: 11, 12, 26, 27, 48, 50, 60, 63, 66, 75, 76, 100, 101, 102, 118, 135, 150, 172

PATE: 23, 62, 107, 115, 149

ROBINSON: 10, 24, 34, 60, 86, 91, 94, 95, 97, 104, 107, 108, 109, 112, 117, 119, 140, 145, 149, 150, 159, 161
ROGERS: 35, 86, 88, 93, 103, 123, 131, 134, 169, 170
RONE: 25
ROWLAND: 38, 39, 44, 162, 166
ROWTON: 76
ROZAR: 40, 96
RUCKER: 3, 10, 18, 22, 48, 104, 149
RUSHING: 2, 3, 15, 30, 48, 96
RUSS: 30, 62, 125
RUSSELL: 3, 5, 12, 30, 59, 69, 72, 79, 82, 86, 101, 138
RUTH: 71, 99, 118, 158, 162
RUTLEDGE: 20, 56, 57, 60, 127, 146

SANDERS: 56, 101, 110, 140, 164, 167
SCALES: 51, 52, 100, 109, 118, 119, 132
SCOTT: 8, 56, 59, 107, 137
SCRUGGS: 7, 9, 23, 66, 85, 95, 113, 117, 135, 136, 151
SCUDDER: 77, 160
SEARCY: 40, 42, 43, 157
SEWELL: 93
SHADDIE: 138
SHANKLIN: 106
SHAPPARD: 40
SHARP (SHARPE): 9, 11, 24, 25, 27, 28, 33, 46, 53, 71, 72, 75, 109
SHAW: 19, 24, 49, 55, 73, 113, 136
SHEARIN (SHEARRIN): 1, 8, 12, 37, 51, 52, 62, 72, 73, 77, 81, 86, 106, 115, 124, 133, 138, 155, 158, 165, 167, 171, 172, 173, 174
SHEPPERSON: 5, 6
SHERWOOD: 83
SHIPP (SHIP): 138, 152
SHOFNER: 2, 7, 13, 34, 35, 39, 59, 65, 66, 79, 93, 131, 138, 156, 160, 173
SHOOK: 4, 10, 28, 43, 144
SHORT: 10, 38, 163
SHRIVER: 1, 14, 16, 117, 118, 121, 124, 126, 157, 159, 160, 162, 163, 166, 171

SIMMONS: 126
SIMPSON: 89, 102, 118, 150, 152
SIMS: 6, 43, 46, 66, 83, 112, 121, 150, 153, 171, 175
SINGLETON: 16, 74, 117, 120, 136, 142
SIVELEY: 22
SKEEN: 138
SKIDMORE: 158
SMALLING: 147
SMILEY: 164
SMITH: 3, 8, 11, 20, 21, 22, 24, 29, 32, 45, 49, 57, 66, 67, 71, 92, 103, 115, 121, 126, 130, 131, 145, 152, 154, 158, 164, 166, 171, 172
SNELL: 12, 17, 28, 44, 49, 57, 58, 104, 105, 130, 133, 171
SNELLING: 1, 17
SNODDY: 57, 68, 70, 95, 156
SOLOMON: 115, 116
SORRELL: 133, 174
SPENCE: 54, 57, 67, 107, 109, 143, 145
SPENCER: 163
SPRINGER: 21, 24, 26, 35, 100, 147
SPROUSE: 127
SPRUCE: 91
STAGGS: 25, 34, 35, 75, 77
STALLINGS: 4, 21, 33, 39, 47, 113, 118, 134, 145, 148, 162, 170
STAMMERS: 19, 34, 41, 42, 90, 167
STANCELL: 40
STANFIELD: 17, 59, 60, 61, 63, 65, 80, 85, 120, 173
STATHAM: 80, 81
STEELE: 7, 10, 11, 12, 15, 17, 18, 22, 24, 27, 29, 35, 37, 38, 39, 40, 45, 56, 63, 67, 74, 78, 84, 90, 111, 113, 118, 119, 123, 134, 135, 146, 172
STEGALL: 39, 64
STEM: 20, 48, 60, 134, 144, 165, 172
STEPHENS: 2, 3, 4, 5, 8, 9, 16, 19, 20, 26, 30, 39, 40, 41, 42, 47, 54, 65, 67, 70, 72, 83, 86, 89, 92, 99, 107, 110, 122, 124, 126, 130, 133, 134, 135, 138, 144, 148, 150, 156, 164, 166, 168, 171, 172, 173
STEPHENS: 4, 57, 58, 69, 110, 112, 153, 162, 174
STEVANS: 4, 30

186

STEVENSON: 92, 166, 169
STEWART: 39, 40, 52, 56, 60, 61,
    63, 69, 90, 108, 110, 140,
    143, 155, 157, 159, 160, 161,
    162, 163, 164, 165, 171, 173
STILLWELL (STILWELL): 133, 154
STOCKARD: 107, 154, 158
STOCKTON: 24, 144
STOKES: 29, 32
STONE: 49, 99
STORY: 22, 75
STOVER: 141
STREATER: 55, 56, 57, 58, 59,
    71, 145
STREETER: 54, 79, 112
STRICKLER: 3, 16, 18, 104
SUGG: 56, 66, 136
SUMNER: 45
SUTTON: 6, 8, 18, 25, 51, 54, 55,
    56, 123, 130, 135, 146, 166,
    172
SWANSON: 121
SWIFT: 6
SWING: 103, 104, 105, 106, 134
SYKES: 144, 153

TALBERT: 15
TARPLEY: 29, 79, 80, 136, 149,
    164
TATUM: 80
TAYLOR (TAILOR): 2, 15, 17, 19,
    22, 26, 33, 34, 48, 55, 67,
    74, 90, 92, 94, 102, 104, 109,
    133, 138, 139, 150, 165, 167,
    168, 170, 171
TEMPLE: 15, 27, 64, 101, 128,
    164
TERRY: 6, 9, 12, 13, 23, 35, 38,
    39, 54, 56, 61, 67, 70, 72,
    73, 78, 98, 114, 134, 135,
    154, 156, 166, 173
THROGMORTON: 2, 6, 29, 126
THOMAS: 23, 42, 56, 65, 85,
    101, 106, 116, 139, 148, 150,
    151, 160
THOMASON: 7, 152
THOMPSON: 4, 11, 12, 21, 25, 27,
    29, 37, 41, 42, 46, 50, 52,
    53, 55, 56, 57, 58, 59, 61,
    63, 64, 68, 70, 71, 72, 73,
    76, 77, 81, 86, 88, 89, 90,
    92, 94, 95, 96, 97, 100, 101,
    102, 106, 107, 110, 113, 115,
    117, 119, 120, 121, 122, 124,
    125, 126, 128, 132, 133, 134,

THOMPSON (continued): 135, 140, 141,
    142, 145, 146, 148, 149, 150,
    151, 152, 153, 154, 155, 157,
    158, 159, 160, 161, 162, 163,
    166, 167, 168, 169, 170, 171,
    172, 173, 174
THORN: 48
THRONEBERRY: 85, 138
TILFORD: 12, 84, 130, 133, 137
TILLMAN (TILMAN): 6, 9, 56, 59, 99,
    104
TOMLINSON: 16
TOWNSEN: 76
TRIBBLE: 5, 16, 47, 144
TRICE: 4, 7, 9, 15, 61, 96, 97, 132
TRIGG: 101, 105, 107, 118, 132, 141,
    168, 172
TROLLINGER (TROLINGER): 14, 24, 63,
    107, 116
TROTT: 174
TROXLER: 22, 101, 115, 117, 120,
    121, 123, 136, 138, 160, 161,
    170
TUCKER: 15, 26, 33, 36, 99, 102
TUNE: 15, 20, 23, 43, 57, 59, 108,
    110, 130, 132, 144, 168, 169
TURMAN: 9
TURNER: 81, 104, 109, 123
TURRENTINE: 25, 138

UNDERWOOD: 43, 83, 107, 162
USELTON: 139
USSERY (USERY): 150, 174

VANCE: 57, 58, 78, 82, 83, 84, 89,
    94, 107, 109, 128, 168
VANNATTA: 8, 43, 69, 120
VANNOY: 59, 62, 66, 67, 68, 72, 75,
    85, 94, 161
VENABLE: 52
VERNON: 88
VICKERY: 126, 127, 164

WADE: 12
WADLEY: 49, 50, 70, 113
WAGSTER: 2, 29
WAID: 153
WAITE: 7, 14, 66, 165
WALKER: 134
WALLACE: 29, 32, 66, 101, 110, 154
WALLIS: 6, 136, 154
WARD: 65
WARNER: 4, 25, 30, 45, 54, 56, 59,
    60, 61, 63, 64, 71, 76, 89, 94,
    101, 105, 117, 121, 122, 126,127, 146

WARREN: 34, 53, 85, 111, 137, 142
WATERS: 12, 21, 73
WATKINS: 37, 38, 39, 44, 53, 85, 94
WATSON: 60, 61, 63, 89, 102, 154, 161, 162, 169
WEAVER: 7, 64, 168
WEBB: 1, 7, 13, 19, 29, 38, 131, 139
WEBSTER: 4, 13, 14, 34, 35, 65, 79
WELCH (WALSH, WALCH): 129, 131, 157, 163, 172, 174
WELLS (WELLES): 130
WEST: 52, 85, 89, 155
WHEELER: 7, 11, 12, 35, 123, 127, 131, 143, 147, 154
WHINNERY: 61
WHITE: 34, 52, 89, 92, 100, 101, 102, 110, 111, 114, 115, 123, 145, 146, 154, 159, 161
WHITESELL (WHITSELL): 1, 3, 5, 14, 15, 24, 34, 54, 55, 59, 60, 63, 75, 88, 90, 116, 174
WHITESIDE: 25, 98, 113, 138, 155, 157, 175
WHITMAN: 4, 10, 14, 57, 110, 117, 132, 154, 155, 156, 157, 173
WHITNEY: 18
WHITSON: 101, 106, 119
WHITTHORNE: 42, 77, 84, 99, 102, 153
WHITWORTH: 8, 19, 30, 54, 74, 124, 128, 129, 164
WHORLEY (WHIRLY): 12, 133
WIGGINS: 50, 61, 64, 112, 114
WILHOITE: 7, 21, 22, 24, 25, 27, 39, 54, 59, 60, 64, 66, 72, 82, 86, 88, 89, 91, 93, 94, 96, 97, 136, 150, 167, 168, 170
WILKES: 165
WILLIAMS: 6, 7, 24, 44, 47, 48, 51, 52, 53, 58, 68, 70, 71, 73, 79, 86, 88, 89, 91, 94, 95, 97, 99, 107, 136, 145, 147, 148, 149, 154, 155, 156, 157, 173
WILSON: 7, 10, 17, 18, 26, 55, 58, 60, 73, 74, 86, 88, 90, 93, 101, 102, 104, 123, 135, 139, 141, 144, 150, 153, 154,

WILSON (continued): 156, 158, 166
WINSETT: 7, 36, 38, 77, 90, 105, 148
WISE: 16, 17, 144
WISENER: 15, 32, 98, 130, 144, 145, 146, 156
WOLF: 31
WOMACK (WOMMACK): 49, 63, 96
WOOD (WOODS): 9, 11, 18, 19, 26, 34, 39, 42, 48, 70, 71, 74, 77, 78, 81, 98, 99, 106, 111, 113, 118, 132, 133, 138, 151, 166, 169
WOODARD: 17
WOODFIN: 85, 141
WOOSLEY: 2, 20, 21, 111
WORD: 1, 3, 6, 13, 19, 23, 29, 40, 54, 56, 61, 65, 66, 67, 70, 72, 73, 74, 79, 93, 98, 101, 106, 108, 113, 150, 153, 154, 156, 158, 160, 162, 167, 171
WORKS (WORKE): 24, 25, 120, 128, 129, 137, 143
WORTHAM: 57, 104, 123, 136, 154, 156, 158, 161, 163
WRAY: 15
WRIGHT: 5, 53, 83, 103, 104, 122, 123, 161
WYNN (WINN): 20, 40, 46, 90, 92, 93, 99, 109, 153

YANCEY (YANCY): 32, 41, 105, 115, 118, 158, 171
YATES: 20, 24
YELL: 86, 91, 97, 131
YORK: 3, 21, 32, 36
YOUNG: 57, 58, 78, 104, 106, 113, 137
YOUNGER: 2

www.ingramcontent.com/pod-product-compliance
Lightning Source LLC
Chambersburg PA
CBHW072131020426
42334CB00018B/1755